THE BASSIST'S BIBLE

HOW TO PLAY EVERY BASS STYLE
FROM AFRO-CUBAN TO ZYDECO

BY

TIM BOOMER

WITH

MICK BERRY

SEE SHARP PRESS ◆ TUCSON, ARIZONA

Boomer, Tim.
    The bassist's bible : how to play every bass style from Afro-Cuban
to Zydeco / by Tim Boomer ; with Mick Berry -- Tucson,
Ariz. : See Sharp Press, 2009, 2013.
        261 p. : ill., music ; 28 cm. + 2 sound discs (digital : 4 3/4 in.) + dvd disc.
        Includes approximately 400 musical examples, organized by style,
with historical information preceding the bass grooves.
Includes bibliographical references.
        ISBN 1-937276-23-6
        ISBN 978-1937276-23-2

1. Bass -- Instruction and study. 2. Bass – Methods 3. Zydeco
music--Instruction and study. 4. Latin jazz -- Instruction and study.
I. Title. II. Berry, Mick.

    786.95   MT662

First Printing—August 2009
First Printing Second Edition—May 2013

The drum tracks on the accompanying compact discs were played by Mick Berry
and Jason Gianni. The bass examples were performed by Tim Boomer, Brandon
Essex (Rockabilly), Stuart Brotman (Klezmer), and Alex Szotak (Slap & Pop). Audio
voiceovers were spoken by Mick Berry. The drum tracks were recorded and mixed
at Trakworx Studios in South San Francisco. The bass tracks were recorded, mixed
with the drum tracks, and mastered at Boomer Studios in Berkeley, California by
Tim Boomer.

To contact the author, go to http://www.bassistsbible.com.

Cover design by Micaela Marsden. Interior design by Chaz Bufe.
Cover photo by Craig Isaacs. Tim Boomer back cover photo by Mateo Carr.

CONTENTS

Appendixes

QUICK REFERENCE

When you need to find a groove in a hurry!

CD TRACKS

CD 1 TRACK ORDER

AFRICAN

NORTH AFRICAN

1.	**Rai**	(example 1)
2.	Rai	(example 2)
3.	Rai	(ex 2 var 1)

SUB-SAHARAN AFRICAN

4.	**Highlife**	(example 1)
5.	**Afrobeat**	(example 1)
6.	Afrobeat	(example 4)
7.	**Juju**	(example 1)
8.	**Soukous**	(example 1)
9.	Soukous	(example 2)
10.	**Bikutsi**	(example 1)

AFRO-CUBAN

11.	**3–2** Son Clave	
12.	**2–3** Son Clave	
13.	**Mambo/Cha Cha**	(example 1)
14.	Mambo/Cha Cha	(ex 1 var 1)
15.	Mambo/Cha Cha	(example 2)
16.	Mambo/Cha Cha	(ex 2 var 1)
17.	Mambo/Cha Cha	(ex 2 var 2)
18.	Mambo/Cha Cha	(example 3)
19.	Mambo/Cha Cha	(ex 3 var 1)
20.	Mambo/Cha Cha	(example 4)
21.	Cha Cha	(example 1)
22.	**Bolero**	(example 1)
23.	**Merengue**	(example 1)
24.	**Cumbia**	(example 1)
25.	**3–2** Rumba Clave	
26.	**2–3** Rumba Clave	
27.	**Afro-Cuban Jazz**	(example 1)
28.	Afro-Cuban Jazz	(example 2)
29.	**6/8 Clave**	
30.	**6/8 Bell Pattern**	
31.	**Afro-Cuban 6/8**	(example 1)

BLUES

32.	**Blues Scale**	
33.	**Jump**	(example 1)
34.	**Shuffle**	(example 1)
35.	Shuffle	(example 2)
36.	Shuffle	(example 3)
37.	**Boogie**	(example 1)
38.	**12/8 (Slow)**	(example 1)
39.	12/8 (Slow)	(ex1 var 1)
40.	12/8 (Slow)	(ex1 var 3)
41.	**Blues Rumba**	(example 1)
42.	Blues Rumba	(ex 1 var 2)
43.	Blues Rumba	(example 2
44.	**Blues Mambo**	(example 1)
45.	Blues Mambo	(ex 1 var 1)
46.	**Blues Rock**	(example 1)
47.	Blues Rock	(ex 1 var 1)

BRAZILIAN

48.	**Samba**	(example 1)
49.	Samba	(ex 1 var 2)
50.	Samba	(ex 2 var 1)
51.	**Baiao**	(example 1)
52.	Baiao	(ex 1 var 1)
53.	**Bossa Nova**	(example 1)
54.	Bossa Nova	(ex 1 var 2)

CAJUN / ZYDECO

55.	**Cajun Two Step**	(example 1)
56.	Cajun Two Step	(ex 1 var 1)
57.	**Cajun Waltz**	(example 2)
58.	**Zydeco Two Step**	(example 1)
59.	Zydeco Two Step	(ex 1 var 1)
60.	**Zydeco Shuffle**	(example 1)
61.	Zydeco Shuffle	(ex 1 var 1)
62.	**Zydeco Waltz**	(example 1)
63.	Zydeco Waltz	(ex 1 var 2)

CARIBBEAN

64.	**Calypso**	(example 1)
65.	Calypso	(example 2)
66.	Calypso	(example 3)
67.	**Soca**	(example 1)
68.	Soca	(example 3)
69.	**Ska**	(example 1)
70.	Ska	(example 4)
71.	**Reggae**	(example 1)
72.	Reggae	(example 3)

COUNTRY

73.	**Bluegrass**	(example 1)
74.	Bluegrass	(ex 1 var 3)

CD #2 (CONT'D)

LATIN ROCK (CONT'D)

54. **Baiao**	(ex 1 var 2)
55. **Rumba**	(example 2)

METAL

56. Example 1
57. Example 1 Variation 1
58. Example 2
59. Example 2 Variation 1
60. Example 2 Variation 3

MIDDLE EASTERN

61. **Saudi**	(example 1)
62. **Sayyidi**	(example 1)
63. Sayyidi	(example 2)
64. **Laz**	(example 1)
65. **Karsilama**	(example 1)
66. Karsilama	(example 2)

(For Rai, see CD 1 examples 1–3)

POLKA

67. **Basic Example**	(example 1)
68. Polish	(example 2)
69. Slovenian	(ex 1 var 1)
70. **Slovenian**	(example 1)

PUNK

71. Example 1
72. Example 1 Variation 1
73. Example 2
74. Example 4

ROCK N' ROLL

75. **Early Rock**	(example 1)
76. Early Rock	(ex 1 var 1)
77. **Shuffle**	(example 1)
78. Shuffle	(ex 1 var 1)
79. **Mersey Beat**	(example 1)
80. Mersey Beat	(example 2)
81. Mersey Beat	(example 3)
82. **Rockabilly**	(example 1)
83. Rockabilly	(ex 1 var 1)
84. Rockabilly	(example 2)
85. **Standard Rock**	(example 1)
86. Standard Rock	(example 2)
87. Standard Rock	(example 3)
88. **Standard Rock (Halftime)**	(example 1)

SURF

89. **Instrumental Surf**	(example 1)
90. Instrumental Surf	(example 3)
91. **Vocal Surf**	(example 1)
92. **Surf Ballad**	(example 1)

TECHNO

93. Example 1
94. Example 1 Variation 2
95. Example 2

DVD Navigation

You can use the Style Menus where the examples are, as you'd expect, grouped by style, or you can use the Example Index to play the examples individually.

The Style Menus have two flavors. If you click on the name of the style itself—say Acid Jazz—it will play every video related to that style. If you choose an individual track it will, predictably, play only that track. In the other menu, Example Index, the tracks are organized sequentially just like the DVD index in the book. (Note that Rai has moved to the Middle Eastern Section.)

When using the remote control on a hardware DVD player, pressing the Right and Left arrow keys (usually used for menu navigation, surrounding the Enter Key) will take you to the major style headings. It will also take you to the Main Menu, Next and Previous buttons at the bottom of the menu. The Down and Up arrow keys will take you sequentially through the tracks.

If you are playing a track and want to go back to the menu, press the Next Chapter key, which is usually labeled Next on the remote located near the Play / Stop / Pause buttons. If you are playing a whole style you will have to press it multiple times. (Oh no, I got stuck in the Wedding Dance section . . . I don't wanna get married.)

The Top Menu (or Title Menu) buttons should take you back to the Main menu, unless you are actually playing a track. In that case press the Next Chapter button. The Menu button should do the same.

DVD TRACKS

AFRICAN

1. Highlife	(example 1)
2. Afrobeat	(example 1)
3. Afrobeat	(example 4)
4. Juju	(example 1)
5. Soukous	(example 1)
6. Bikutsi	(example 1)

AFRO-CUBAN

7. Mambo/Cha Cha	(example 1)
8. Bolero	(example 1)
9. Merengue	(example 1)
10. Cumbia	(example 1)
11. Afro-Cuban Jazz	(example 1)
12. Afro-Cuban 6/8	(example 1)

BLUES

13. Jump	(example 1)
14. Shuffle	(example 1)
15. Shuffle	(example 3)
16. **Boogie**	(example 1)
17. 12/8 (Slow)	(ex1 var 3)
18. Blues Rumba	(example 1)\
19. Blues Mambo	(example 1)
20. Blues Rock	(example 1)

BRAZILIAN

21. Samba	(example 1)
22. Baiao	(example 1)
23. Bossa Nova	(example 1)
24. Bossa Nova	(ex 1 var 2)

CAJUN / ZYDECO

25. Cajun Two Step	(example 1)
26. Cajun Waltz	(example 2)
27. Zydeco Two Step	(example 1)
28. Zydeco Shuffle	(example 1)
29. Zydeco Waltz	(example 1)

CARIBBEAN

30. Calypso	(example 1)
31. Soca	(example 1)
32. Ska	(example 1)
33. Ska	(example 4)

34. Reggae	(example 1)
35. Reggae	(example 3)

COUNTRY

36. Bluegrass	(example 1)
37. Bluegrass Waltz	(example 1)
38. Western Swing	(example 1)
39. Two Step	(ex 1 var 1)
40. Country Shuffle	(example 1)
41. Train Beat	(example 1)
42. Country Rock	(ex 1 var 1)
43. Country Rock	(ex 1 var 2)

DISCO

44. Disco Bass Fill

DRUM N' BASS / JUNGLE

45. Example 1
46. Example 5
47. Example 6

FLAMENCO

48. Example 1
49. Example 2

FUNK

50. Legba Beat	(example 1)
51. New Orleans	(example 1)
52. Motown	(example 1)
53. Stax	(example 1)
54. Early Funk	(ex 1 var 1)
55. Later Funk	(example 3)
56. Funk Rock	(example 2)
57. Slap & Pop	(example 1)

GOSPEL

58. Polka	(example 1)
59. Rock	(example 1)
60. Slow Blues	(example 1)
61. Shout	(example 1)

DVD (CONT'D)

HIP HOP / RAP

62. Example 1
63. Example 4
64. Example 5

JAZZ

65. N.O. Second Line	(example 1)
66. Dixieland	(example 1)
67. Big Band	(ex 1 var 1)
68. Small Band	(example 1)
69. **Jazz Waltz**	(example 1)
70. Jazz Waltz	(ex 1 var 1)

LATIN ROCK

71. Cha Cha	(example 1)
72. Cha Cha	(ex 1 var 1)
73. Baiao	(ex 1 var 2)
74. Rumba	(example 2)

METAL

75. Metal	(example 1)
76. Metal	(ex 1 1 Var 1)
77. Metal	(ex 2 var 3)

MIDDLE EASTERN

78. Rai	(example 1)
79. Sayyidi	(example 1)
80. Laz	(example 1)
81. Karsilama	(example 1)

POLKA

82. Polish	(example 2)
83. Slovenian	(example 1)

PUNK

84. Punk	(example 1).
85. Punk	(ex 1 var 1)

ROCK N' ROLL

86. Early Rock	(example 1)
87. Shuffle	(example 1)
88. Standard Rock	(example 1)

SURF

89. Instrumental Surf	(example 1)
90. Instrumental Surf	(example 2)

TECHNO

91. Techno	(example 1)
92. Techno	(ex1 var 2)
93. Techno	(example 2)

ACKNOWLEDGMENTS

A GREAT MANY PEOPLE helped us with this book.

We'd particularly like to thank Jazz legend Ron Carter (www.roncarter.net), who has appeared on over 2500 albums with everyone from Miles Davis to Quincy Jones, for encouragement and information on Jazz. Funk master Paul Jackson (www.pauljackson-bass.com), bassist for Herbie Hancock and the Head-hunters, was good enough to write the Introduction and help with Funk. Stuart Brotman, bassist for Brave Old World and Veretski Pass (www.veretskipass.com), and formerly of Canned Heat, helped greatly with Klezmer and generously played the recorded examples in that chapter.

Some other bassists were also exceptionally helpful in ways that we could not have anticipated. Gary Brown (www.mindspring.com/~mellowtone) jumped into Brazilian at a moment's notice and provided more help than we could have asked. Brandon Essex, (www.brandonessex.com) bassist with Doppler Trio and Terrence Brewer, contributed to Jazz, Rock, and the Standup vs. Electric appendix, and played the Rhythm Changes track. Ann Marie Harrop of Brave Combo was a big help with the Polka chapter—she showed us that there's more to Polka than roots and fifths. Dave Belove, bassist for Pete Escovedo, helped get the Afro-Cuban chapter right. James Singleton (www.jamessin-gletonmusic.com), bassist for Astral Project, helped with Funk and Jazz and showed us the Big 4. And Harvey Brooks (http://harveybrooks.net), bassist for Miles Davis, Jimi Hendrix, Bob Dylan, and The Doors, et al., was good enough to look through the book at the last moment (while he was moving!) and provide a quote for the back cover.

We greatly appreciate all the support we've received from members of the bass community, and also from guitarists and keyboard players. Many experts generously provided comments on individual chapters.

They include Clay Parnell (www.myspace.com/claiborneparnell), bassist for Biodesel (Acid jazz, Drum & Bass, Hip Hop); Ken Okulolo (www.africanmusic-source.com), bassist for King Sunny Ade and West African Highlife Band (African); Rebeca Mauleón (www.rebecamauleon.com), author of *The Salsa Guidebook* (Afro-Cuban); Karl Sevareid, bassist for the Robert Cray Band (Blues); Butch Landry of Tout Les Soir (www.toutlessoir.com) (Cajun/Zydeco); Roy Vogt (www.royvogt.com), co-author (with Brian Fullen) of *Contemporary Country Styles for the Drummer and Bassist* (Country); Ric Wilson, session guitarist for Huey Lewis & the News (Country); Tracy (Trae) Pierce (www.myspace.com/traepfeattstone), bassist for the Blind Boys of Alabama (Gospel); Brett Stranne (Gospel); Alex Szotak (Funk); Michael Lucas, co-author of *Rock Stardom For Dumbshits* (Punk); Paul J. Olguin (www.myspace.com/paulolguin), bassist for Maria Muldaur (Rock); and Allen Whitman, bassist for The Mermen (www.mermen.net) and What+What=What (Surf). And last but not least, Chuck Gee, pianist and music editor, made valuable suggestions about Afro-Cuban, Brazilian, Blues, and Jazz.

Finally, we would like to thank Jason Gianni (www.jasongianni.com), instructor at The Drummers Collective, who recorded a great many of the drum tracks on *The Drummer's Bible* (www.drummersbible.com) CDs, which are used here as accompaniment for the bass tracks on this book's CDs.

Our sincere apologies to anyone we haven't properly acknowledged. It wasn't intentional.

And for the second edition: Thanks to everyone who offered criticism and corrections.

INTRODUCTION

THE BASS IS A DEEP INSTRUMENT. The styles with the most impact have bass. The deeper the foundation the more stable the building—and the higher you can go. It is almost a language when you play bass, and each person speaks their own dialect. It's something that you can develop.

I was in junior high school the first time I saw Paul Chambers (bassist for Miles Davis) play at the Black Hawk in San Francisco. It completely amazed me. I went straight to the school music department, picked up a bass, and the first time I played a note I realized I didn't want to do anything else. I had a great bass teacher and got to take my bass home to practice. I walked over a mile every day with an upright bass.

Al Tanner, my first mentor, taught me how to play changes. He would play the chords on piano, and he showed me the bass notes I could use with his left hand.

Having a book like *The Bassist's Bible*, that has this kind of thing in it—having it all written down along with the examples on the CDs—is a great tool, something I wish I had had when I was coming up. I am helping with this book because I feel an obligation to pass on what I know, and this is a way to do it.

I was an early reader. We had two encyclopedias, and I used them, just checking out different things. *The Bassist's Bible* is the same kind of tool. You can use it randomly, checking out different styles, or you can look up specific things you need to know. Learning about styles that you don't know will only make you play better.

And the history of the styles is just basically cool. Knowing the history of music can only help you as a musician, as music *is* cultural.

Even if you don't read music, what the book gives you is important, because not only does it describe the styles, but the authors give you nearly 400 musical examples—and play nearly 200 of them. Even if you don't read music you can listen to the examples and read about them in the book to better understand what you are hearing. And the more you know, the better you'll play.

You can see all of the work here. Tim has done a really great job. I could jump on him for a few things, but it's just not worth it because the book is so comprehensive.

This book is very important and I think every bassist should own it.

—Paul Jackson

PREFACE

TO THE FIRST EDITION

THIS BOOK IS A SURVIVAL GUIDE, an introduction to all of the styles within. It provides historical background, common grooves, common chord progressions, and typical tone settings for almost every popular style played in the Western world. If you need a crash course in an unfamiliar style, this is the book for you. It will provide the information you need to play virtually any type of music with which you're unfamiliar—from playing a song at a wedding for a friend, to an audition with a band that plays an unfamiliar genre, to subbing at a gig. To make learning a new genre easier, every track on both CDs contains both the bass line and the corresponding drum groove. Even if you just want to see if you like a style, we've included not only the audio tracks, but also the names of bassists/bands in every genre, a discography, and a bibliography listing both books and web sites.

But, we repeat, this is a survival guide, an introductory work. There are many good books on individual styles, and we recommend that you dive into them if you plan in-depth study of particular styles. This book provides enough info to get you started on every style covered, and to play authentic grooves at gigs. But there are many fine points that we simply can't deal with due to the very large number of styles we cover and space limitations.

We assume that you're playing a 4-string bass, as that is the standard instrument. Most styles can be played either on an electric, a standup/upright, or an electric upright bass with a clean mid-power to loud combo amp or an amp head with a 1x15-inch, 2x12-inch or 4x10-inch speaker cabinet. (See the "Equipment" appendix for information about amps and instruments. See the "Electric vs. Standup" appendix for info on what gear is appropriate to individual styles.) If you are playing with a particularly loud band (for example, one with a lot of percussion), adding a cabinet with 10-inch speakers to your regular amp/speakers can help you cut through sonically.

This is not to say that you can't play a style with, say, a 6-string bass and a stack of Marshall amps, or even with an electric upright bass with MIDI and a rack full of samplers or synthesizers. This is all about your expression, taste, and what your bandmates (or the band leader) might think appropriate for the music (and whether you get asked to play again).

The tone settings mentioned in the "Characteristics" sections of individual chapters are for round wound strings on an electric bass, as you can always cut the midrange and treble, but it is much more difficult to add them when they're lacking (as is the case with flat wound strings).

The specific tone suggestions in this book are just that: suggestions. They're best used with an amp that can change the center frequency of the midrange (as in "mids +3 dB @ 500 Hz"). Not all amplifiers allow you to do that, and most amps have distinctive "voicing," meaning that the bass, mids, and treble controls cover different frequency ranges on each amp. Even so, just turning the "mids" up or down (when indicated) will give you a result that approximates the specified tone, even if you can't dial it in exactly.

The ability to read bass clef and chord symbols is helpful to fully understanding the written examples in this book. We have added tabs, as well, for bassists who prefer that format. The tabs (set up for electric bass) suggest an easy or authentic position on the neck, often below the 5th fret, but your taste and tone preferences may guide you to play in another position. If you play by ear—especially if you play well by ear—you can still make good use of this book: just listen to the CDs to learn the grooves. As most examples in this book are simple, you can also use the examples as an aid in learning to read music.

Chord progressions are notated using Roman numerals, the same notation used by blues and jazz players. This system is related to its country cousin—the Nashville numbering system, which uses standard Arabic numbers rather than Roman numerals. These informal transcription methods use the scale degree that a chord is built on to describe the chord rather than a chord's formal name.

Example: I - IV - V - I

This means that if the progression is in C, the chords are C - F - G - C. The Roman numerals indicate the degree of the scale the corresponding chord is built from. For example, in C the IV chord is built on the fourth degree of the scale: F. The dashes in the above example separate the four measures in the example.

Here are the specifics:

• Major chords use upper case numerals: I II III

• Minor chords use lower case numerals: i ii iii

• Multiple chords per measure use slashes as in: I - I/IV - V In this case the second measure chords are on beats 1 and 3 (unless otherwise specified)

• Flat chords use the "b" symbol as in bii, a flat minor second chord or Dbm (in the key of C)

Arabic numbers following Roman numerals refer to the degree of the chord as in the following examples, key of C:

• Imaj7 is a tonic major 7th (CM7—the notes C, E, G, B)

• ii7 is a minor 7th (Dm7—the notes D, F, A, C)

• V7 is a dominant 7th (G7—the notes G, B, D, F)

• V9 is a dominant 9th (G9—the notes G, B, D, F, A)

• V7#9 is a dominant 7th with a sharp 9th (G7#9—the notes G, B, D, F, A#)

• vi dim (or vi°) is diminished (A dim or A°—the notes A, C, Eb, Gb)

There are many good resources at your local library and on the Internet. For example, www.basstalk.com hosts a forum of bassists talking about bass technique, history, gear, instruments, and styles. Another more general, but still very useful, site is www.harmony-central.com, which has a section devoted to bass. And don't forget to make use of the bibliography and discography in the back of this book. If you're on a budget, your local public library will likely have many of the CDs listed.

A good way to expand what you learn about the styles covered in this book is to immerse yourself in the genres you want to learn. Get on the 'Net and use Google to search and gather information, using queries like "Blues chord progressions," "Blues history," "Blues bassist," or "Blues scale," and see what you find. Then try replacing the word "Blues" with something like "Jazz" or "Klezmer." There is a larger world out there than you—or we—can imagine.

No one knows everything. While writing this book, we gathered as much information as we possibly could to show you the wealth, diversity, and, yes, similarities of bass playing in different styles. We did our best to get it right. We did our best to give you good, easily playable, working examples. (Rest assured that these grooves work—if you're playing an unfamiliar style, you can rely on them.) There are obviously many more grooves than we provide—in fact a near-infinite number. But this book gives you accurate grooves and enough information to play professional gigs in all styles covered.

PREFACE

TO THE SECOND EDITION

THIS SECOND EDITION includes several new features, most importantly tablature (tabs) for nearly every written musical example, and a DVD showing how to properly play nearly 100 of the examples. The video examples were shot using three camera angles sequentially, so you can see both hands individually and simultaneously.

The recorded examples on the CDs are approximately two to three times the length of the recorded examples in the original edition's CDs, to help you learn the grooves. The e-book editions of the book have all of the audio and video tracks embedded.

We've also revised and in some cases expanded the history and style characteristics sections of almost all chapters, and have also added dozens of new grooves. We also show typical bass lines applicable to an entire genre at the beginning of some chapters. And we've added summary musical examples for some styles to show how to play patterns across entire chord progressions.

In a number of chapters we've added essential drum grooves in standard drum notation from our companion book, *The Drummer's Bible*, to help you understand how bass patterns correspond to the their matching drum grooves.

We decided to make some of these changes ourselves, while other changes were suggested by bassists who were involved in editing the original edition of this book, and still others by reviewers and individual users of the first edition. We thank you all for your help in making this a better and more accurate book.

THE ART OF BASS

I WROTE THIS BOOK because I wanted to own it. It solves problems I've run into while playing music for a living over many years.

Although we use the word "Bible" in the title, everything in this book is a suggestion or, at most, a guideline. There are no Ten Commandments here. Our goal is to help you learn bass styles, not replicate pieces of history. But, of course, some styles are more rigid than others. In traditional Country, for instance, it's unusual to play anything other than root and fifth half notes on beats one and three, and in Cha Cha Chas it's rare to play anything other than a pattern involving notes on the "and" of beat two and on beat four. Other styles are more open. The thing to remember is that our suggestions are a starting point. What you do with them is up to you (and your bandmates).

The most common role for a bassist is, of course, to support his or her band rhythmically and harmonically. Bassists are not limited to any specific role, however, as we can do considerably more, such as playing the hook (or the melody) and soloing, improvising, and comping.

Providing a solid foundation for a band is still, however, the usual role of the bassist—especially if you play in a dance band. The bassist is the bridge between the melodic players and the rhythm section. You live in both worlds: melody and rhythm. You are that bridge.

There is truth in the saying that "You make most of your money below the fifth fret." You establish the chord being played and the basis of the pulse simultaneously by playing the root note of the chord on the first beat of a measure (and at most chord changes). Next in importance to the root, usually, is the fifth, then the third or seventh. Pretty simple stuff, but it works.

It is also common to play patterns. Bass lines. This does not prevent you from varying the pattern in a musical way by slightly changing the notes played, note duration, or by adding a little syncopation, but over the course of a song there will still typically be a pattern. This might seem obvious, or easy, but you need to lock in with the drummer, be aware of solos, notice when the lead singer changes the form, watch

the dancers on the floor, try not to knock over your drink, and still keep it interesting.

You can learn a lot by watching the dancers and seeing the effects of your playing. A groove is a pattern, a predictable sound that dancers can follow. Watch them. Bassists (and the rest of the band) may get bored playing the same lines over and over again, so, of course you'll fill and vary the pattern in other ways, but if you break the groove too often, dancers will get out of sync, the thread will be broken, and the dancers will stop.

One way to be creative, and keep dancers happy, is to understand playing "in the pocket." This is often described as playing in such a way that the groove is very solid. The bassist locks in with the drummer and never wavers. Using the standard rock beat as an example, the drummer plays kick drum on beat one (the downbeat) and also on beat three, and the snare on beats two and four. The bassist also plays precisely on the downbeat, followed by a pattern. That pattern can be a little ahead of the beat or behind the beat or exactly on the beat. As long as the drummer and bassist are in sync with each other, and play/feel the downbeat at the same time, they are in the pocket. You know it when you're in it, as it feels like the music is playing you, or the entire band is one instrument.

If you are not playing for dancers, you can leave the groove at any time—but returning to it provides resolution in a song. For instance, in jazz, the bassist (or more often a horn player or pianist) plays the "head" (the melody played in the first verse of a multi-verse song) after several choruses of solos to bring the tune to a close. And the audience will recognize it—"Oh look, they're playing that theme again"—and any improvisation that came before the final statement of the head will seem intentional.

In the same way, once you have established the basic foundation of a song, look for holes where nothing much is happening—a sustained note or chord perhaps, or a straight groove. You can then find a space to develop an idea—either melodically or rhythmically. You can repeat a note, syncopate, or play (a) note(s) outside of the pattern you've established.

You can also intentionally leave holes by resting, as in Reggae bass lines. This sets up a pattern that extends across measures rather than a pattern that repeats within a single measure. It still allows complexity, but in a relaxed context. It also allows your bandmates a lot of space. Study Miles Davis to learn about the spaces in music.

Developing your own style has a lot to do with knowing when to play and when not to. In a few words: "If in doubt, lay out." Typically, if there are vocals, you simplify and come down in volume to allow the focus to be on the vocalist.

Another important aspect of playing bass is to learn to use fills tastefully. Fills are usually played at the end of four- (or eight- or twelve-) measure patterns that lead to a new section of a song or the repeat of a verse. They are not played in random places.

This doesn't mean that a bassist must strictly follow rules. Jazz musicians and jam bands often break rules, and often get away with it—sometimes with brilliant results. It is simply helpful to know that some styles sound better when you play patterns typical of them.

The bass now encompasses everything from stand-up bass to electric bass to synthesized and sampled bass. Basses themselves now feature not just 4 strings, but 5, 6, and even 12 strings; they're produced with up to 28 frets. There are both fretted and fretless basses, acoustic bass guitars, piccolo basses, and onboard-MIDI basses. And it's certain that more variations are waiting in the wings.

The technique of playing these instruments has also evolved greatly over the years. Bass technique is virtually unlimited now. You can combine nearly any style with any other, from anywhere in the world. You can use effects, tap, slap, pluck, pick, thump, play with a bow (or an e-bow). You can lay down an unmistakable heavy groove or take extended solos in a jam format. You can also just play roots, fifths, and octaves on a standup or a P-bass and be happy.

We hope this book is useful to the bass community. As one of my deepest influences, John Entwistle from The Who, said when asked what he thought when he saw another bass player, and what he felt about the camaraderie of bassists: "The first thing I think of is poor fellow" (and, paraphrasing, "poor bastard"). We are underrated and underappreciated, but essential.

I love bass. Thank you all for being bassists. We need more of us.

—Tim Boomer

1 ACID JAZZ

ACID JAZZ draws on many musical styles—Funk (mainly 1970s Funk), House, Soul, R&B, Hip Hop, Afro-Cuban, Brazilian, and Jazz—and it has no standard grooves. It originated in the late 1980s in the UK, but achieved greater popularity in the 1990s, especially in San Francisco and New York.

Prominent Acid Jazz artists include Alphabet Soup, the Mo'Fessionals, Galactic, Brand New Heavies, Groove Collective, Digable Planets, Jamiroquai, and St. Germain. Artists recognized as forerunners to Acid Jazz include Roy Ayers, Grant Green, and Donald Byrd. Acid Jazz artists in Japan include Mondo Groso (aka Shinichi Osawa), Gota (aka Gota Yashiki) and Simply Red. In Poland, Skalpel are prominent, as is Moscow Grooves Institute in Russia.

More recently, Thievery Corporation uses a complex mix of samples and live musicians, both in the studio and in live performaces, combining elements of Acid Jazz, Dub, Reggae, Brazilian, and classical Indian music. Though they do not play with a live trap set drummer, they do use a live bassist who syncs his playing to sampled drum loop sequences, as well as live and sampled percussion such as tablas and congas as well as to the other live musicians.

For a bassist, the style is best approached by creating a strong, supportive groove, often locked into a click track. The challenge is in playing in the characteristic relaxed groove of this style while not losing sync to the looped parts (which may be created on the fly) and looking out for the fades, breakdowns, and mutes that are characteristic of the DJ techniques used in the genre.

Instrumental parts are as important as the vocals and lyrics in Acid Jazz, and the style is characterized by danceable grooves and lengthy, repetitive vamping. A typical Acid Jazz ensemble blends horns, a full rhythm section (often percussion in addition to a drum set), a vocalist (singing and/or rapping), and even a DJ. Acid Jazz ensembles also use digital samples extensively, both in recording sessions and live performances.

The style itself has crossed over into modern Hip Hop and Electronica, which are often characterized by melodic lines backing up a singer/rapper. (For the purposes of easy classification and historical accuracy, we've retained the term "Acid Jazz" here.)

ACID JAZZ CHARACTERISTICS

GROOVES: Bass lines in Acid Jazz are usually repetitive dance grooves.

TONE: Many tracks are sampled from original upright and electric bass sources. Other tones are synthesized. Effects and distortion can be used. For more choices, refer to chapters on specific styles.

GEAR: When performed live (in studio or on stage), conventional instruments can be used. Much of the material comes originally from upright bass sounds, sometimes sampled and looped. Amplified acoustic or electric upright bass can be used to great effect.

ACID JAZZ CHARACTERISTICS (CONT'D)

PROGRESSIONS: No limits. From simple one-chord "progressions" to the most complex chord patterns. (Here, as in all of the others chapters, the progressions are only examples taken from songs that we listened to while researching the style.)

1) i7 - i7 - iv7 - ii7/bii7
2) I - II7 - III7 - I
3) i7 - bVII - bIII - bVI
4) i7 - ii7 - i7 - ii7
5) i7 - V7 - i7 - V7
6) i7 - ii7 - bII7
7) i - bIII - iii
8) i7 - i7/iv7
9) Imaj7 - ii7

TEMPO: Acid Jazz tempos vary according to the style of music being played.

EXAMPLE 1 (HIP HOP/RAP)

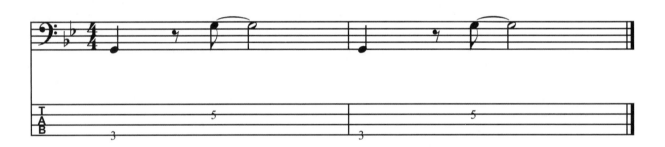

EXAMPLE 2 (HALF-TIME STANDARD ROCK—CD 2 TRACK 88)

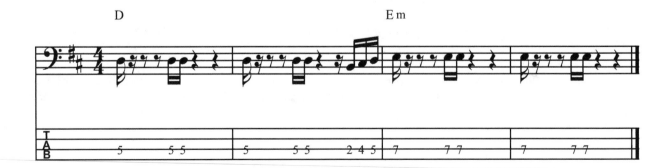

EXAMPLE 3 (SWING—CD 2 TRACK 41, DVD TRACK 68)

EXAMPLE 4 (BOSSA NOVA—CD 1 TRACK 53, DVD TRACK 23)

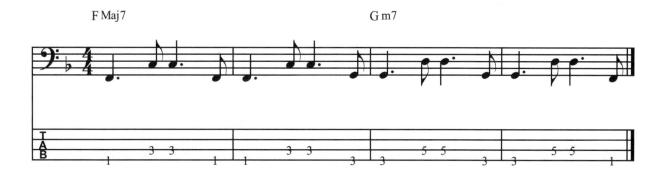

EXAMPLE 5 (MAMBO—CD 1 TRACK 14)

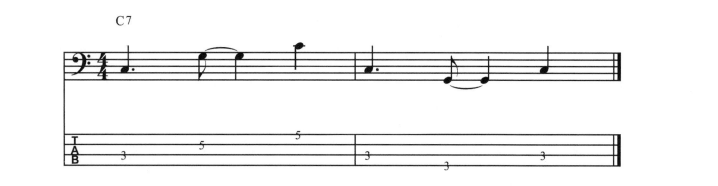

EXAMPLE 6 (EARLY FUNK—CD 2 TRACK 10, DVD TRACK 54)

2 AFRICAN

AFRICA HAS ONE-FIFTH THE LAND MASS and one-seventh the population of the planet, and literally hundreds of cultures. Musical styles number in the thousands. Although a bassist may encounter other African styles, those presented in this chapter are the most common.

Contemporary sub-Saharan African music began with the sounds and rhythms of Afro-Cuban (son) music in the 1920s and 1930s, which was introduced via radio airplay; its clave-based phrasing soon found it's way into Congolese and West African bands, which were beginning to create African Pop and Jazz. With the introduction of radio throughout Africa after World War II, and later through television, African music became popular across the continent.

As Western instruments (most importantly the electric guitar and electric bass) became cheaper through mass production, African musicians began to use them. This enabled composers to easily incorporate new developments in Western music (e.g., Rock n' Roll, Reggae, and Funk) into African music.

Today, African music is popular globally, influencing many other genres while continuing to develop in its own directions. The styles below represent the broader category of Afropop or sub-Saharan African popular music, which while incorporating elements of it, is quite different from African traditional music, and is also quite different from the Algerian Rai style, which is more similar to Middle Eastern pop music.

◼ WESTERN AFRICAN STYLES

Western African styles include Juju, Afrobeat, and Highlife. These styles originated in the early 20th century in Ghana and Nigeria, and eventually reached their peak in Africa toward the middle of the century. These styles blend African tribal songs with popular music from the West. They originally incorporated the sounds from Big Band horn sections and later adopted grooves from the Caribbean as well as Rock and Soul.

Because Western African genres incorporate musical influences from North America and the Caribbean, it's helpful to be thoroughly versed in Reggae, Ska, Soca, and Rock when playing West African styles.

Afrobeat is characterized by the "endless groove" created by repetitive bass, guitar, and percussion lines. In Juju and Highlife, although many of the bass lines are repetitive, there is ample room for improvisation. In some compositions the bass plays unison (or octave) lines with the other musicians or vocalists.

When interviewed in 1998, by Jason Gross, King Sunny Ade said, "A bass guitar is more or less like a thumb piano from the old days, in a box with some

metal on top. A bass can play that so what's the use of carry[ing] the boxes all around?"

A resurgence of Western African music, also called World Beat, in the 1980s created a global following attracted to the music's celebratory and joyful nature. Important West African musicians include Fela Kuti (Afro Beat), Fela's sons Femi and Seun Kuti (who now leads Fela's band), Fela's musical director Tony Allen, King Sunny Ade (Juju and Afrobeat), Chief Udoh Essiet (Highlife), Rex Jim Lawson (Highlife), and Prince Nico Mbarga (Highlife).

Orchestra Baobab play an African/Afro-Cuban fusion that is reminiscent of Cuba's Buena Vista Social Club. After re-release of cassettes made in Senegal in 1982, the band now tours the world.

The San Francisco Bay Area's Albino! is an example of Afrobeat in America. Another prominent Bay Area musician is bass player Baba Ken Okulolo, a native of Nigeria, who moved to the Bay Area in 1985 and formed three Highlife bands—The West African Highlife Band, Kotoja, and The Nigerian Brothers.

WEST AFRICAN CHARACTERISTICS

BASS GROOVES: Afrobeat and Juju use repetitive lines appropriate to dance music with hypnotic grooves, often using one- or two-bar phrases. Juju is typically played as a lyrical, uplifting, unending jam, whereas Afrobeat is heavier, funkier, and pounds deep grooves while featuring solo sections. Highlife is more lyrical and allows more improvisation on bass. The bassist can be in the background or can be featured as a prominent melodic player in Highlife.

TONE: Bass flat to +3 dB, Mids flat to +6 dB @ 700 Hz, Treble flat to -3 dB. Few or no effects. No distortion. Relatively soft dynamics are an integral part of these styles.

GEAR: The plentiful use of percussion makes electric bass more appropriate than upright in most African styles, but some styles, such as African/Afro-Cuban fusion (Orchestra Baobab), are quieter and use upright. The use of 2x10" or 4x10" cabinets helps to cut through the percussion.

CHORD PROGRESSIONS: Afrobeat and Juju use a lot of one- and two-chord vamps. Highlife is more progression oriented than the other styles.

1) I/IV - V/I
2) I - V
3) I - IV/V
4) I - IV - ii7/V7 - I
5) I - V/I - I/IV - V/I

6) I - ii7
7) I - ii7 - I - V
8) IV - V - I
9) I - I/IV - IV/ii7 - V7/I
10) I - V - IV - V

QUARTER NOTE = 100 – 138 BPM

HIGHLIFE EXAMPLE 1 (CD 1 TRACK 4, DVD Track 1)

Example 1, Example 1 Variation 1, and Example 2 courtesy of West African Highlife Band, Ken Okulolo bass.

HIGHLIFE EXAMPLE 1 VARIATION 1

HIGHLIFE EXAMPLE 2

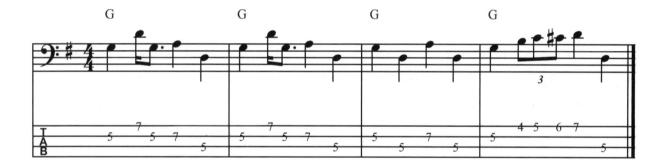

AFROBEAT EXAMPLE 1 (CD 1 TRACK 5, DVD Track 2)

Afrobeat Example 2

A m7

Afrobeat Example 3

D m

Afrobeat Example 4 (CD 1 Track 6, DVD Track 3)

F m

AFROBEAT EXAMPLE 5

JUJU EXAMPLE 1 (CD 1 TRACK 7, DVD Track 4)

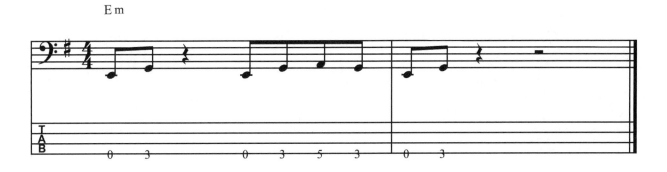

JUJU EXAMPLE 2

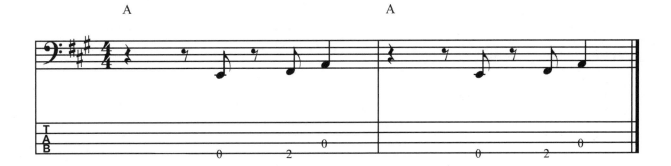

A

SOUKOUS

Soukous is a type of dance music that emerged in the Congo region in the early 1960s. Soukous (*secousser*, "shake" in French) is one of the most popular styles of contemporary African music in Africa, Europe, and North America. The roots of this style go back to the post-World War II era when radio stations in the Congo region played Cuban Rumba music. African musicians adapted it and created what was originally called "African Rumba" or "African Jazz."

Prominent Soukous bands and musicians include Zaiko Langa Langa, Franco (François Luambo Makiadi), Tabu Le (Tabu Ley Rochereau), and Chief Shaba Kahamba. In the 1970s, bands such as Super Mezembe and Kanda Bongo Man became popular

In the 1980s, Soukous migrated to London and Paris. Bands, sometimes including up to 20 players, often had a lineup of three or four guitars, bass, vocals, percussion, and horns.

Vocalist Papa Wemba is a prominent Soukous player. He performs with his band Viva La Música in Kinshai, The Republic of the Congo, and also with the band Viva Tendence in Paris. Other current performers include Koffi Olomide and the groups Extra Musica and Wenge Musica.

SOUKOUS CHARACTERISTICS

BASS GROOVES: Soukous grooves usually have a 16th-note feel.

TONE: Bass +3 dB, Mids flat to +6 dB @ 700 Hz, Treble flat to -3 dB. Few or no effects. No distortion.

GEAR: Electric upright bass will work, but this is more of an electric style than a standup style.

CHORD PROGRESSIONS: Chord progressions tend to be simple and are based on the I, IV, and V chords.

1) I - I - IV - IV
2) I - IV - V
3) I - I - V - V
4) I - IV/V
5) V/IV - I
6) I/IV - IV/I
7) I - V - I - V
8) V/IV - I

QUARTER NOTE = 100 – 138 BPM

SOUKOUS EXAMPLE 1 (CD 1 TRACK 8, DVD TRACK 5)

SOUKOUS EXAMPLE 1 VARIATION 1

SOUKOUS EXAMPLE 2 (CD 1 TRACK 9)

■ BIKUTSI

Bikutsi developed in the Beti culture in Cameroon. The origin of the word stems from "Bi" (more than one), "Kut" (to strike) and "Si" (the ground), translating to "strike the ground repeatedly." Whereas Soukous began as an African Jazz interpretation of Afro-Cuban music, Bikutsi is a contemporary development based in African musical ideas. Bikutsi became popular in Western Africa by the middle of the 20th century, but only found wide exposure in the mid-1980s through music videos. It rivals Makossa as Cameroon's most popular style.

The "father of modern Bikutsi music," Messi Me Nkonda Martin, front man for Los Camaroes, simulated the traditional "balafon" instrument on an electric guitar, muting the strings by using cotton cord to tie the strings together. One of the more popular contemporary Bikutsi bands in Cameroon is Zélé le Bombardier.

Following its popularization in the mid-1980s, elements of Bikutsi began to appear in the music of American and European musicians, notably in Paul Simon's 1990 recording, "Rhythm of the Saints." Individuals and groups responsible for Bikutsi's success include journalist/promoter Jean-Marie Ahanda, Theodore Epeme (Zanzibar), and Les Tetes Brulees.

BIKUTSI CHARACTERISTICS

BASS GROOVES: Much like Soukous, Bikutsi is primarily dance music, and so the bassist's primary job is that of timekeeper. Although occasionally played in 9/8, Bikutsi music usually has a quick 6/8 feel and the drummer usually plays the bass drum on every beat, which allows the bassist opportunities for improvisation around the consistent pulse.

To complicate matters, Bikutsi is often written in 4/4 rather than 6/8. In practice, this means that when Bikutsi is written in 4/4 two 6/8 "measures" are played within every 4/4 measure.

TONE: Bass flat +3 dB, Mids flat to +6 dB @ 700 Hz, Treble flat to -3 dB. Few or no effects. No distortion.

GEAR: Electric upright bass will work, but this is more of an electric style than a standup style. Effects such as flange and chorus can be used.

CHORD PROGRESSIONS: Chord progressions tend to be simple and are based on the I, IV, and V chords.

1) I - V - I - V
2) I/V - I/V - I/V - I/V
3) I - IV - I - IV

QUARTER NOTE = 116 – 168 BPM

BIKUTSI EXAMPLE 1 (CD 1 TRACK 10, DVD Track 6)

The following Bikutsi examples are all courtesy of West African Highlife Band, Ken Okulolo bass.

BIKUTSI EXAMPLE 2

BIKUTSI EXAMPLE 2 VARIATION 1

3 AFRO-CUBAN

SALSA

WITHIN 50 YEARS after Columbus discovered the New World, the Spaniards instituted slavery in Cuba. Most of the slave trade was concentrated in the western part of the island, so Afro-Cuban music developed mostly in the two largest cities there, Matanzas and Havana.

The Spaniards permitted their slaves to worship (in the Catholic religion) through music and dance, which led to the merging of the two cultures in both secular and religious aspects, establishing the foundation of Afro-Cuban music. What has survived is primarily a combination of the Spanish and West African cultures (Congolese, Yoruban, and Dahomean).

The styles presented here developed individually, so it's important to recognize the uniqueness of each and its appropriate application in Afro-Cuban music. It's even more important to recognize and understand the differences between Afro-Cuban music (commonly referred to as "Salsa") and Brazilian music, because they're often lumped together under the vague term "Latin Music." The information in this chapter and the Brazilian chapter will clarify the differences between these very different styles. (Among other things, as we'll see shortly, the foundation of Afro-Cuban music is clave rhythms; and there are no clave rhythms in Brazilian music.)

This chapter focuses on the most commonly played Afro-Cuban styles: Mambo, Cha Cha Chá (usually referred to as Cha Cha), Merengue, Cumbia, Afro-Cuban 6/8, and Afro-Cuban Jazz. (Although Merengue and Cumbia originated in The Dominican Republic and Colombia respectively, they are often thought of as Afro-Cuban genres, largely due to their being dance-oriented Latin styles.) There are many other Afro-Cuban and Latin styles, but those presented in this chapter are the most important for bass.

Salsa is the most prominent and recognizable style of Afro-Cuban music. Various stories credit the name to different sources: 1) It first appeared in the late 1940s song "Échale Salsita" by Ingacio Pineiro; 2) Cuban musician "Bigote" Escalona introduced bands as playing with "salsa"; 3) Tito Puente coined the term. Whatever its derivation, Salsa is now established as the name for Afro-Cuban music performed in a dance setting. The terms "Salsa" and "Mambo" are often used interchangeably, which is close to being accurate. Mambo is the most important Salsa style, while Salsa includes other musical forms such as Bolero.

MAMBO'S & CHA CHA'S RHYTHMIC ROOTS

As percussion is the foundation of the Salsa styles, the following information on percussion is essential. The bassist, in order to fully execute and feel the music, must listen to and lock in with the percussionist(s).

The traditional Afro-Cuban percussion section consists of a Conga player (conguero), a timbale player (timbalero), and a bongo and hand bell player (bongocero), who may also play güiro on Cha Chas. Additional hand percussion, usually played by singers, includes claves and maracas.

When the traditional percussion section is not present, the drum set takes its place, with the drummer handling all of a percussion section's tasks simultaneously.

The primary Afro-Cuban rhythmic parts consist of:

1) Clave (pronounced cla - vay, with the "a" in "cla" being soft and the "a" in "vay" being hard, and with the accent on the first syllable)
2) The Cáscara rhythm
3) The Campana rhythm (bongo bell)
4) Montuno (played by the piano)
5) Tumbao (pronounced toom-ba-oh)(played by the conguero)
6) Tumbao (played by the bassist)

The interplay between these rhythmic parts is complex. Because this chapter is an introduction to Afro-Cuban bass playing—a basic how-to guide—we will only cover those rhythmic parts most directly useful to bass players: clave and tumbao rhythms.

■ CLAVE

CLAVE ("KEY") is the underlying rhythm of Afro-Cuban music. A repetitive two-measure pattern, clave has become a near-universal rhythm, whose influence extends beyond Cuba to North American Jazz, Rock and Roll (e.g., the familiar "Bo Diddley beat"), and even Funk. It is essential for all instrumentalists to understand the rhythm and role of the clave in Afro-Cuban music. The clave has two major forms, the Son and the Rumba. The Son is covered here, the Rumba in the Afro-Cuban Jazz section of this chapter.

SON CLAVE

Son (pronounced with a hard "o" as in "tone") clave (also called "3–2 clave") is a two-measure phrase; the first measure is syncopated and the quarter notes in the second measure are played on beats 2 and 3. Son clave always falls in the order of three beats in the first measure, two in the second.

3–2 CLAVE (CD 1 TRACK 11)

It may be played in reverse order, in which case it is no longer referred to as "Son clave" or "3-2 clave" but simply "Reverse clave" or more commonly "2–3 clave."

2–3 CLAVE (CD 1 TRACK 12)

■ TUMBAO

TUMBAO is the term for the rhythm played by the bass player and conguero (conga player) in Mambo and Cha Cha. The importance of this rhythm cannot be overstated: it is *the* basis of Afro-Cuban bass playing. (The Tumbao rhythm is often doubled or enhanced by the trap set's kick drum, predominantly on the "and" of beat 2.)

The two most common rhythmic patterns played in the bass Tumbao follow. The Tumbao rhythm is clave derivative, but is not identical to the clave pattern. That is, the first half of a 3–2 clave is the same rhythm as in a Tumbao, but the Tumbao does not vary—it's the same in every measure, regardless of clave order. However, the bassist must be able to hear the clave pattern while playing a Tumbao, as all parts of a Salsa song are built around the clave rhythm.

(While this chapter covers basic Tumbao, the more complex Tumbaos of modern Cuban music and advanced Afro-Cuban Jazz bass playing are still completely clave based; in these advanced styles, the Tumbao bass rhythm will not necessarily be the same in both measures.)

TUMBAO EXAMPLE 1

TUMBAO EXAMPLE 2

NOTE: Rather than "Son" and "reverse clave," the terms most often used for Son Clave are 3–2 and 2–3. Both orders can be found in Salsa. It is essential that all musicians agree on the order of the clave so that the rhythms played by the ensemble do not clash.

Sometimes, within the same song, the order of the clave is reversed. This is done in one of two ways: 1) by finishing a song section with an odd number of measures, then beginning the next phrase on the first ensuing measure (in which case the clave does not change, but the music flips to the other direction); 2) by actually reversing the clave: i.e., 2–3 is completed, and then the clave itself reverses to a 3–2 order. In either case, all of the musicians need to be aware of the switch and adjust their playing to the new feel of the clave.

■ MAMBO & CHA CHA CHA

ALTHOUGH BASED ON A DANCE that developed in the early 1940s in Havana, Mambo's name comes from an instrument originally used in Bantu rituals. It first appeared as an "open section" of the Danzon in the late 1930s as a non-vocal interlude with a repetitive figure (vamp) played in an extended improvisational section. As a result of its popularity, the Mambo section began to be played separately and was soon recognized as its own style. It reached New York City by the late 1940s and reached its greatest popularity by the mid-1950s.

Today, Mambo's influence is found in virtually all Salsa music. While Cuban artists such as Cuban master bassist Israel "Cachao" López, Arsenio Rodríguez, and Orestes López created the Mambo, musicians such as Tito Puente, Pérez Prado, and Dizzy Gillespie (in songs such as "Manteca" [translation: "Lard"]) did much to develop it through fusing Swing with Cuban rhythms.

The Mambo is a two-measure, up-tempo pattern based on a Son clave; it can be started on either the "2" or "3" side of the clave. Bassists use Tumbao patterns in the bass lines for Mambos.

Cha Cha Cha (more familiarly Cha Cha) is a variation of Mambo. The primary difference between the two is tempo: Cha Chas are played at a much slower tempo than Mambos. The term "Cha Cha" comes from the Salsa dance known as the "Cha Cha Chá" which refers to the sound of the "three-note rhythm" in the dance step. Enrique Jorrín is credited with inventing and naming the Cha Cha in 1951. Its popularity reached a peak during that decade in dance clubs in Cuba and the United States. Two of the most widely recognized Cha Chas in Latin and American pop music are "Oye Como Va" ("Listen to How It Goes," written by Tito Puente and popularized by Carlos Santana) and "Morning," by Clare Fischer.

All Tumbao bass patterns played in Mambo are transferable to Cha Cha. One important rhythmic difference between the two is that bass lines in Cha Cha employ beat 1 more often than Mambo (where beat 1 is normally played only in the first measure and then never played again).

As it's a variation of Mambo, Cha Cha may employ both directions of clave: 3–2 and 2–3.

MAMBO & CHA CHA CHA CHARACTERISTICS

GROOVES: Even though Mambo/Cha Cha (plus Merengue and Bolero) are normally played and often notated in cut time (2/2), all examples here are presented in 4/4 for ease of learning. The important thing to remember is that the pulse is two beats per measure.

TONE: Bass +3 to +9 dB, Mids flat, Treble flat. (These settings hold true for all styles in this chapter.)

GEAR: Electric or upright electric is preferred in Salsa due to the loudness of the horns and percussion. The tone is soft, mimicking the sound of an upright bass or Ampeg Baby Bass. (The Ampeg Baby Bass is the classic bass of Salsa.) Upright works well for early Cuban music (as in Buena Vista Social Club). Cabinets with 10-inch speakers (2x10, 4x10) help cut above the percussion.

TECHNIQUE: Finger style, with tied/sustained notes blending into each other.

CHORD PROGRESSIONS:

1) I7 - ii7 - V9 - I7
2) vi7 - II9 - V7 - I9
3) I - IV - V - IV
4) I/IV - V/IV - I/IV - V/IV
5) V7 - I7 - V7 - I7

6) V/IV - I/IV - V/IV - I/IV
7) I - V - V - I
8) I/IV - V/IV - V/IV - I/IV
9) i7 - V7 - i7/bIII - bVII/IV - i7 - V7 - i7 / bIII - bVII/IV
10) I7 - I7 - III7/VI9 - II7/V9

QUARTER NOTE = 200+ BPM (MAMBO)
QUARTER NOTE = 110+ BPM (CHA CHA)

MAMBO / CHA CHA EXAMPLE 1 (CD 1 TRACK 13)

Although the bassist usually does not play on beat 1, getting used to playing it provides a good start in feeling the Tumbao rhythm.

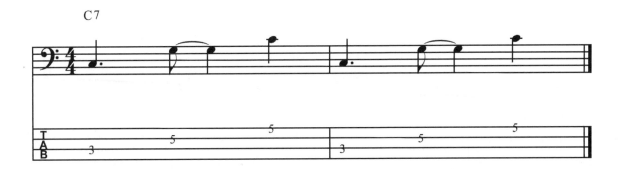

NOTE CHOICE: The root and fifth are the strongest choices for most Afro-Cuban bass playing. The root is almost always played (actually, held) on beat one, and the fifth is the most common choice for the "and" of beat 2 when there is one chord per measure. As long as the bass notes remain within the chord, there are no incorrect choices; the notes played are a matter of taste.

MAMBO / CHA CHA EXAMPLE 1 VARIATION 1 (CD 1 TRACK 14)

MAMBO / CHA CHA EXAMPLE 1 VARIATION 2

MAMBO / CHA CHA EXAMPLE 2 (CD 1 TRACK 15, DVD TRACK 7)

MAMBO / CHA CHA EXAMPLE 2 VARIATION 1 (CD 1 TRACK 16)

MAMBO / CHA CHA EXAMPLE 2 VARIATION 2 (CD 1 TRACK 17)

PLAYING ON THE "1": It's common in Tumbao patterns to play on beat 1 in the first bar of a song, and then to seldom if ever play it again, while continuing to play on the "and" of beat 2 and on beat 4. There is no secret way to do this. Many kinds of music, including R&B, Funk, and even straight ahead Jazz, have a "down on 1" feel for the drums and bass. In the three Tumboa patterns on the previous page, you do play on the "1." *But this is not usual.*

In *most* Tumbao patterns (as above), you will play the "1" only in the first measure, and then never play it again, but you must learn to know and feel where the "1" is. That is the only way you can play the "and" of beat 2 and beat 4 in their proper places when you do not play the "1" (in other words, when you hold over beat 4 from the previous measure). Practice with a metronome and try to tap your foot on beats 1 and 3 or 2 and 4. If you still can't feel it, tap your foot on all four beats and count aloud "one and two *and* three and *four* and" to nail the "and" of 2 and beat 4. With practice you will get it.

MAMBO / CHA CHA EXAMPLE 3 (CD 1 TRACK 18)

MAMBO / CHA CHA EXAMPLE 3 VARIATION 1 (CD 1 TRACK 19)

MAMBO / CHA CHA EXAMPLE 4 (CD 1 TRACK 20)

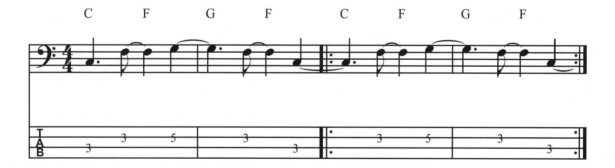

NOTE: When there are two chords per measure (on the first and third beats), the root of the chord on beat 1 is anticipated, as is usual in Tumbao patterns, on the fourth beat of the previous measure, and the root of the chord on the third beat is anticipated on the "and" of beat 2.

CHA CHA EXAMPLE 1 (CD 1 TRACK 21)

Note the lack of a tie from beat four of the second measure to beat 1 of the following measure. This device, which is fairly common in Cha Cha, should be used as an occasional alternative to the Tumbao pattern. And we stress "occasional": it would sound redundant to play the "1" in every measure.

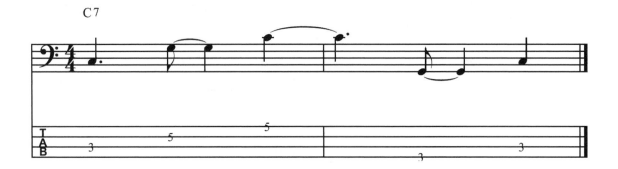

NOTE: When playing Tumbao patterns you are free to play roots and fifths in any position you want with two caveats: 1) the decision to move up or down must make musical and technical sense (the bass line must flow—don't make large interval jumps); and 2) don't play too high (12th fret or above) on the neck for too long—you lose the fat bottom up there and the music requires it.

Although you have this freedom of movement, keep in mind that your function is to establish a repetitive foundation, as Salsa is predominantly dance music. Radical changes of Tumbaos within a song should usually be reserved for Afro-Cuban Jazz.

BOLERO

BOLERO IS A BALLAD STYLE with slow tempos and sentimental lyrics. The term "Bolero" stems from the Spanish verb "volar," meaning "to fly," exemplified in the elegant moves of Bolero dancers. The first Bolero is said to have been invented by Spanish dancer Sebastiano Carezo in 1780. Originally in a triple meter ("Bolero" by Maurice Ravel is the best known example of triple-meter Bolero), it morphed into a duple meter form in Cuba. As Afro-Cuban musical styles matured toward the end of the 19th century, Cuban musician Pepe Sanchez composed the first known Cuban Bolero, "Tristeza" ("Sadness"). By the early 1900s, the immensely popular Bolero reached Mexico and Latin America, eventually becoming popular in North America by the late 1920s. Significant Bolero composers include Bugy Cárdenas and Agustín Lara in the early 1900s and, more recently, José Feliciano.

BOLERO CHARACTERISTICS

BASS GROOVES: Bolero bass grooves tend to be simple. Note the absence of the Tumbao pattern in the following example and variation.

CHORD PROGRESSIONS: Progressions vary considerably. Some are fairly simple, such as the two below, while some are quite complex and bear considerable resemblance to Jazz progressions.

1) i7 - i7 - bVI9 - V9 - i7 - i7 - bVI9 - V9
2) i7- i7 - i7 - i7 - V7 - V7 - V7 - V7 - i7 - i7 - i7 - i7 - V7 - V7 - bVI7 - V7

QUARTER NOTE = 74 – 120 BPM

20

BOLERO EXAMPLE 1 (CD 1 Track 22, DVD Track 8))

BOLERO VARIATION 1

■ MERENGUE

Merengue is the national dance of the Dominican Republic, officially promoted as such by the dictator Rafaél Leonidas Trujillo-Molina (in power, 1930–1961). Like most Salsa music, Merengue traces its roots back to African slaves. Due to French occupation of the island of Hispaniola (the Dominican Republic shares it with Haiti), the music of the Dominican Republic combined African dance with the French Minuet, resulting in the first forms of Merengue in the late 18th and early 19th centuries. Traditional Merengue instrumentation consisted of tambora (rope-tuned drum with goatskin head), güira (shaker), and accordion. After becoming established as the Dominican national dance in the early 20th century, Merengue made its way to the United States, primarily through New York City, in the 1950s. It is now a well established form of dance music throughout the world.

Although it is not of Cuban origin, Merengue is often played in a Salsa setting. So, it's important for a working bassist to be familiar with the style.

MERENGUE CHARACTERISTICS

BASS GROOVES: Merengue bass grooves tend to be simple. Note the absence of the Tumbao pattern in the following example and variations.

TECHNIQUE: Finger style. The notes lean more to staccato, with a distinct quarter-note percussive sound and feel, in contrast to the legato notes of Mambo and Cha Cha. In Merengue, it's fairly common to play the fifth rather than the root on beat 1.

CHORD PROGRESSIONS: Merengue progressions are simple: nearly always a I chord and a V chord in two-bar combinations.

1) I7 - V7 - I7 - V7
2) V7 - I - V7 - I
3) I - I - V7 - V7
4) V7 - V7 - I - I

QUARTER NOTE = 240+ BPM

MERENGUE EXAMPLE 1 (CD 1 TRACK 23, DVD TRACK 9)

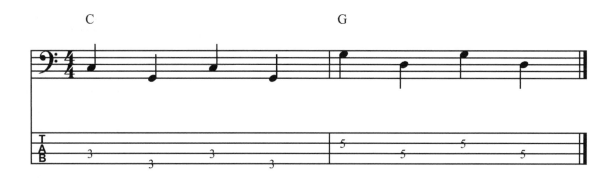

MERENGUE EXAMPLE 1 VARIATION 1

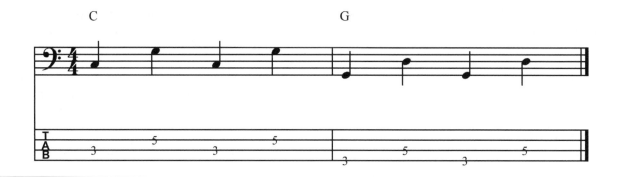

MERENGUE VARIATION 2

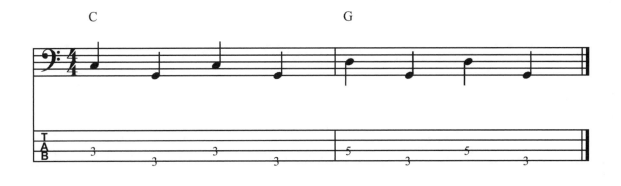

CUMBIA

CUMBIA DATES TO THE EARLY 1800s and is from the Caribbean coast of Colombia. Its roots can be traced to Gaitero music—folk music played on cactus-wood flutes, maracas, African hand drums, and other instruments. Similar in evolution to other Afro-Cuban genres, Cumbia developed through the mixing of African slaves and their descendants with local tribes and settlers in the new world.

Rhythmically, Cumbia is characterized by a constant pattern on a high drum, wood block, or bell, with intricate rhythms in the maracas and other hand drums. Over the years, lyrics were added to Cumbia song arrangements, and eventually orchestral and electronic instruments were added. Today, Cumbia is popular throughout the Americas, and is frequently included in the repertoire of Afro-Cuban ensembles.

CUMBIA CHARACTERISTICS

BASS GROOVES: Cumbia bass grooves tend to be simple. Note the absence of the Tumbao pattern in the following example and variations.

TECHNIQUE: Finger style, with the downbeat sustained; beats 3 and 4 are played in a more staccato manner.

CHORD PROGRESSIONS: Cumbia progressions are simple, like those of Merengue—nearly always a I chord and a V chord in two-bar combinations. As in Merengue, it's common to play the fifth rather than the root on beat one.

1) I - V - I - V
2) V - I - V - I
3) I - I - V - V
4) V - V - I - I

QUARTER NOTE = 160 – 252 BPM (with a double-time feel)

CUMBIA EXAMPLE 1 (CD 1 TRACK 24, DVD TRACK 10)

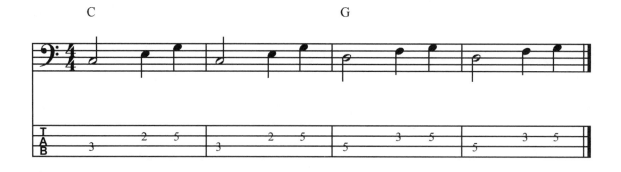

■ AFRO-CUBAN JAZZ

THE DIFFERENCE BETWEEN AFRO-CUBAN JAZZ and Salsa is the difference between music for listening and music for dancing. In Jazz, a listening music, you can be freer in your approach, whereas in Salsa the rhythmic feel must always be clear.

The predominant styles in Afro-Cuban Jazz are derived from the Mambo, Cha Cha, and Afro-Cuban 6/8. Songs that fall into the Afro-Cuban Jazz genre are of two kinds: 1) those written as Afro-Cuban Jazz songs (with clave already defined); 2) those adapted to the style (clave to be determined). In the first case, the lead sheet of the song will indicate the kind of clave and the order to be used (e.g., "2–3 Rumba"). In the second case, the order and type of clave will be determined by the musicians.

Just as in Salsa, the music is still based upon the clave. Once again, determining the order (3–2 or 2–3)

depends upon which way the song sounds best—that is, how the accents of the rhythm of the melody fit with the clave pattern.

In addition to the 3–2 Son clave (and its reversed order, the "2–3 clave"), the Rumba clave is also sometimes used.

RUMBA CLAVE

The sole difference between the Rumba and Son claves is the placement of the third note on the three side. Whereas in Son clave the third note is played directly on beat 4, in Rumba clave it is played on the "and" of beat 4. If Rumba clave is to be used, it must be stated as such: 3–2 Rumba, or 2–3 Rumba. Otherwise, musicians will assume that the third accent of the three side is on beat 4, as in Son clave.

3–2 RUMBA CLAVE (CD 1 TRACK 25)

2–3 RUMBA CLAVE (CD 1 TRACK 26)

AFRO-CUBAN JAZZ CHARACTERISTICS

BASS GROOVES: All of the above bass lines for Mambo/Cha Cha can be used in Afro-Cuban Jazz. When playing Mambo patterns in a Jazz setting, the bass line may vary much more than in Salsa. When there are three chords per measure, the easiest thing to do is to play the roots of the chords as they appear, and then return to a Tumbao pattern when there are only one or two chords per measure. When there are four chords per measure, the easiest choice is to play roots on each quarter note. However, it is best not to think of this as walking bass (as in Blues or Jazz), as the notes are more legato (sustained) than is typical when walking.

CHORD PROGRESSIONS: Afro-Cuban Jazz progressions vary greatly, overlapping considerably with conventional Jazz progressions (e.g., use of partial cycle of fifths). (See Jazz chapter for more progressions.)

    1) vii7 - III7 - iii7 - VI7 - vi7 - II7 - ii7 - V7
    2) i7 - i7/IV9 - bVII7 - bVII7 - bVII7 - bVII7/bIII9 - bVI7 - bVI7
    3) i7/IV9 - i7/IV9 - i7/bVII - i7/bVII7 - bIII9 - bVI7 - bvi7/bII7/iv7/bVII7 - bIII7
    4) I7 - II7/V7 - I7 - iv7/bVII - bIII/I7 - iv7/bVII - bIII/bVII - bIII
    5) i7 - IV - i7 - IV - iv - bVII - i7 - IV - v7 - v7 - iv7 - bVII
    6) I7 - II9 - bVII9 - V9
    7) i7/IV9 - i7/IV9 - i7/IV9 - i7/IV9 - iv7/bVII9 - iv7/bVII9 - i7/IV9 - i7/IV9 - v7 - iv7 - i7/IV9 - i7/IV9

QUARTER NOTE = 100 – 200+ BPM

AFRO-CUBAN JAZZ EXAMPLE 1 (CD 1 TRACK 27, DVD TRACK 11)

Notice the similarity of this pattern to the familiar Tumbao pattern from Mambo/Cha Cha.

AFRO-CUBAN JAZZ EXAMPLE 1 VARIATION 1

AFRO-CUBAN JAZZ EXAMPLE 2 (CD 1, TRACK 28)

Notice that the clave pattern reverses at bar 2 in this example.

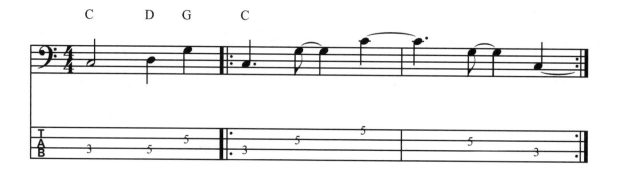

AFRO-CUBAN JAZZ EXAMPLE 2 VARIATION 1

AFRO-CUBAN JAZZ EXAMPLE 3

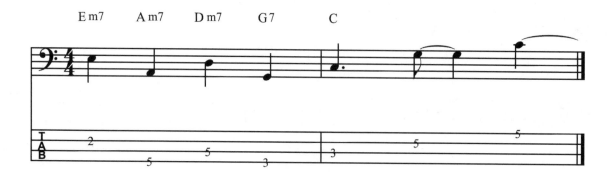

■ AFRO-CUBAN 6/8

IN ADDITION TO THE DUPLE METERS covered in this chapter, 6/8 is a common groove in Afro-Cuban music. Although not often used in a Salsa setting, it frequently appears in Afro-Cuban Jazz. It is also immensely adaptable; it can be used as a two-measure pattern with all Jazz songs in 3/4.

The roots of both the duple-meter Son and Rumba claves can be found in the two-part 6/8 clave pattern. Unlike the duple rhythm of Son clave and Rumba clave, the 6/8 rhythm is based on a triple feel.

6/8 CLAVE (CD 1 TRACK 29)

It is now quite common to hear 6/8 rhythmic styles interchanged with duple-time Cuban styles such as Cha Cha, Mambo, Guaguanco, Songo, etc. So, it is highly useful to develop the ability to flow from one feel to the other.

The 6/8 bell pattern contains the clave pattern (plus two additional notes) and is easier to feel than the clave pattern. Even though the 6/8 clave may be hard to hear, concentrating on the 6/8 bell pattern will serve to hold down a 6/8 groove.

These patterns are counted in 4/4 on the CD, but they're easier to see and understand written in 6/8.

6/8 BELL PATTERN (CD 1 TRACK 30)

As stated above, any Jazz song in 3/4 may easily be adapted to the 6/8 feel by playing the groove with a two-measure 3/4 pulse. Writing the clave pattern in 3/4 clearly shows how the two parts of the pattern are played on and off the beat. Feeling the pattern in 3/4 creates an entirely different groove, though the rhythm remains exactly the same.

6/8 CLAVE PATTERN IN 3/4

Writing the 6/8 bell pattern in 3/4 clarifies even further how the accents fall on and off the beat.

6/8 BELL PATTERN IN 3/4

Once you recognize and understand 6/8 bell and clave patterns, you'll find it much easier to play authentic Afro-Cuban 6/8 bass lines. In many of the grooves, the 6/8 pattern can be heard on the percussionist's bell or trap set ride cymbal. Listening for and locking in with it allows you to lay down the characteristic solid 6/8 bass groove, even if you don't play the clave pattern.

AFRO-CUBAN 6/8 CHARACTERISTICS

BASS GROOVES: Unlike Mambo and Cha Cha grooves, Afro-Cuban 6/8 bass lines do not anticipate beat one by tying beat 4 from the previous measure to it.

QUARTER NOTE = 100+ BPM

6/8 EXAMPLE 1 (CD 1 TRACK 31, DVD TRACK 12)

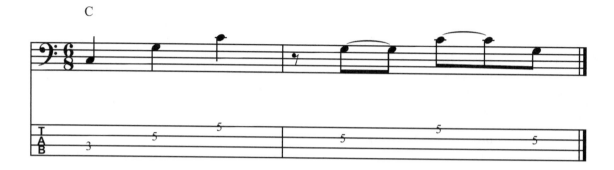

6/8 EXAMPLE 1 VARIATION 1

6/8 EXAMPLE 2

6/8 EXAMPLE 3

6/8 EXAMPLE 4

4 BLUES

IN THE POST-CIVIL WAR UNITED STATES, a mixture of field hollers, spirituals, and dance music gave birth to the Blues, and by the early 20th century Blues had emerged as its own genre. However, it was not a Blues man but a classically trained musician who first brought Blues to worldwide attention. In 1903, W.C. Handy heard a Blues musician while waiting for a train in Mississippi. He later called Blues "the weirdest music I ever heard." Despite his first impression, Handy composed many Blues songs, notably "Memphis Blues" and his immensely popular "St. Louis Blues."

Blues' infectious spirit is exemplified through legendary stories. For instance, upon hearing "Good Night Irene," the governor of Louisiana was so moved that he granted the song writer, convicted murderer Huddy "Leadbelly" Ledbetter, a full pardon. In the 1930s, guitarist/vocalist/songwriter Robert Johnson recorded many songs that would become Blues standards for Columbia Records. At about the same time, musicologist Alan Lomax traveled through the southern United States recording a huge amount of Blues music for the Smithsonian Institution. Lomax's work and the popularity of Johnson and other Blues artists, especially Bessie Smith (also recorded by Columbia) brought Blues national popularity.

Although there were bassists among the early bands (including a few "brass bass" tuba players in New Orleans styles), the bass line was normally played on the lower strings or keys on a guitar or piano. Early street corner Blues groups sometimes used washtub bass, but by the 1920s standup was the norm in groups with bassists (which were relatively few).

In the 1920s and 1930s, Blues was still primarily an acoustic music played by individual guitarists/vocalists (or sometimes pianists and vocalists) and occasionally small ensembles utilizing guitar, harmonica, and percussion instruments such as washboard, spoons, and even the musician's own body ("hambone").

The Blues changed greatly in the 1940s. In the postwar period, Chicago-based Blues artists such as Muddy Waters (McKinley Morganfield), Howlin' Wolf (Chester Burnett), Elmore James, the bassist/composer/session musician Willie Dixon, and the West Coast-based guitarist/songwriter T-Bone Walker (Aaron Thibeax Walker) began playing "electric" Blues featuring the electric guitar, amplified vocals, bass (still upright at the time), and the drum set. In 1946, Willie Dixon formed The Big Three Trio with pianist Leonard "Baby Doo" Caston and guitarist Bernardo Dennis. Other Chicago Blues legends of the 1950s and 1960s include Buddy Guy, Freddie King, and Paul Butterfield.

By the 1950s, Blues had matured into its standard 12-bar form played in swung 4/4 time (I-I-I-I-IV-IV-I-I-V-IV-I-I). The vocal melody and lyrics were organized in an A-A-B structure. A well known example is "T-bone Shuffle," by T-Bone Walker, which has been recorded by innumerable artists. (Of course, there are many Blues songs in nonstandard forms; to cite but one example from this general period, pianist Floyd Dixon's famous "Hey Bartender" is a 16-bar Blues featuring eight bars of the I chord at the beginning of the pattern).

At about the same time, a fusion took place between Swing and Blues, resulting in Jump Blues, which features horn sections, fast tempos, swung time, and walking bass. The most prominent exponents of this enormously popular style were Louis Jordan, Junior Parker (Herman Parker, Jr.), and T-Bone Walker.

When Leo Fender introduced the Fender Precision Bass (P-bass) in 1951, the role of the Blues bassist began to change, primarily because the amplified instrument was loud enough to be heard above the drums. Dancers could feel the powerful low end, along with the drum grooves, chords, horn lines, and vocals.

By the mid-1950s, Rock n' Roll (which is characterized by straight eighth notes) had begun to achieve mass popularity, and Blues artists such as Chuck Berry (Charles Edward Anderson) and Bo Diddley (Ellas Otha Bates) began to explore the straight feel, while keeping the 12-bar form.

Bo Diddley also established what has come to be known as the "Bo Diddley Beat," copied directly from a Son clave. (See Afro-Cuban chapter, page 15.) In addition, Rock and Roll also altered the 12-bar Blues form. An example is Chuck Berry's famous "Johnny B. Goode" (which is nonstandard in that the V chord at the 9th bar "hangs" on through the 10th bar rather than descends to the IV at the 10th bar).

In the 1960s, white musicians and bands (especially in England) began playing the Blues. Prominent Blues-influenced British bands and musicians of that and later eras include John Mayall, The Yardbirds, Eric Clapton, Cream, Savoy Brown, and The Rolling Stones, while in the U.S., white artists such as Paul Butterfield and Canned Heat began playing the Blues. Ironically, they had much greater success than the African-American musicians who had pioneered the form. But they did bring Blues to a far wider audience than it had ever had, and some of the established African-American Blues players benefited from this in the form of recording contracts and concert gigs. They included Albert King, Freddie King, B.B. King, and John Lee Hooker.

With the death of Jimi Hendrix in 1971, and the end of the late-1960s/early-1970s cultural upheaval, Blues lost much of its audience despite the arrival of new Blues performers such as Son Seals and the spectacular success of Eric Clapton's one-off, Derek and the Dominoes. With the rise of Disco and Punk, Blues appeared all but dead by the end of the decade.

However, in the mid-1980s, Stevie Ray Vaughan, with his blistering guitar virtuosity, almost single handedly brought Blues to greater popularity than ever before. At the same time, Robert Cray resurrected and modernized West Coast Blues, updating the style popularized by T-Bone Walker in the 1940s and 1950s.

Despite the death of Vaughan in 1990, Blues has retained its popularity. There are now annual Blues festivals in many American cities, and Blues is one of the most popular forms of music in the U.S.

BLUES BASSISTS

As the primary Blues instrument is unquestionably guitar, it is fitting that one of the first prominent Blues bassists was guitarist/songwriter Willie Dixon. He appeared with a host of players on Chess Records recordings, including Howlin' Wolf, Sonny Boy Williamson, Muddy Waters, Little Walter, Bo Diddley, John Lee Hooker, and Chuck Berry. Other noted Blues bassists of the classic Chicago period include Leonard Ware (with Elmore James), Mac Arnold (with John Lee Hooker), Edgar Willis (on many Ray Charles sessions), and Ernest "Big" Crawford, who appeared on many classic Chess Records recordings.

Blues guitar legend B.B. King (Riley B. King) originally recorded with Tuf Green on bass in 1949. Additional B.B. King bassists include Willie Weeks and Ray Brown, with Gerald Jemmott on B.B. King's famous "The Thrill is Gone" sessions. B. B. King's later recordings featured bassist Nathan East, who also recorded and toured with Eric Clapton.

Other notable Blues bassists include Barry Oakley of The Allman Brothers, who helped bring an improvisational feel to the Blues, incorporating Jazz and Rock into traditional Blues forms. His legacy continued after his tragic death with Allen Woody and later Oteil Burbridge joining the Allmans. Current notable Blues bassists include Tommy Shannon (formerly with Stevie Ray Vaughan) and Karl Sevareid (formerly of the Robert Cray Band).

GROOVES

In Blues, there are seven prominent grooves: Jump; Shuffle; Boogie; 12/8 Slow Blues; Blues Rumba; Blues Mambo; and Blues Rock. The following comments apply to all.

BLUES CHARACTERISTICS

SCALES: Bassists will normally use the Blues Scale in minor keys.

A BLUES SCALE (CD 1 TRACK 32)

E Blues Scale

Blues Characteristics (CONT'D)

SCALES (CONT'D): Bassists will, however, normally add the major 3rd (e.g., G# in the key of E) when playing in major keys. The use of other tones, especially in walk-ups, is also common.

GROOVES: Notes are primarily determined by chord structure. For example, if the band plays a G7 chord, the bassist would primarily use the notes G, B, D, and F as well as notes from the Blues scale as mentioned above. The bassist virtually always plays the root on the first beat of a measure.

Most classic Blues bassists played repeating lines, which is one reason for the genre's popularity—such lines help make the music danceable. Simple, uncluttered lines work better than lines with a lot of fills or improvising. It's best to leave the focus on the singer and the soloists rather than the bass.

TONE: Bass +3 to +9 dB, Mids flat to +3 dB @ 300 Hz, Treble flat to -6 dB. In Blues, bass tone varies, but is not bright. Flat wound strings, matching those played by the original Blues bassists, are sometimes used by those seeking a "classic" sound, though round wound strings are the norm. Depending on your preferences and those of your bandmates, you can add more mids and cut back the bass boost slightly.

TECHNIQUE: Finger style predominates, although it is possible to play Blues with a pick.

CHORD PROGRESSIONS: The major chords in Blues progressions are almost always dominant 7th-type (V7-type) or (especially on the IV and V chords) dominant 9th-type (V9-type) chords. The minor chords will almost always be minor 7th chords. Except in Jazz Blues (see "Small Band" section of the Jazz chapter), it's very unusual to find altered chords in Blues, except for the V7#9 chord which is found fairly often as the final chord in turnarounds. (See "Turnarounds" on the next page.)

12-Bar Blues

1) I7 - I7 - I7 - I7 - IV7 - IV7 - I7 - I7 - V7 - IV7 - I7 - I7
   (Note that V7 [or V7#9] is often substituted for the I in the final bar, either for the entire bar or the final two beats. Also, IV9 and V9 are often substituted for the IV7 and V7 chords.)

2) I7 - I7 - I7 - I7 - IV9 - IV9 - I7 - I7 - V9 - bVI9/V9 - I7 - I7

3) I7 - IV7 - I7 - I7 - IV7 - IV7 - I7 - I7 - V7 - IV7 - I7 - I7
   (The "fast four" [on bar 2] is a very common 12-bar variation. Again, IV9 and V9 are often substituted for the IV7 and V7)

4) i7 - i7 - i7 - i7 - iv7 - iv7 - i7 - i7 - v7 - iv7 - i7 - i7
   (Again, the V7 or V7#9 is often substituted for the i on the final two beats of the final bar.)

5) i7 - i7 - i7 - i7 - iv7 - iv7 - i7 - i7 - V7 - iv7 - i7 - i7

6) i7 - i7 - i7 - i7 - iv7 - iv7 - i7 - i7 - V9 - bVI9/V9 - i7 - i7

7) I7 - I7 - I7 - I7 - IV7 - IV7 - I7/ii7 - iii7/biii7 - V9 - bV9I/V9 - I7/IV9 - I7/V7#9
   (This variation is relatively uncommon and is mostly found toward the jazzier side of Blues.)

BLUES CHARACTERISTICS (CONT'D)

8-BAR BLUES

1) I7 - I7 - IV7 - I7 - V7 - IV7 - I7 - V7

(The final two bars are often replaced by the turnaround I/IV - I/V.)

2) I7 - V - IV - IV - I7 - V - I7 - I7

(This is the "Key to Highway" progression which is unique to that song. It's included here solely because it's so famous that some might assume that it's the standard 8-bar Blues progression.)

16-BAR BLUES

1) I7 - I7 - I7 - I7 - I7 - I7 - I7 - I7 - IV9 - IV9 - I7 - I7 - V9 - IV9 - I7 - I7

2) I7 - I7 - I7 - I7 - IV7 - IV7 - I7 - I7 - IV7 - IV7 - I7 - I7 - V7 - IV7 - I7 - I7

BOOGIES

1) i7 - i7 - i7 - i7 (etc.)

2) I7 - I7 - I7 - I7 (etc.)

3) i7 - i7 - i7 - i7/i7/bIII/IV - i7 - i7 - i7 - i7/i7/bIII/IV

(This pattern is usually played in E, as is the next progression.)

4) I7 - I7 - I7 - I7/I7/bIII/IV - I7 - I7 - I7 - I7/7I/bIII/IV

TURNAROUNDS

Turnarounds are very common in Blues; they replace the I chord in the last two bars of a progression. In turnarounds, the chords usually change every two beats. In such cases, the bass normally plays half notes on the roots of all the chords.

Turnarounds are more common in fast songs than in slow songs. They also tend to be far more common in songs in major keys than in songs in minor keys.

The first turnaround listed is the most common.

1) I7/IV7 - I7/V7 or I7/IV9 - I7/V7#9 or in minor keys i7/iv7 - i7/V7#9

Other common ones include:

2) I7 - I7/V7 or I7 - I7/V7#9 or in minor keys i7 - i7/V7#9

3) I7/vi7 - ii7/V7

Less common ones include:

4) I/bIIImaj7 - IImaj7/bIImaj7

(This is normally found only in Jazz Blues.)

5) I7/bVI9 - V9/bV9

(Rare)

EXTENDED AND FALSE ENDINGS: It's common to play the final four bars of a song three times before ending it. It's much less common, but it is done, to apparently come to a final ending, pause, and then begin playing again, restating the head or the hook in one or two additional verses before actually ending the song.

JUMP BLUES CHARACTERISTICS

GROOVES: Jump Blues bass lines emulate walking lines played by a keyboard player's left hand. When walking, the bassist plays all four quarter notes of every measure. In Jump Blues, it's fairly common for the bassist to play quarter-note arpeggios. For more on walking see the Jazz chapter's Big Band section.

QUARTER NOTE = 160 – 200 BPM Note that, as in all Blues with swung eighth notes, the tempo is actually that of a dotted quarter. In this case, **dotted quarter = 160 – 200 BPM**. This oddity is due to the fact that Blues, even though usually swung, is usually written in 4/4 time.

JUMP BLUES EXAMPLE 1 (CD 1 TRACK 33, DVD TRACK 13)

JUMP BLUES EXAMPLE 1 VARIATION 1

JUMP BLUES EXAMPLE 1 VARIATION 2

SHUFFLE CHARACTERISTICS

BASS GROOVES: When playing a shuffle, a bassist commonly plays the first and third eighth-note triplets of every triplet grouping on every beat. The downbeat triplets are usually accented louder than the offbeat triplets. At very fast tempos it's more practical to walk than to shuffle notes.

In "Chicago Shuffles," with a slow and relaxed feel with a "four on the floor" bass drum pattern, a bassist will normally walk in order to match the quarter notes on the bass drum rather than play a shuffle pattern. (See Jump Blues example and variations on pages 34 and 35; also see the section on walking in the Jazz chapter.)

There are three feels in playing shuffles: 1) Staccato—e.g., Example 1; 2) Legato—e.g., Example 2 Variation 1; 3) Short-long—e.g., Example 4.

Because it's helpful to bassists to understand the drum set shuffle pattern, we've placed it at the top of the next page. It (and the many variations on it) is used in all swung Blues styles.

QUARTER NOTE = 80 – 200+ BPM Again, note that the tempo is actually that of a dotted quarter. The fastest tempos are normally found in Stevie Ray Vaughan-type songs.

SHUFFLE DRUM PATTERN

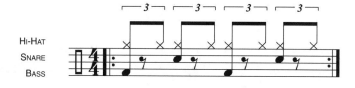

SHUFFLE EXAMPLE 1 (CD 1 TRACK 34, DVD TRACK 87)

SHUFFLE EXAMPLE 1 VARIATION 1

SHUFFLE EXAMPLE 2 (CD 1 TRACK 35, DVD TRACK 14)

SHUFFLE EXAMPLE 2 VARIATION 1

SHUFFLE EXAMPLE 2 VARIATION 2

SHUFFLE EXAMPLE 3 (CD 1 TRACK 36, DVD TRACK 15)

SHUFFLE EXAMPLE 4

SHUFFLE EXAMPLE 5

The following groove is suited to a hard "rock shuffle." When using it, a bassist could retain the pattern throughout or could shift to simply shuffling the roots of the IV and V chords while retaining this pattern for the I chord.

SHUFFLE SUMMARY (12-Bar Pattern)

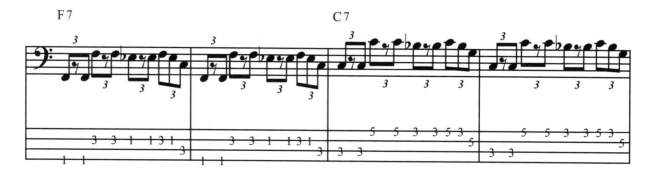

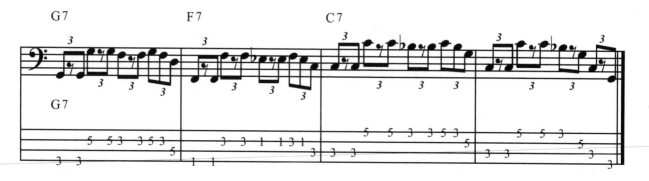

BOOGIE EXAMPLE 1 (CD 1 TRACK 37, DVD TRACK 16)

BOOGIE EXAMPLE 1 VARIATION 1

BOOGIE EXAMPLE 1 VARIATION 2

BOOGIE EXAMPLE 2

This classic line is played as a 2-bar phrase.

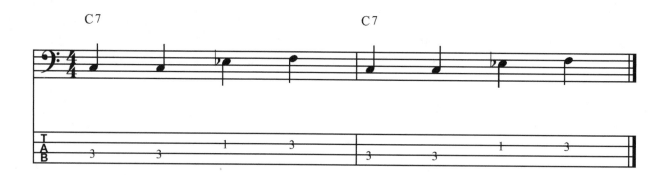

12/8 SLOW BLUES CHARACTERISTICS

BASS GROOVES: Rhythmic patterns in 12/8 Slow Blues grooves vary considerably, ranging from steady eighth notes to a dotted-half-note pulse. The following bass lines can be used not only as grooves in separate songs, but within the same song, depending on the tempo and the song itself.

QUARTER NOTE = 50 – 80 BPM

SLOW BLUES EXAMPLE 1 (CD 1 TRACK 38)

SLOW BLUES EXAMPLE 1 VARIATION 1 (CD 1 TRACK 39)

Slow Blues Example 1 Variation 2

A 7

Slow Blues Example 1 Variation 3 (CD 1 Track 40, DVD Track 17)

E

Slow Blues Example 1 Variation 4

In 12/8 Slow Blues, a bassist will sometimes play all 12 eighth notes. This is usually done only in the slowest tunes.

E

Slow Blues Example 2

Slow Blues Example 3

Slow Blues can also be notated/felt in 4/4.

Slow Blues Example 4

E 7

A 7   E 7

B 7   A 7   E 7

BLUES RUMBA CHARACTERISTICS

BASS GROOVES: Unlike other forms of Blues (except Blues Rock and Blues Mambo), Blues Rumbas are played with straight eighth notes. It is helpful for a bassist to understand the Rumba drum pattern, reproduced on the following page.

QUARTER NOTE = 108 – 160 BPM

BLUES RUMBA DRUM PATTERN

BLUES RUMBA EXAMPLE 1 (CD 1 TRACK 41, DVD TRACK 18)

G7

BLUES RUMBA EXAMPLE 1 VARIATION 1

G7

BLUES RUMBA EXAMPLE 1 VARIATION 2 (CD 1 TRACK 42)

G7

BLUES RUMBA EXAMPLE 2 (CD 1 TRACK 43)

BLUES RUMBA SUMMARY (12-BAR PATTERN)

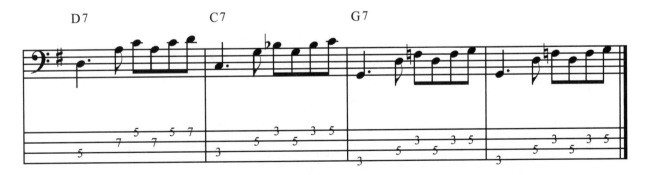

BLUES MAMBO CHARACTERISTICS

BASS GROOVES: Although the terms "Blues Mambo" and "Blues Rumba" are often used interchangeably, the terms refer to very different grooves (even though both are Afro-Cuban styles and both use straight eighths). In addition to having different rhythmic patterns, Blues Mambo has a narrower tempo range than Blues Rumba. It is helpful for a bassist to understand the Mambo drum pattern, reproduced below.

QUARTER NOTE = 96 – 120 BPM

BLUES MAMBO DRUM PATTERN

BLUES MAMBO EXAMPLE 1 (CD 1 TRACK 44, DVD TRACK 19)

BLUES MAMBO EXAMPLE 1 VARIATION 1 (CD 1 TRACK 45)

BLUES MAMBO EXAMPLE 1 VARIATION 2

BLUES MAMBO EXAMPLE 1 VARIATION 3

BLUES ROCK CHARACTERISTICS

BASS GROOVES: Blues Rock is essentially Rock that utilizes the 12-bar Blues pattern and variations on it as a harmonic structure. Blues Rock uses straight eighths, and the drum groove is normally the very familiar standard Rock pattern, reproduced below.

QUARTER NOTE = 80 – 160 BPM

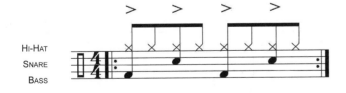

Blues Rock Example 1 (CD 1 Track 46, DVD Track 20)

Blues Rock Example 1 Variation 1 (CD 1 Track 47)

Blues Rock Example 1 Variation 2

BLUES ROCK EXAMPLE 1 VARIATION 3

BLUES ROCK EXAMPLE 1 VARIATION 4

BLUES ROCK EXAMPLE 2

BLUES ROCK EXAMPLE 3

BLUES ROCK EXAMPLE 4

5 BRAZILIAN

"LATIN MUSIC" is often used as a genric term, as if there were no distinctions between Afro-Cuban and Brazilian styles. But there are major distinctions, and it's important to understand them. By becoming familiar with the bass lines in this chapter and those in the Afro-Cuban chapter, a bassist will be able to recognize and play appropriate bass lines in almost any Latin style.

The roots of Brazilian go back over 400 years to when Brazil was a Portuguese colony. To manage the abundant slave population, the government supported the rule of slave kings and queens in each tribe. Their coronation ceremonies and celebrations were called "Maracatu." With the abolition of slavery in 1888, and with it slave royalty, Maracatu emerged as the musical ensemble and dance for street celebrations in the northeastern state of Pernambuco. The festivals evolved to include dancers and a "bateria" (percussion battery).

This legacy continues today, as Brazilian music is often performed in the tradition of the Maracatu (with a bateria comprised of instruments such as ago-go bells and surdo drums) far beyond the borders of Brazil. Large ensembles, rhythmic and percussion dominance, costumes, and dancers all create a celebratory atmosphere.

In contrast, in dance bands a single drum set player produces the different rhythms of the bateria, while the bass player augments the percussion, supporting it with a non-deviating steady pulse.

Prominent Brazilian bass players, and non-Brazilian bass players accomplished in the style, include Luizao Maia, Sizao Machado, Nico Assumpçao, Nilson Matta, Tommy Williams, and Ron Carter.

BRAZILIAN CHARACTERISTICS (ALL STYLES)

TONE: **Bass +3 to +9 dB, Mids flat, Treble -3 to -6 dB.** Emulates upright.

GEAR: Brazilian styles are well suited to upright bass, especially Samba with finger slaps between notes. Electric bass and fretless electric bass can also be used.

SAMBA

SAMBA IS THE MOST FAMOUS Brazilian musical style. The term is derived from the West African fertility dance "Semba," meaning "dance of the bellybutton." The styles presented in this section are derivatives of the Samba styles played in Carnaval.

What we now recognize as Samba developed in working class areas in Bahia and Rio de Janiero during the early part of the 20th century. Stemming from the tradition of the Maracatu, Samba ensembles had large percussion sections. Samba became popular nationally in the 1930s via radio broadcasts. It gained worldwide recognition around 1940 when it became a featured musical style in Hollywood films, most notably those starring Portuguese singer/musician Carmen Miranda. In the 1950s and 1960s, artists such as Stan Getz and Sergio Mendez introduced Samba to the Jazz genre.

The bass playing ideas presented here can be applied to Jazz performed in a Samba style or to authentic Brazilian music. The consistent and driving bass line pattern in Samba mimics the rhythm of the surdo drum, which matches the rhythm played in modern ensembles on the bass drum.

SAMBA CHARACTERISTICS

BASS GROOVES: 1) Play mainly roots and fifths; 2) Make use of repetitive patterns, both melodic and rhythmic—typically dotted quarter note with eighth note; 3) Play legato rather than staccato. Even though Samba is normally played and often notated in cut time (2/2), all examples here are presented in 4/4 for ease of learning. The important thing to remember is that *the pulse is two beats per measure.*

TECHNIQUE: Finger style. There are numerous opportunities for soloing and standing out.

CHORD PROGRESSIONS: There are no common chord progressions in Samba. However, commonalities do exist: 1) Dominant 9th-type chords are common (as opposed to the major 7th chords characteristic of Bossa Nova); 2) Chord progressions are generally simpler and more repetitive than those of Bossa Nova, due in part to much faster tempos.

1) **ii7 - iii7 - VI9 - VI9 - ii7 - iii7 - VI9 - VI9**
2) **V9 - I7 - V9 - I7 - I7 - I7 - IV9 - IV9 - II7 - II7 - V7 - V7**
3) **i9 - i9 - i9 - i9**
4) **Imaj7 - vi7 - ii7 - V7 - Imaj7 - vi7 - II7 - #IIdim7 - iii7 - vi7 - vii7 - III7 - VImaj7 - VImaj7 - ii - V7**

QUARTER NOTE = 170 – 260 BPM

SAMBA DRUM PATTERN

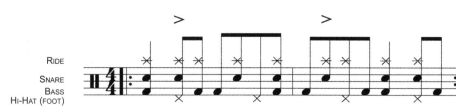

SAMBA EXAMPLE 1 (CD 1 TRACK 48)

The following example and its two variations show the most common rhythmic figure in Samba bass lines.

SAMBA EXAMPLE 1 VARIATION 1

D7

SAMBA EXAMPLE 1 VARIATION 2 (CD 1 TRACK 49, DVD TRACK 21)

D7

SAMBA EXAMPLE 2

D7

SAMBA EXAMPLE 2 VARIATION 1 (CD 1 TRACK 50)

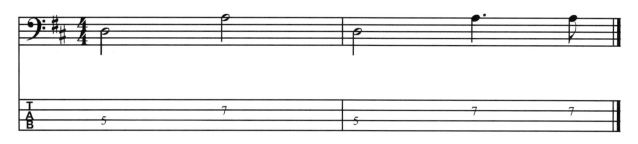

SAMBA EXAMPLE 3

SAMBA EXAMPLE 3 VARIATION 1

■ BAIAO

THE ROOTS OF BAIAO (pronounced "by owe" or "by own") can be traced back to the northeastern Brazilian state of Paraiba. Though Baiao developed from the stylized dances of European settlers accompanied by Brazilian instruments, it allegedly originated with the dancing of Cangaceiros (Brazilian bandits). The pri-

mary percussion instrument was originally a zabumba (a large bass drum) played on both sides in a syncopated rhythm.

Baiao's development was greatly influenced by radio appearances in the 1930s and 1940s of musician Luis Gonzaga. Prior to this, Baiao was mainly an instrumental form, traditionally incorporating the zabumba, accordion, vocals, pandeiro (a tambourine without the jangles) and triangle. With air play, Baiao became popular throughout Brazil. At the same time, Baiao ensembles began to include the guitar. By the 1960s, Baiao rhythms made their way to the United States and into popular music in songs like Burt Bacharach's "Do You Know the Way to San Jose?" Baiao can now be found in American Jazz in compositions by artists such as Joe Henderson and Chick Corea.

BAIAO CHARACTERISTICS

GROOVES: Even though Baiao is often played and notated in cut time (2/2), all examples here are presented in 4/4 for ease of learning. The important thing to remember is that the pulse is two beats per measure.

Because it's helpful to bassists to know the Baiao drum pattern, we've included it here. Notice the resemblance of Baiao bass lines and Baiao's bass drum pattern (**one** and two **and** three and **four** and) to those of some New Orleans and Afro-Cuban styles, and the absence of the characteristic Samba/Bossa Nova bass drum pattern (**one** and two **and three** and four **and one** and two **and three** and four **and one** . . .).

CHORD PROGRESSIONS: Baiao progressions are similar to those of Samba.

1) I9 - I9 - ii7 - V7 - iii9 - VI7 - ii7 - bII
2) I7 - I7 - I7 - I7 - IV7 - IV7 - I7 - I7 - V7 - IV7 - I7 - bIII7
3) I9 - I9 - I9 - I9 - bVI7 - V7 - IV7 - IV7 - III7 - bIII7 - bVI7 - bVI7 - v7 - v7 - I9 - I9

QUARTER NOTE = 170 – 240+ BPM

BAIAO DRUM PATTERN

BAIAO EXAMPLE 1 (CD 1 TRACK 51)

BAIAO EXAMPLE 1 VARIATION 1 (CD 1 TRACK 52, DVD TRACK 22)

BAIAO EXAMPLE 1 VARIATION 2

BAIAO EXAMPLE 1 VARIATION 3

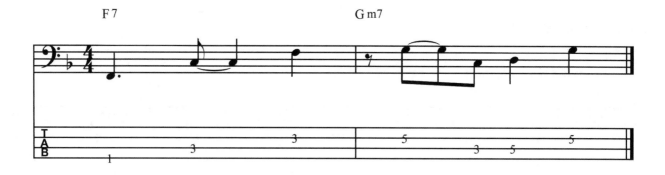

F7

BOSSA NOVA

WHILE SAMBA MUSIC traditionally dealt with the hardships of the Brazilian working class, Bossa Nova focused on the idyllic atmosphere of the prosperous neighborhoods along the beaches of Rio de Janeiro. Similarly, Bossa Nova composers and musicians tended to come from the middle and upper classes. To reflect its luxurious-lifestyle theme, Bossa Nova borrowed the rich chord structures found in American Jazz while retaining the drum rhythms of Samba, but at a slower and more relaxed tempo.

Bossa Nova was born in the 1950s, early examples being guitarist Joao Gilberto's song "Bim Bom" and, later, Antonio Carlos Jobim's "Chega de Saudade", and very quickly became popular in Brazil. In 1963, "The Girl from Ipanema" ("Garota de Ipanema"), written by Vinicius de Moraes and Antonio Carlos Jobim, established the style worldwide. Since the song was first recorded, over 300 recording artists have covered it.

By the mid-1960s, Bossa Nova had become accepted as a common style within American Jazz. As with Samba, American Jazz standards are often composed or played in Bossa Nova style (e.g., "Blue Bossa," by Kenny Dorham, with saxophonist Joe Henderson and bassist Butch Warren). In addition, variations on Bossa Nova can even be found in Rock music in songs such as "Break On Through" and "Light My Fire" by the Doors, and "Aja," by Steely Dan.

The Bossa Nova grooves which follow will work with both American Jazz standards and authentic Brazilian Bossa Nova. The constant bass pattern is identical to the one played in Samba, once again matching the rhythm of the bass drum in the first two examples. The drummer's ride hand commonly plays a consistent sequence of eighth notes, while the snare hand plays a rim click pattern often mislabeled as the "Brazilian Clave."

BOSSA NOVA CHARACTERISTICS

GROOVES: The grooves are written and felt in 4/4, unlike in Samba and Baiao.

CHORD PROGRESSIONS: There are no common chord progressions in Bossa Nova. However, commonalities do exist:

1) Major 7th chords are commonly used (often as the I chord).
2) Chord alterations (flatted fifths, sharp fifths, etc.) are common.
3) Step-wise and chromatic motion is common.
4) A chord progressing to another a tritone away is fairly common.
5) Cycle of fifths movement is very common.

Bossa Nova Characteristics (cont'd)

Chord Progressions (cont'd):

Since chord patterns vary a great deal, the most useful approach is to look at standard Bossa Novas, such as "Black Orpheus," "Desafinado," "Girl from Ipanema," "One Note Samba," etc. (See Listening Appendix.)

When b5 and #5 chords (e.g., 7b5 or 7#5, or 9b5 or 9#5) appear, as they will in Bossa Nova and standard Jazz, you need to take them into account. The easiest thing to do is to play the b5 or #5 where a normal fifth would appear in your bass line. In the case of b9 or #9 chords, you should ignore the alterations unless you're using them in the only way possible: as passing tones on weak beats or offbeats.

1) Imaj7 - Imaj7 - ii7 - VI7 - ii7 - ii7- iv7 - bVII7 - iii7 - biii7 - ii7 - V7
2) I13 - I13 - bVIIsus4 - VII7 - I13 - I13 - iii7 - VI7
3) i7/IV13 - i7/IV13 - i7/IV13 - i7/IV13 - Imaj7 - bvidim7 - III13 - V9
4) I - i7 - II7 - II7 - V7 - V7 - I - ii7b5/V9
5) Imaj7 - Imaj7 - II7 - II7 - ii7 - bII7b5 - Imaj7 - bII7b5
6) Imaj7 - Imaj7 - bIImaj7 - bIImaj7 - bV7 - bV7 - bii7 - bii7

Quarter Note = 100 – 168 BPM

Bossa Nova Drum Pattern

Bossa Nova Example 1 (CD 1 Track 53, DVD Track 23)

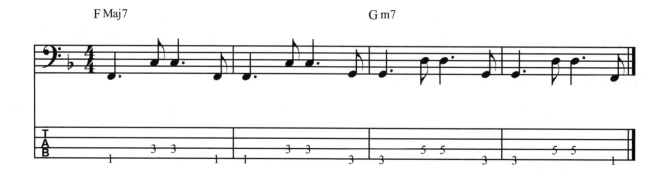

BOSSA NOVA EXAMPLE 1 VARIATION 1

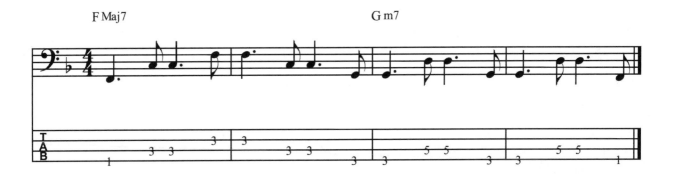

BOSS NOVA EXAMPLE 1 VARIATION 2 (CD 1 TRACK 54, DVD TRACK 24)

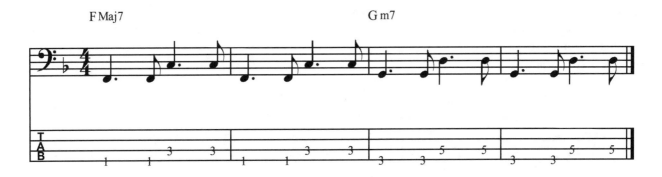

BOSSA NOVA EXAMPLE 2

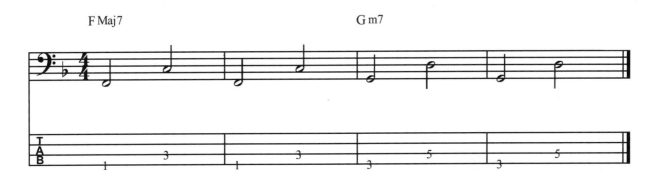

BOSSA NOVA EXAMPLE 2 VARIATION 1

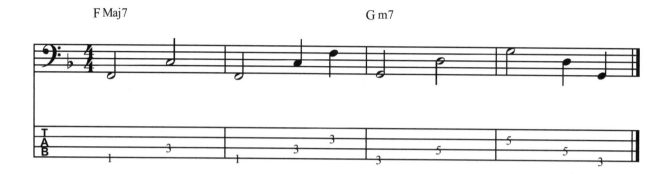

BOSSA NOVA EXAMPLE 3

Notice the flatted fifth in the third measure. The only time you'd play a flatted fifth is when the chord contains one. Most typically this would be in a 7b5 chord, although you'll also find flatted fifths in other altered chords such as 7b5b9 and 9b5 chords.

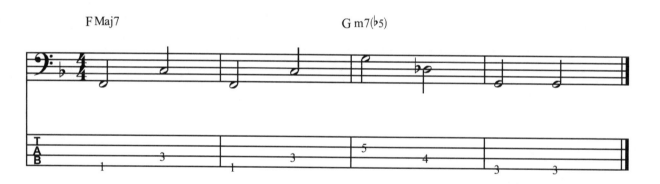

6 CAJUN / ZYDECO

THE TERMS "CAJUN" AND "ZYDECO" refer to two distinct styles, both stemming from French cultures in southern Louisiana. Traditionalists say *lache pas la patate* ("don't drop the potato"), meaning "don't let go of the old culture," more specifically, don't allow Cajun music to become a hybrid musical form. However, as current Cajun and Zydeco musicians often perform both genres, it's appropriate to include both in this chapter. An appreciation and understanding of the differences between the two will aid in accurate and authentic performance of both.

Cajuns ("Acadians," French-Canadians exiled from Nova Scotia) came to central and southwest Louisiana in the 18th century. Originally, Cajun music revolved around the fiddle and stomping the floor on beats 1 and 3 (in 4/4 time) while playing a homemade triangle called the *"tit fer"* (little iron). Following World War II, Cajun musicians began using the accordion, after American servicemen brought back the German-style (diatonic, single-row button) accordion from Europe. Similar to a harmonica with bellows, the German-style accordion has a fixed, limited tonal range, so, it lends itself harmonically and structurally to simple music. Its volume soon made it one of the primary instruments within the genre.

In addition to 4/4 tunes, Cajun music features many songs in waltz time (3/4), often subdivided into a 9/8 feel (3/4 with a triplet pulse).

Zydeco has its roots in African and Caribbean music and the Creole culture (Creoles being the racially mixed offspring of Europeans, American Indians, and Africans), and is still sometimes referred to by its early names, Swamp Pop and Swamp Rock. The term Zydeco is attributed to accordion legend Clifton Chenier, who popularized the song *"Les Haricots Sont Pas Sales"* ("The Beans Are Unsalted"). *"Les Haricots"* (pronounced "layzarico") evolved into the term Zydeco.

The two leading instruments in Zydeco are the accordion (multi-row button or keyboard varieties, both of which can play sharp and flat accidentals) and a percussion instrument called a *"frottoir,"* a rub board often worn on the chest. Invented in the 1940s by Willie Landry and Clifton Chenier (with his brother Cleveland Chenier), the rub board has become Zydeco's signature rhythmic voice. With it up front and dictating the rhythm, the style is up tempo, with the drummer and bass player powerfully driving the band. Zydeco music is predominantly played in 4/4 (shuffled or straight), with fewer 3/4 (and far fewer 9/8) tunes than in Cajun music.

Although the two musical styles maintained marked differences well into the 20th century, Cajun and Zydeco cultures began to blend as far back as the early 1900s, when rural African-American laborers invented "Juré," a style which mixed singing, praying, hand clapping, and dancing. Shortly after its invention, Juré began to fuse with Cajun music to form *"La La"* (a Creole French slang term for "House Dance"). These early styles featured percussion instruments such as spoons, washboard played with a notched stick, the fiddle, and the accordion.

Country music began to influence Cajun music in the late 1930s and early 1940s, which resulted in the introduction of bass and steel guitars. This Country music influence, along with that of Rhythm & Blues in the early 1950s, brought the electric guitar, electric bass, and drum set into both Cajun and Zydeco ensembles. Although Cajun and Zydeco music developed separately, by the mid-1980s both styles were often played by the same bands, some of which brought Cajun/Zydeco to worldwide attention. Both styles' popularity continues, as evidenced by Cajun/Zydeco festivals and the success of bands and musicians such as Beausoleil, Queen Ida, Buckwheat Zydeco, Zachary Richard, and C.J. Chenier (son of Clifton Chenier).

Other notable bands within the Cajun genre include Steve Riley and The Mamou Playboys, Jackie Caillier and the Cajun Cousins, Jay Cormier and the Cajun Country Band, and Rodney Thibodeaux and Tout Les Soir. Other prominent Zydeco bands include Beau Joque, Boozoo Chavis, Rockin' Doopsie, Geno Delafosse, and Grammy award winner Terrance Simien.

The examples and variations below provide a thorough representation of Cajun/Zydeco bass grooves, most notably the Two-Step groove found in both styles. The most important characteristic in distinguishing between Cajun and Zydeco is that the Zydeco rhythm section is more active than the Cajun rhythm section. Cajun/Zydeco bands often mix both genres freely when performing, but almost never within the same song.

CAJUN CHARACTERISTICS

TONE: Bass +3 to +9 dB, Mids +3 to +6 dB @ 350 Hz, Treble -6 dB.

GEAR: Older Cajun forms were played on upright. In contemporary Cajun, the electric bass is normally used.

TECHNIQUE: Finger style. Not much sustain. The bassist plays relatively softly.

CHORD PROGRESSIONS: Cajun progressions tend to be simple, usually consisting of two or three chords: the I, IV and/or V (or i, iv and/or v). As well, not all Cajun progressions are in four-measure phrases. The number of bars can vary depending on the vocals and the melody. One oddity is that Cajun tunes occasionally start on the IV rather than on the I. Blues progressions can be found, but are relatively uncommon. Simple major and minor chords are the norm in Cajun, although dominant 7th-type chords are also common. Cajun songs tend toward the major keys.

1) i - i - v - i
2) I - I - IV - I
3) I7 - I7 - V7 - I7
4) I - IV - I - V - I - IV - I / V - I
5) I7 - I7 - I7 - V7 - V7 - V7 - V7 - I7
6) IV - IV - I - I - IV - V - I - I
7) I7 - I7 - IV7 - IV7 - I7 - I7 - V7 - V7 - I7 - I7
8) IV - I - V - I
9) I7 - I7 - I7 - I7 - IV 7 - IV7 - I7 - I7 - V7 - V7 - I7 - I7

QUARTER NOTE = 120 – 176 BPM (TWO-STEP)
QUARTER NOTE = 120 – 152 BPM (WALTZ)

CAJUN TWO-STEP EXAMPLE 1 (CD1 TRACK 55, DVD TRACK 25)

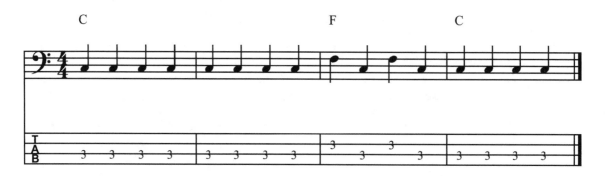

Cajun Two-Step Example 1 Variation 1 (CD1 Track 56)

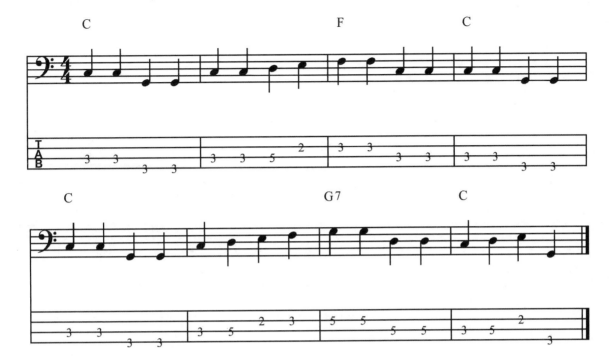

Cajun Two-Step Example 1 Variation 2

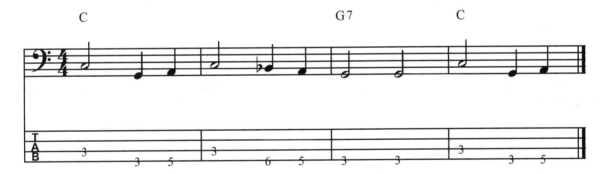

Cajun Waltz Example 1

CAJUN WALTZ EXAMPLE 2 (CD 1 TRACK 57, DVD TRACK 26)

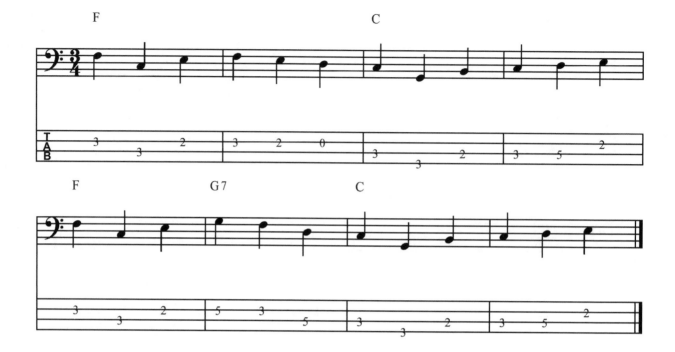

CAJUN WALTZ EXAMPLE 2 VARIATION 1

ZYDECO CHARACTERISTICS

BASS GROOVES: Zydeco Two-Step bass grooves are often more rhythmically active than Cajun Two-Step grooves, and are sometimes slightly syncopated. A bassist will normally not shuffle notes in Zydeco shuffles, but will instead play quarter notes and half notes, and will occasionally play a fifth on the first beat of the final bar of a 4-bar phrase.

TONE (TRADITIONAL): Similar to Blues. **Bass +6 to +9 dB, Mids flat to +3 dB @ 300hz, Treble -6 dB.**

TONE (CONTEMPORARY): More mid boost and treble for a crisper sound. **Bass +6 to +9 dB, Mids flat to +6 dB @ 300 to 500hz, Treble flat to +3 dB.**

GEAR: Older forms were played on upright. In contemporary Zydeco, the electric bass is normally used.

TECHNIQUE: Finger style, sometimes incorporating slap and pop. (See Funk chapter.)

CHORD PROGRESSIONS: Many newer Zydeco tunes are vamps on a single chord. Blues progressions are very common in Zydeco. Other progressions are simple Cajun-type progressions built on the I, IV and V. Major keys are the norm, as are dominant 7th-type chords.

1) I7 - I7 - I7 - I7
2) I7 - I7 - I7 - I7 - IV7 - IV7 - I7 - I7 - V7 - IV7 - I7 - I7
3) I7 - IV - I7 - V
4) I7 - I7 - I7 - I7 - V7 - V7 - I7 - I7

QUARTER NOTE = 156 – 236 BPM (TWO-STEP)
QUARTER NOTE = 126 – 160 BPM (WALTZ)
QUARTER NOTE =   80 – 160 BPM (SHUFFLE)

ZYDECO TWO-STEP EXAMPLE 1 (CD 1 TRACK 58, DVD TRACK 27)

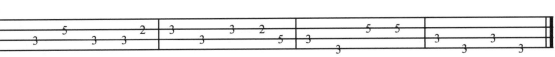

ZYDECO TWO-STEP EXAMPLE 1 VARIATION 1 (CD 1 TRACK 59)

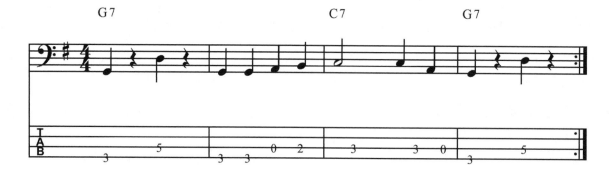

ZYDECO TWO-STEP EXAMPLE 2

ZYDECO SHUFFLE EXAMPLE 1 (CD 1 TRACK 60, DVD TRACK 28)

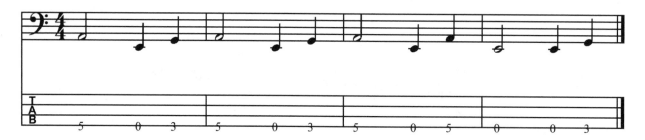

ZYDECO SHUFFLE EXAMPLE 1 VARIATION 1 (CD 1 TRACK 61)

ZYDECO WALTZ EXAMPLE 1 (CD 1 TRACK 62)

ZYDECO WALTZ EXAMPLE 1 VARIATION 1 (CD 1 TRACK 63, DVD TRACK 29)

7 CARIBBEAN

CARIBBEAN MUSIC IS THE RESULT of the fusion of many different musical cultures, including South American, Cuban, African, North American, and even European. The compositions, rhythms, and instruments (such as the signature steel drums) which characterize Caribbean music, sometimes referred to as "Island Music," usually reflect a celebratory atmosphere. In keeping with Island Music's upbeat, danceable nature, most Caribbean music is rather simple rhythmically and does not usually stray outside of 4/4.

This chapter explores the most commonly played styles within the broad Caribbean-music classification: Calypso, Soca, Ska, and Reggae.

The role of the bassist in all of these styles is supportive—there is always a strong groove that reflects the music's upbeat mood. As well as providing a solid foundation, some Carribean bass lines can be melodic, duplicating the guitar or vocal lines, most typically in Soca and Reggae.

CALYPSO

CALYPSO'S ROOTS are in the song forms of French Patois culture (a French-Creole dialect in the Caribbean, notably in Trinidad). While Calypso started as a type of folk music, it developed into a verbal call-and-response form, alternating between the leader (the "griot") and the ensemble. While the style originally featured political and social commentary, it has evolved into dance and party music. Trinidadian musicians Rupert Grant (Lord Invader), Aldwyn Roberts (Lord Kitchener), Egbert Moore (Lord Beginner) and Omni Mundle (Lord Composer) were primary exponents of Calypso in its early days. It became widely popular outside of the Caribbean in the 1950s and 1960s with the success of musician/composer Harry Belafonte, who like Lord Composer also played Mento, a precursor of Calypso.

To fully appreciate Calypso and the related style, Soca, it is important to become familiar with the history of steel drums, which are largely responsible for both genres' characteristic sounds. During British colonial rule of Trinidad in the 1800s, hand drums were used as a form of communication by neighborhood gangs. However, due to a steady increase in violence, culminating in the Canboulay Riots of 1881, the government outlawed the use of these drums. As a result, Trinidadians turned to a variety of materials to take the place of the banned drums. One common replacement was bamboo sticks ("tamboo bamboo") which were pounded on the ground during parades and ceremonies. These were soon prohibited as well.

Regardless, the people continued searching for objects they could use to create music, including garbage can lids, old car parts, and empty oil barrels. Eventually, these metallic found-instruments became the basis of musical gatherings called "Iron Bands." In the late 1930s, someone discovered that hitting a dented section of an oil barrel produced a particular tone, and people began to experiment with different shapes, resulting in the original steel drums, now referred to as "pans," which were convex like a dome rather than concave like a dish. Ellie Manette, a steel drum maker still active in the United States, was the first to hammer out a pan and give the drum its familiar concave form. Over many years, steel drum makers have perfected the quality, tone, and appearance of the instrument, which has led to its finding acceptance in the present-day percussion family. Three of the most prominent contemporary steel drum artists are brothers Andy and Jeff Narell, and The Mighty Sparrow. Jonathan Scales, a young American steel pannist, has played with bassists Oteil Burbridge and Victor Wooten.

CALYPSO CHARACTERISTICS

BASS GROOVES: Calypso grooves are often felt as 2/4 but are written both as 4/4 and 2/4. True Calypso songs tend to have a walking bass line, although they often contain fills.

TONE: Bass +3 to +9 dB, Mids flat, Treble -6 dB. Emulates upright.

GEAR: Any bass can be used: electric, fretless electric, upright, or electric upright.

TECHNIQUE: Finger style.

CHORD PROGRESSIONS: Calypso progressions tend to be simple, revolving around the I, IV and V.

1) I - IV - V - I
2) I - I - I - V7/I
3) I - I/V - V - V/I
4) I - I - V - I - VI - ii - V - I
5) i - i - iv - V - i - i - V - i
6) vi - ii - V - I

QUARTER NOTE = 80 – 120 BPM

CALYPSO EXAMPLE 1 (CD 1 TRACK 64, DVD TRACK 30)

CALYPSO EXAMPLE 2 (CD 1 TRACK 65)

◼ SOCA

CREATED IN TRINIDAD in the mid-1970s, this adaptation of Calypso is credited to Garfield Blackman (aka "Ras Shorty I" and "Lord Shorty"), who had a career spanning four decades. He played in steel bands as a child, then progressed into Calypso, and then invented Soca.

Its incorporation of African and East Indian musical elements initially made Soca controversial among purists who considered it a corruption of Calypso. Soca is distinguished from Calypso by its faster tempo, a heavier beat with a "four on the floor" bass drum pattern, and a more syncopated bass line. However, the newer Soca style retains Calypso's party-type lyrics. A well known example of Soca is "Hot Hot Hot," written by Montserrat musician Arrow, and later covered by David Johnsen (aka "Buster Poindexter"), which sold 12 million copies.

Soca found immediate success with its dance audience, and has retained its popularity. Some Calypso players, such as Lord Kitchener, made a successful transition to Soca. Others, such as Lord Pretender, hold it in low esteem. When interviewed for the Calypso/Soca film, "One Hand Don't Clap," Lord Pretender expressed his contempt for the paucity of lyrics in Soca: "A man sing a line, the music play five minutes."

Soca now embraces a variety of substyles such as Chutney Soca, Ragga Soca, and Rapso (a combination of Rap and Soca), all having a similar rhythmic foundation. Popular Soca artists include Super Blue, Iwer George, Colin Lucas, and Ronnie McIntosh, Shadow, The Mighty Sparrow, and more recent artists such as Machel Montano, Shurwayne Winchester, Denise Belfon, Destra Garcia, Maximus Dan and Michel Montano.

SOCA CHARACTERISTICS

BASS GROOVES: Soca grooves are syncopated, with room for improvisation. The bass may play along with horn punches or play in octaves with the vocalist. Of course, the bass line fits the "four on the floor" drum pattern.

TONE: Bass +3 to +9 dB, Mids -3 to +3 dB @ 500 Hz, Treble flat to +6 dB. Soca players use very modern, sometimes electronic-sounding tones. Flange and chorus effects are common.

GEAR: Soca is more suited to electric bass than standup. Active electronics help with the bright Soca sound.

TECHNIQUE: Finger style.

CHORD PROGRESSIONS: Soca progressions tend to be simple, revolving around the I, IV and V. As in Calypso, chords tend to be simple triads. The first progression, I - V - V - I (and variations on it), is very common.

SOCA EXAMPLE 1 (CD 1 TRACK 67)

SOCA EXAMPLE 2

This pattern builds toward the root of the tonic, which, when it's played, is not on the downbeat.

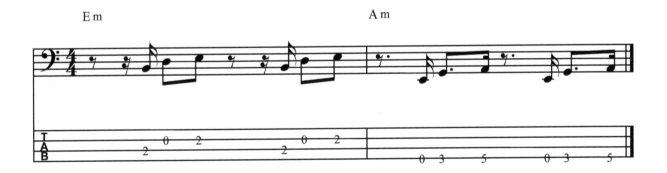

SOCA EXAMPLE 3 (CD 1 TRACK 68, DVD TRACK 31)

SOCA EXAMPLE 4

■ SKA

DURING WORLD WAR II, American service men stationed in Jamaica brought big band Jazz/Swing to the island. Local big bands such as Eric Dean's Orchestra (with Ernest Ranglin, guitar) soon became popular. When R&B displaced Swing in the 1950s in the U.S., with Rock and Roll following, Jamaican music adapted. Radio broadcasts from New Orleans introduced the music of Fats Domino, Lloyd Price, and other New Orleans singer/songwriters to Jamaica.

New Orleans Second Line (see Jazz chapter), along with early Rock n' Roll, Jazz, and R&B blended with Mento, a type of Jamaican folk music. The result was a new Jamaican sound, which came to be known as Ska.

At the time, "sound-systems" (dances with DJs spinning records) were the primary source of music in Jamaica, principally because a single DJ or "toastmaster" was cheaper than a band of musicians, and more reliable. People who couldn't afford radios came to rely on DJ-hosted dances as their only access to new music. The constant need of the sound-systems for new tunes created a huge opportunity for Jamaican musicians—initially big band Jazz players—to make records.

Jamaican guitarist Ernest Ranglin says that musicians created the word Ska "to talk about the skat! skat! skat! scratchin' guitar that goes behind." Prince Buster (Cecil Campbell), a Jamaican producer, is credited with having his guitarist Jah Jerry (Skatalites) emphasize the "afterbeat," thus laying the foundation of Ska. Another way that a guitarist might refer to this is "backwards comping," in which the guitar strongly and equally accents all offbeats (the "ands" of beats) in comping patterns. This pattern is largely what gives Ska its characteristic sound.

Initially Ska was optimistic and enthusiastic, reflecting the achievement of self-governance in Jamaica in 1962. This upbeat mood was reflected in the bass lines of the time: a free walking style at relatively fast tempos. As the culture became darker, the sound reflected the change in mood. The tempo slowed and Ska morphed into Rock Steady (which later became Reggae).

The first successful Ska musicians were Jimmy Cliff, The Maytals, The Wailers, Cecil Bustamente Campbell (Prince Buster), Kentrick Patrick (Lord Creator), and the Skatalites. The core musicians of the Skatalites played on the majority of the recording sessions for these bands, although they were not credited.

As Jamaicans emigrated to the UK, Ska clubs appeared in the cities in England in which they settled (Blackburn, Lancashire, and Margate), and the second wave of Ska, or two-tone Ska, was born. Second wave bands, such as The English Beat, The Specials, Selecter, Bad Manners, Madness, The Police, and Men At Work, brought Ska international popularity in the late 1970s and the 1980s. Currently third wave bands such as No Doubt, 311, The Mighty Mighty Boss Tones, and Sublime have continued the Ska tradition.

The noticeable differences between Ska and Reggae are Ska's characteristic guitar comping pattern, its "straight" feel, its use of a "four on the floor" bass drum pattern (in contrast to Reggae's "one drop" [on beat 3] pattern), and its greater use of horns.

SKA CHARACTERISTICS

BASS GROOVES: Early Ska featured laid back walking grooves. Modern Ska has a more driving feel. In it, the bass stresses the downbeat to offset the guitar's upbeats, which are more pronounced than in early (Jamaican) Ska. Because it's useful to bassists to understand the Ska drum pattern, we've included it here.

TONE: Bass +3 to +6 dB, Mids flat to +3 dB @ 500 Hz, Treble flat to +3 dB.

GEAR: Ska is almost invariably played on electric bass.

TECHNIQUE: Finger style.

CHORD PROGRESSIONS: Ska progressions are primarily based on Blues and R&B. Ska bands will often take songs from other genres (e.g., Bad Manners' cover of the "The Guns of Navarone Theme") and "Ska them up." Ska songs often have bridges based on I - IV or I - V changes.

1) i7 - i7/iv7/iv7/V7 - i7 - i7/iv7/iv7/V7
2) I7 - I7 - ii7 - V7 - I7 - I7 - ii7 - V7
3) i7 - i7/i7/i7/bVII7 - i7 - i7/i7/i7/bVII7 - bIII7/bVII7/bVI7/V7 - i7 - bIII7/bVII7/bVI7/V7 - i7
4) I7 - I7 - I7 - I7
5) i7 - i7 - i7 - i7 - iv7 - iv7 - i7 - i7 - v7 - iv7 - i7 - i7
6) I - IV - V - I
7) I7 - I7 - V7 - I7 - VI7 - ii7 - V7 - I7
8) i7 - i7 - iv7 - V7 - i7 - i7 - V7 - i7

QUARTER NOTE = 116 – 192 BPM

SKA DRUM PATTERN

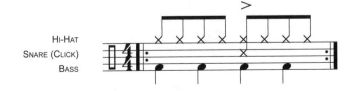

SKA EXAMPLE 1 (CD 1 TRACK 69, DVD TRACK 32)

This is a classic example of first wave Ska, but will also work well with second and third wave Ska.

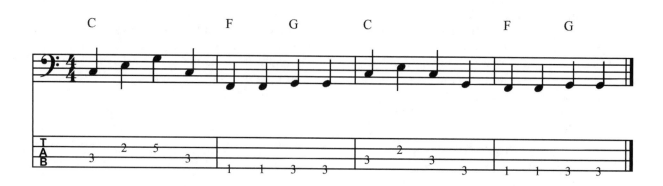

SKA EXAMPLE 1 VARIATION 1

SKA EXAMPLE 1 VARIATION 2

Using a little syncopation can result in a relaxed feel.

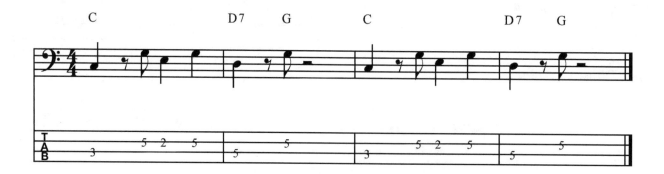

SKA EXAMPLE 2

This example is representative of second and third wave Ska.

SKA EXAMPLE 3

SKA EXAMPLE 4 (CD 1 TRACK 70, DVD TRACK 33)

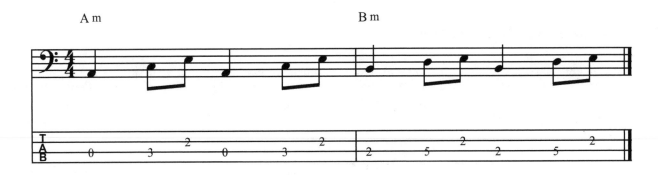

■ REGGAE

THE ORIGIN OF THE WORD REGGAE is unclear. Some claim that the word stems from "Regga," which refers to a group of natives from the Lake Tanganyika region in Africa. Bob Marley claimed it was a Spanish term for "The King's Music" (in Spanish, *la música del rey*"), which is unlikely enough that one suspects that Marley was pulling someone's leg—although it is barely possible that the word "Reggae" is a corruption of the word "*rey*" (king). Toots Hibbert of the Maytals says he came up with it, too. Yet another, more likely, explanation is that of Jamaican studio musician Hux Brown: "It's a description of the beat itself. It's just a fun, joke kinda word that means ragged rhythm and the body feelin'. If it's got a greater meanin', it doesn't matter."

Reggae incorporates Rhythm & Blues, New Orleans Second Line "in the crack" (between swing and straight) feels, African rhythms, Jamaican folk traditions, and Rastafarian culture (a religion developed in Jamaica which deifies former Ethiopian emperor Haile Selassie). Although its roots extend back to the 1950s, the genre's success is partially due to the breakthrough of Calypso and Ska in the late 1950s and early 1960s.

Reggae gained popularity in the 1960s through musicians such as Alton Ellis, Delroy Wilson, Toots and the Maytalls, Jimmy Cliff, and, most importantly, Bob Marley and the Wailers. Even though he died in 1981, Bob Marley still stands as the leading voice of Reggae. The influence of Reggae extends into popular music through Johnny Nash, Stevie Wonder, The Clash, Elvis Costello and the Attractions, and Paul Simon ("Mother and Child Reunion," which is considered by many as the first attempt at Reggae by a white musician). Contemporary artists include Ziggy Marley (son of Bob Marley), Third World, The Mighty Diamonds, Burning Spear, Sly and Robbie, and the still-active Jimmy Cliff. Many older Reggae bassists, with careers dating from the early days of Caribbean music, are still recording and touring today. As well, The Easy Star All Stars from New York City have been recording covers of famous albums in Reggae style, such as "Dub Side of the Moon" and "Easy Star's Lonely Hearts Dub Band," covering the classics by Pink Floyd and The Beatles respectively.

Bass lines transitioned from the double-time of Ska to Reggae's precursor Rock Steady in 1966. One story, possibly apocryphal, involves an Alton Ellis studio session. When the bassist didn't show up for the session ("Get Ready — Rock Steady"), Alton had the keyboardist (Jackie Mittoo, founding member of the Skatalites) play the bass line on piano with his left hand while he played the keyboard part with his right hand. As Mittoo couldn't play both parts simultaneously at the fast Ska tempo, they slowed the tune down. The result was so unusual that when the bassist recorded his part, Alton insisted that the bassist play it the same way as the pianist. This resulted in a syncopated, repetitive line that no longer had the quarter-note walking feel of Ska. The bass style moved from continuous, steady movement to cluster-like patterns, with more space between phrases.

Understanding Reggae bass requires understanding the "One Drop" drum groove. Reggae drumming resembles that of the New Orleans Second Line, in which the feel of the music falls "in the crack." This requires playing between a swung and a straight feel. Bass lines, of course, should also be played "in the crack."

Because it's impossible to notate this feel with complete accuracy, all of the following patterns are approximations, and as such are open to interpretation.

REGGAE ONE DROP DRUM PATTERN

The distinguishing features of a Reggae beat are the simultaneous rim click and bass drum kick played as one note on beat 3 of each measure (hence the name "One Drop") and the "in the crack" hi-hat pattern.

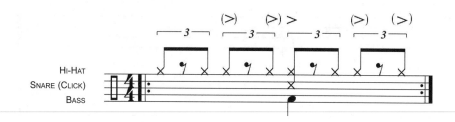

REGGAE CHARACTERISTICS

BASS GROOVES: A Reggae bassist plays simple lines with an extremely laid back feel. At the same time that the bass playing must be relaxed, it also needs to be active and syncopated, given the relatively slow tempo of Reggae and the slow rate of chord changes—it's common in Reggae songs to hang on chords for four bars.

TONE: Bass +6 to +12 dB, Mids flat to -15 dB @ 500 Hz, Treble flat to -12 dB.

GEAR: Electric is the norm. Upright can be used, but is not common.

TECHNIQUE: Finger style.

CHORD PROGRESSIONS: (Some of these are compressed — some chord repetitions are not included so that the entire progression can be shown.) The chords themselves tend to be simple triads.

1) I - IV/V - I - IV/V
2) i - iv - i - v|
3) i - i - i - i - iv - iv - iv - iv
4) I/VI - IV/I - I/VI - IV/V/I/I
5) i - IV - bVI/v - i
6) I - IV - I - IV - I - V - I/IV - I/V
7) V - V - IV - IV - V - V - IV - IV - III - III - vi - vi - V - IV - I - I

QUARTER NOTE = 88 – 126 BPM

REGGAE EXAMPLE 1 (CD 1 TRACK 71, DVD TRACK 34)

The eighth-note triplets should be played "in the crack."

REGGAE EXAMPLE 2

REGGAE EXAMPLE 3 (CD 1 TRACK 72, DVD TRACK 35)

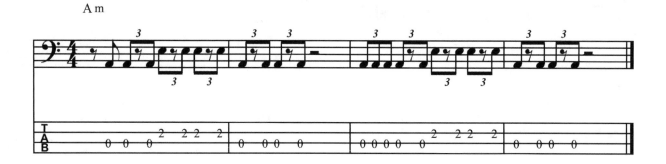

REGGAE EXAMPLE 4

REGGAE EXAMPLE 5

REGGAE EXAMPLE 6

REGGAE EXAMPLE 7

8 COUNTRY

COUNTRY MUSIC IS POPULAR around the world and serves an age-old function: storytelling. Its themes of love, heartache, and the promise of salvation in the afterlife are exceedingly popular. It stems from the Appalachian region, where during the 18th and 19th centuries most people were of Scotch or Irish descent. These physically isolated mountaineers performed the Scotch-Irish folk songs of their ancestors. The folk-based formula consisted of ABAB rhyming quatrains citing personal experiences combined with the vocal/harmonic characteristics and subject matter of religious hymns.

Appalachian/Scotch-Irish music centered on the fiddle, and this remained so even after the intrusion of railroads in the 19th century brought new musical influences and instruments to the region. Traveling minstrel shows imported the banjo, providing a unique sound to accompany the fiddle. By the early 1900s, now-affordable, mass-produced guitars gave singers a broader chordal and rhythmic base than the less harmonically versatile banjo and fiddle. This pairing of vocals with guitar accompaniment became the foundation of contemporary Country music.

In the 1920s, radio broadcasts, most notably Nashville's "The Grand Ole Opry" (first broadcast in 1925), brought Country music to a mass audience. Recognizing its commercial potential, recording pioneer Ralph Peer announced auditions in 1927 in the Bristol, Tennessee newspaper. The indigenous musicians straddling the Virginia-Tennessee border showed up in droves. They included Jimmie Rodgers and The Carter Family.

Bluegrass pioneer Bill Monroe replaced the jug player for his Bluegrass Boys with upright bassist Amost Garret in 1939. After Garret, Monroe hired "Cousin" Wilbur Wesbrooks in 1940, and in 1944 Howard "Cedric Rainwater" Watts, who appears on all the major Monroe recordings featuring Lester Flatt, Earl Scruggs, and Chubby Wise. In 1948, Watts left Bill Monroe to join Flatt and Scruggs. Watts also played with The Drifting Cowboys backing up Hank Williams Sr., Ray Price, and, decades later, a reformation of The Drifting Cowboys in support of Hank Williams Jr.

In the 1930s, Texas musicians (most notably Bob Wills, with brother Billy Jack Wills on bass) combined the vocal harmonies of Country with the swing feel and improvisation of big band Jazz, while using more complicated harmonies than those of traditional Country music, creating Western Swing. As the name implies, the primary feel was swung, as opposed to the straight feel of most other forms of Country music.

Not surprisingly, the upright bass proved indispensable, along with its counterpart, the drum set. Western Swing's rhythmic base consisted of a swung drum pattern and a walking bass line. However, the drum/bass instrumentation of Western Swing was not wholly accepted within the confines of Country, as evidenced in Bob Wills' appearance on the stage of "The Grand Ole Opry" on December 30, 1944. Although the Opry lifted its ban on drums for that performance, it immediately reinstated it afterwards.

At about the same time, another relative of Country music appeared in the West, as Roy Rogers and Gene Autry pioneered Western music. Western music differed considerably from both Appalachian hillbilly (Country) music and Western Swing in that it downplayed instrumental virtuosity, was primarily vocally oriented, and more especially crooner oriented.

The subject matter of Western songs also differed greatly from that of Country music. Instead of Country's strange duality of gritty and religious songs, Western artists sang pop songs (e.g., Gene Autry's 1941 version of "You Are My Sunshine"), while their original Western songs portrayed a heavily romanticized American West (e.g., "Cool Water" and "Tumbling Tumble Weeds," both written by bassist Bob Nolan).

Western music's greatest star in the latter half of the 20th century was Marty Robbins ("El Paso"), who used bassists Hillous Butrum and Colin

Cameron. The Sons of the Pioneers (founded by Roy Rogers) are Western music's most durable group, still active even today; the group's bassists have included Bob Nolan and Pat Brady.

Western groups often avoid use of the bass entirely, with bass lines usually played instead on the acoustic guitar. When the bass is used in Western groups, it's invariably acoustic.

By the 1940s, Country music had made its way into the night life of cities and their run down bars. In the latter part of that decade, Country music's first post-war superstar, Hank Williams, developed the Honky Tonk style with his back-up band the Drifting Cowboys. The band featured bassists Herbert "Lum" York and Howard Watts, and for a time, due to the typically rough venues in which they played, bodyguard "Cannonball" Nichols.

The Honky Tonk style inspired what has become the standard Country instrumental line-up: acoustic guitar, electric guitar, electric bass, drums, vocalist, and often pedal steel guitar and/or fiddle, and occasionally piano.

In the 1950s, Ray Price, with his drummer Buddy Harman, developed the Country Shuffle, and the heavier back-beat influence of Rock n' Roll emerged in Rockabilly. This hybrid Country-Rock style was popularized by Country artists such as Carl Perkins and Johnny Cash, as well as Rock and Rollers such as Jerry Lee Lewis and, of course, Elvis Presley.

Of all the early Country bass players, perhaps the most prominent was Bob Moore. He not only recorded with Ray Price, Chet Atkins, Elvis Presley, Jerry Lee Lewis, and Johnny Cash, but he played on over 17,000 recordings with a staggering diversity of artists, including Ernest Tubb, Loretta Lynn, Flatt and Scruggs, Burl Ives, Simon & Garfunkel, Bob Dylan, and Pete Fountain.

Country went "pop" in the late 1950s with the Nashville Sound (which dominated Country for decades). This was essentially an attempt to reach a mass audience by taking the "twang" out of Country. The distinguishing features of the Nashville Sound are a very smooth, heavily produced sound, background strings, vocal choirs, and electric, rather than acoustic, bass. Early examples of this sound are the recordings of Chet Atkins and the more over-produced songs (by influential producer Owen Bradley) of Patsy Cline, in which Bob Moore played on songs such as "Crazy" (written by Willie Nelson), "I Fall to Pieces," and "Walkin' After Midnight."

As a reaction against the pop Nashville Sound, the Country-Shuffle-influenced Bakersfield Sound arose in the early 1960s. Its primary exponent was Buck Owens, who wrote and sang "Tiger by the Tail" and "Act Naturally." Buck's first bass player was Merle Haggard, who is credited with naming Buck's back-up group "The Buckaroos." Buck's later bassists included Doyle Holly and Doyle Curtzinger. The distinguishing feature of the Bakersfield Sound was that the "twang" returned—with the exclusion of strings and vocal choirs. In contrast to earlier Hank Williams-style Country, there was more emphasis on the electric guitar (with a tone owing much to Surf music), and song styles included Western Swing and Country Shuffle. Today, the primary exponent of the Bakersfield Sound is Dwight Yoakam.

The Outlaw Movement of the 1970s was a further reaction against the Nashville Sound. Outlaw music used both Hank Williams-style Country and the Bakersfield Sound, differing from them primarily in its lyrical content, which dwelt on the dark side, emphasizing heavy drinking, barroom brawls, and infidelity. David Allan Coe ("Now I Lay Me Down to Cheat") was one of the Outlaw standouts. Others included Merle Haggard, Waylon Jennings (who had played bass for Buddy Holly in 1959), and Willie Nelson (who had played bass for Ray Price in the early 1960s). Nelson's and Jenning's influential 1976 album, "Wanted: The Outlaws," featured up-and-coming Nashville bassist Gary Tallent, who went on to record with such notables as Emmylou Harris and Solomon Burke, and who became the primary bassist for Bruce Springsteen.

Another notable trend in the early 1970s was the emergence of Country Rock. On the Rock side, performers included The Byrds, Gram Parsons, The Flying Burrito Brothers, Marshall Tucker, and, most prominently, The Eagles. On the Country side, the musicians included Willie Nelson, Waylon Jennings, and Hank Williams, Jr.

In the 1980s, still another reaction against the Nashville Sound arose with the New Traditionalists, led by Dwight Yoakam and Steve Earle. These artists returned to the stripped-down sounds of early Country, the Bakersfield Sound, and, to a limited extent, Bluegrass.

Alt-Country rose in the 1990s as yet another reaction to the Nashville Sound. It's musically ill defined and embraces elements of many styles, including traditional Country, Folk, Rock, Western Swing, Rockabilly, Bluegrass, and even Mariachi. Its lyrics are what set it apart. They avoid Country cliches, are often humorous, often dark, and occasionally overtly leftist (in stark contrast to mainstream Country). Alt-Country's best-known performers (not that all of them would accept the label) include Steve Earle, Junior Brown, the Austin

Lounge Lizards, Calexico, Roger Clyne, Al Perry and the Cattle, The Mavericks, Jim White, James McMurtry, John Hiatt, and Hank Williams III.

But Country Rock is the dominant Country style today, with its performers including Garth Brooks, Clint Black, Shania Twain, Tim McGraw, Toby Keith, Alan Jackson, and Kenny Chesney. The dis-

tinguishing features of Country Rock are its use of Country harmonies and melodies, Rock and Country instruments, and Rock drumming and bass grooves.

Although it appears deceptively easy, Country music boasts some of the best musicians ever to pick up an instrument, bass included.

■ BLUEGRASS

GROWING OUT OF THE INSTRUMENTATION of early 20th century string bands and the influence of Blues, Bluegrass (originally called "Old Time Country," "Mountain Music," or "Hillbilly Music") first received radio exposure in the 1930s. Developed in Kentucky, it eventually came to symbolize the state through its unofficial nickname, "The Bluegrass State." The style became immensely popular after Bill Monroe and his Blue Grass Boys performed at The Grand Ole Opry in 1939, establishing them as the seminal force of this high-energy, primarily instrumental music.

Traditional Bluegrass instrumentation is all acoustic and consists of a 5-string banjo, flat-top guitar, fiddle, mandolin, dobro, and upright bass. In 1960, Earl Scruggs and Lester Flatt added the drum set to their

Bluegrass group at a recording session. But use of drums is still unusual in Bluegrass groups.

Currently Ricky Skaggs and the Dixie Chicks play a modernized form of Bluegrass, while Bluegrass's more traditional forms have had a resurgence of popularity in recent years, in part due to the soundtrack from the movie "O Brother, Where Art Thou?" Evidence of Bluegrass's renewed popularity—and that its popularity extends far beyond the area in which it originated—can be seen in the annual Bluegrass festivals held in many U.S. states.

Bluegrass songs may—unlike songs in almost all other styles—intentionally speed up ("passing a break," in Bluegrass terms) to add flare to solos and to a song's finale.

BLUEGRASS CHARACTERISTICS

BASS GROOVES: Bluegrass bass patterns tend to be simple. The bass usually plays quarter and half notes and roots and fifths. Example 1 and Example 1 Variation 1 on the following page are very probably the most common Bluegrass grooves.

TONE: Bass +3 to +6 dB, Mids flat, Treble flat to -6 dB. Emulates upright.

GEAR: Upright is standard in Bluegrass, although electric bass can be used.

TECHNIQUE: Finger style. The tone is usually staccato rather than legato, but with a soft touch. The bass occasionally stands out in solos.

CHORD PROGRESSIONS: Bluegrass progressions tend to be simple, revolving around the I, IV and V.

  1) I - I - IV - IV - I - I - V - V
  2) I - I - I - V/I
  3) I - I - I - I - vi - vi - I - I - vi - vi - I - I - V - V - I - I
  4) I - I - IV - I - vi - V - I - I
  5) I - I - I - I - IV - IV - I - I

QUARTER NOTE = 100 – 160 BPM (Bluegrass is normally played in cut time—2 beats per measure.)

COUNTRY BASS GROOVES

Country bass grooves are usually simple, and the simplest Country bass grooves use a root-fifth movement and half-notes or quarter notes on the beat. Syncopation is unusual in Country bass lines. However, many lines that appear the same can sound very different depending on what the drummer is playing.

The following two Bluegrass root-fifth grooves (Example 1 and Example 1 Variation 1) can be used in all 4/4 Country styles.

BLUEGRASS ROOT-FIFTH EXAMPLE 1 (CD 1 TRACK 73, DVD TRACK 36)

BLUEGRASS ROOT-FIFTH EXAMPLE 1 VARIATION 1

BLUEGRASS ROOT-FIFTH EXAMPLE 1 VARIATION 2

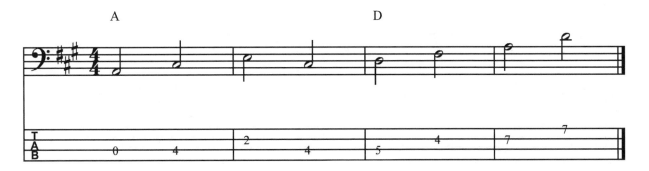

BLUEGRASS EXAMPLE 1 VARIATION 3 (CD 1 TRACK 74)

BLUEGRASS EXAMPLE 1 VARIATION 4

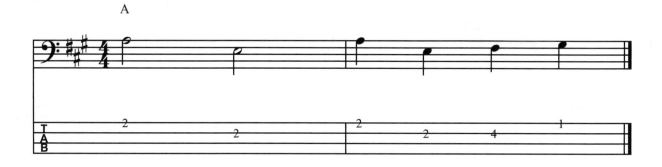

BLUEGRASS WALTZ EXAMPLE 1 (CD 1 TRACK 75, DVD TRACK 37)

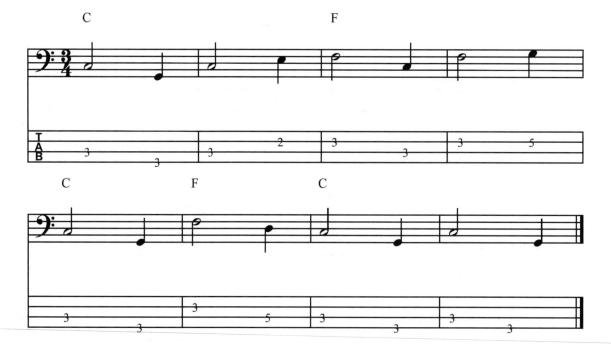

WESTERN SWING

In the late 1930s and early 1940s, Bob Wills and his Texas Playboys popularized Western Swing. It featured swung rhythms and instruments from the Big Band rhythm section, particularly upright bass and, for the first time in Country Music, the drum set. In addition, Western Swing was also the first Country style to utilize electric guitar and pedal steel guitar. In Western Swing, the vocals are sometimes, but far from always, secondary to the instrumental music; vocal-dominated counter examples abound, such as the most famous Western Swing song, "San Antonio Rose," by Bob Wills. Fiddle legend Johnny Gimble has kept this style alive for the past six decades, paving the way for modern-day Western Swing musicians such as Asleep at the Wheel and Dan Hicks.

WESTERN SWING CHARACTERISTICS

BASS GROOVES: Walking lines are very common. The root-fifth grooves on page 82 are also common. The bassist usually plays quarter notes and half notes, and does not shuffle notes. Using half-note lines under the vocals and quarter note walking lines under solos can add interest.

TONE: Bass +3 to +6 dB, Mids flat, Treble flat to -6 dB. Emulates upright.

GEAR: The original Western Swing bands used upright. Today, some Western Swing bassists still use upright, although electric bass is common.

TECHNIQUE: Finger style. More staccato than legato. Uprights can be played either pizzicato or arco. The upright bassist will sometimes employ slaps. (See Rockabilly section of Rock chapter.)

CHORD PROGRESSIONS: Western Swing progressions are sometimes fairly simple, but can be complex, reflecting the style's Big Band roots.

1) I7 - I7 - I7 - I7 - IV7 - IV7 - I7 - I7 - V7 - IV7 - I7 - I7
2) VI7 - II9 - V7 - I7
3) I - I - ii7 - ii7 - V7 - V7 - I - I
4) I - vi - ii - V
5) I - I - V7 - V7 - V7 - V7 - I - I
6) I - I - I - I - I - I - V - V - V - V - V - V - V - V - I - I
7) I - I - IV - II - V7 - V7 - I - I

QUARTER NOTE = 132 – 216 BPM (but may be slower for ballads)

WESTERN SWING EXAMPLE 1 (CD 1 TRACK 76, DVD TRACK 38)

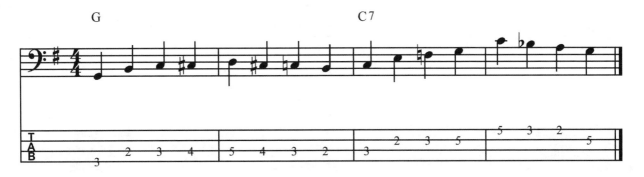

WESTERN SWING EXAMPLE 1 VARIATION 1

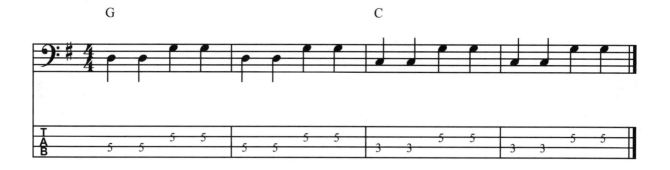

WESTERN SWING EXAMPLE 1 VARIATION 2

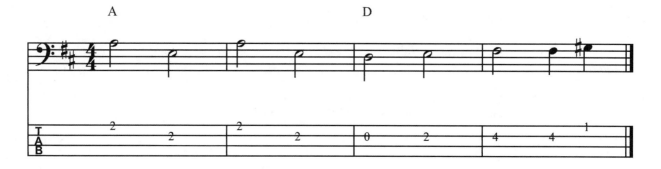

WESTERN SWING EXAMPLE 1 VARIATION 3

NOTE: When Western Swing songs are built on a Blues progression, the bass player's most logical choice is the standard Boogie bass line shown above in Example 1 Variation 3.

WESTERN SWING EXAMPLE 2

Due to the pronounced accents on the downbeats (which is not normal in walking), this line drives much more than a typical walking bass line.

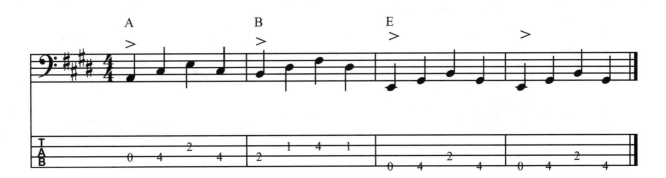

WESTERN SWING EXAMPLE 2 VARIATION 1

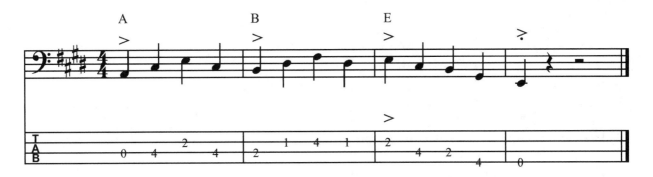

BOB MOORE ROOT-FIFTH EXAMPLE

One minor problem—not that anyone but a bassist would ever notice—in playing half-note root-fifth patterns in Western Swing and other Country styles is that when the chord pattern shifts up a fifth (or down a fourth), as in C to G, the traditional half-note root-fifth pattern anticipates the new chord on the third beat of the preceding measure. To avoid this, legendary Country bassist Bob Moore played the root of the preceding chord twice, on both beats one and three, as in the following example.

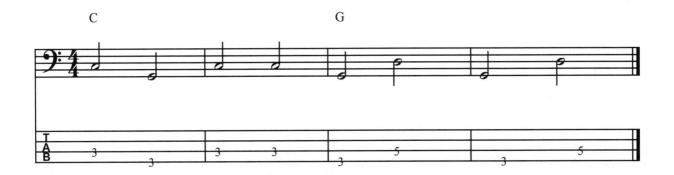

TRADITIONAL COUNTRY CHARACTERISTICS

BASS GROOVES: The root-fifth half-note grooves on page 82 are very common.

TWO-STEP: 1) Play half notes, quarter notes, and occasional eighth notes; 2) Usually play roots and fifths; 3) Play more legato (with sustain) than staccato.

COUNTRY SHUFFLE: 1) Play half notes, quarter notes, and occasional shuffled eighth notes; 2) Usually play roots and fifths; 3) Play more legato than staccato.

TRAIN BEAT: 1) Play half notes, quarter notes, dotted quarter notes, and occasionally use syncopation; 2) Usually play roots and fifths; 3) Play more staccato than legato.

TONE: Clean. **Bass +3 dB, Mids flat, Treble flat.**

GEAR: The original Country bassists used upright. Today, electric is used almost universally.

TECHNIQUE: Finger style.

PROGRESSIONS: Country progressions tend to be simple, revolving around the I, IV and V. Blues progressions are fairly common. Abrupt modulation (no pivot chords or other preparation) upward of either a half-step or a whole step—usually a whole step—is common in Country songs, always at the beginning of a verse or chorus.

1) I7 - I7 - I7 - I7 - IV7 - IV7 - I7 - I7 - V7 - IV7 - I7 - I7
2) I7 - I7 - IV7 - I7 - I7 - V7 - IV7 - I7
3) V - I - vi - I - vi - I - V - I
4) I - I7 - IV - IV - V7 - V7 - I - I
5) I - I - I - I - II7 - V7 - I - V7
6) I - I - IV - IV - V - V - I - I (bridge) I - IV/I - II - V
7) I - I - II7/V7 - I
8) I - I - I - V7 - I7 - IV - IV - IV7 - I - VI7 - II7 - V7

QUARTER NOTE = 80 – 132 BPM (TWO-STEP)

QUARTER NOTE = 80 – 126 BPM (COUNTRY SHUFFLE)

QUARTER NOTE = 100 – 132 BPM (TRAIN BEAT)

TWO-STEP

THOUGH NOT ITS OWN GENRE, the Two-Step (Country Two-Beat) is found throughout Country music, from early artists such as Hank Williams, Sr. to contemporary artists such as Reba McEntire and Lyle Lovett, and is a staple of Traditional Country. Two-Step bass lines have a "two feel," emphasize the upbeat throughout each measure, and are usually notated in 4/4.

TWO-STEP EXAMPLE 1

TWO-STEP EXAMPLE 1 VARIATION 1 (CD 1 TRACK 77, DVD TRACK 39)

TWO-STEP EXAMPLE 1 VARIATION 2

COUNTRY SHUFFLE

COUNTRY SHUFFLE differs from Blues Shuffle in name, its generally slower tempo, its less active bass lines, and that the drummer sometimes plays the Jazz ride pattern in place of the Shuffle pattern on the hi-hat.

Since its introduction by Ray Price in the 1950s, the Country Shuffle has been adopted in Honky Tonk, The Nashville Sound, the Bakersfield Sound, and Modern Day Country. Early examples of the Country Shuffle include "Crazy Arms" and "City Lights."

Country Shuffle's primary characteristics are its swung eighth-note feel borrowed from Jazz and Blues, its use of Blues Shuffle and Jazz ride patterns, its relatively slow tempo, and its solid pulse in the bass line, which often consists of half notes or walking quarters.

COUNTRY SHUFFLE EXAMPLE 1 (CD 1 TRACK 78, DVD TRACK 40)

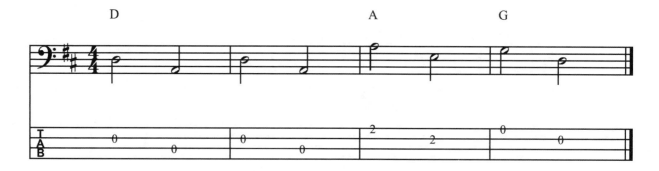

COUNTRY SHUFFLE EXAMPLE 1 VARIATION 1 (CD 1 TRACK 79)

COUNTRY SHUFFLE EXAMPLE 2

Though not common, you can play shuffled eighth-note triplets on the fourth beat, and more rarely on the third and fourth beats.

NOTE: Country Shuffle bass lines normally consist of quarter notes and half notes, not shuffled eighth notes (as in Blues). This leaves the shuffle feel to the drums, guitar, and vocals (and occasionally piano).

TRAIN BEAT

THE TRAIN BEAT is an indispensable groove in Country. Though its roots lie in Bluegrass, it is now used throughout Country music (Willie Nelson's "On the Road Again" being a good example). Train Beat bass lines consistently emphasize beats one and three. They may sometimes be syncopated in ways similar to Brazilian Baiao rhythmic patterns. (See Brazilian chapter.) One of the reasons for this is that Train Beat drum tends to have a medium to medium-fast tempo, allow-ing room for syncopated rhythms. This contributes to Train Beat being felt in 4/4 rather than cut time or "two feel." However, the abundance of notes on the snare drum, from which the groove derives its name, simulates a fast, double-time feel, reminiscent of a train.

Because it's helpful for a bassist to understand the Train Beat drum pattern, we've reproduced it here. **The tempo range is 100 – 132 BPM.**

TRAIN BEAT DRUM PATTERN

TRAIN BEAT EXAMPLE 1 (CD 1 TRACK 80)

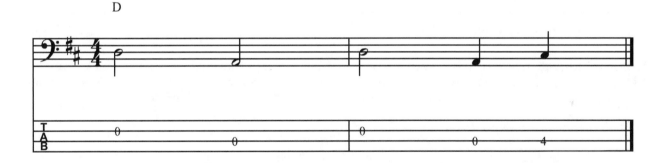

TRAIN BEAT EXAMPLE 1 VARIATION 1 (CD 1 TRACK 81, DVD TRACK 41)

This variation and the following one have a Brazilian Baiao feel.

■ WESTERN

WESTERN MUSIC'S IDENTIFICATION in the 1930s and 1940s with Country music (as in the archaic term "Country and Western") stemmed from its sounding somewhat similar to traditional Country and the use of the guitar as the primary instrument in both genres. Nowadays, a bassist may need to play Western songs in a nontraditional Country setting. The Country Shuffle is the groove in almost all Western songs, with the distinguishing feature being the slow tempo. A "slow shuffle" feel results. Bass lines tend to be even simpler than those of Country, as the style's expressiveness tends to rest solely in the vocals.

WESTERN CHARACTERISTICS

BASS GROOVES: The bass holds down the beat, as it's often the sole instrument in the rhythm section. (There are normally no drums in Western.) The bassist plays quarter-note and half-note roots and fifths. The bassist never shuffles notes or plays all of the triplets. The root-fifth grooves on page 82 are common.

TONE: Clean. **Bass +3 dB, Mids flat, Treble flat.**

GEAR: Upright was originally used in this style, and is still the standard instrument. Acoustic bass guitar can also be used, as can electric bass.

TECHNIQUE: Finger style. Pizzicato (plucked).

PROGRESSIONS: Early Western progressions tend to be surprisingly complex, often involving chromaticism and diminished chords, reflecting the style's origins in the pop music of the 1930s. Later Western progressions (as in Marty Robbins) tend to be simpler.

  1) IV - IV7 - III - III7 - IV - I/bii dim - V - I
  2) I - I - I/#IV dim - V7
  3) I - I - ii - ii - V7 - V7 - V7 - I
  4) I - I - IV - V - V - V - V- I
  5) I - I - V7 - I - I - IV - V7 - I
  6) i - i - III - III - i - i - III - III - i - i7 - i7 - IV - bVI - bVI - IV - i

QUARTER NOTE = 80 – 92 BPM

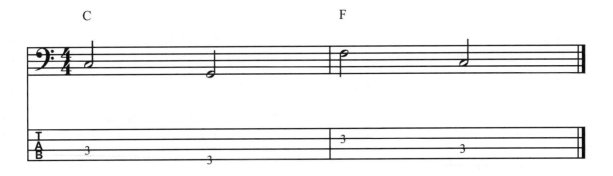

WESTERN EXAMPLE 1 VARIATION 1

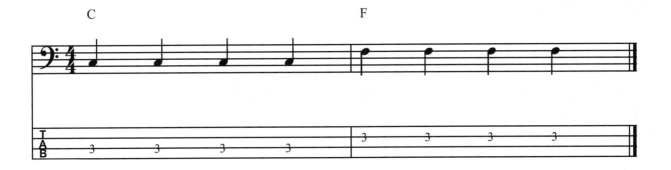

WESTERN EXAMPLE 1 VARIATION 2

ROCKABILLY

Rockabilly bass playing has much in common with that of Western Swing and Honky Tonk, and many Country artists have crossed the line into Rockabilly. However, the genre owes as much to Rock n' Roll as it does to Country, and it appeals mainly to Rock n' Roll enthusiasts. For this reason, Rockabilly bass is covered in the Rock n' Roll chapter.

COUNTRY ROCK AND MODERN-DAY COUNTRY

BEGINNING IN THE 1970s, Country music began incorporating the sounds and influence of mainstream Rock n"Roll. Artists such as Charlie Daniels, Linda Rondstadt, Alabama, Willie Nelson, and Waylon Jennings were pioneers of this marriage of styles. Current Country Rock artists such as Garth Brooks, Shania Twain, Faith Hill, and Clint Black are popular worldwide.

Because of the heavy contemporary Rock n' Roll influence on the style, most Country Rock grooves may be straight or shuffled. The main difference between Country Rock grooves and Modern Day Country grooves is that Country Rock bass lines tend to be more active than Modern Day Country lines, which are similar to Traditional Country grooves.

Country Rock and Modern Day Country are often put in the same category due to their similar musical characteristics. However, Country Rock tends to incorporate a dynamic rhythm section with loud guitars and bigger drum sounds, similar to those in a Rock n' Roll band, while Modern Day Country relies on heavy, in-studio production (including drum loops and sequencing). There are crossover artists, such as Tim McGraw and Americana, who explore both styles. Similar bass lines and grooves appear in both, and both sometimes draw from the more traditional Country bass styles covered elsewhere in this chapter. The following lines are primarily Country Rock lines, but will also work with Modern Day Country.

COUNTRY ROCK / MODERN-DAY COUNTRY CHARACTERISTICS

BASS GROOVES: 1) Play half notes, quarter notes, eighth notes, eighth-note triplets, and sixteenth notes, while including syncopation; 2) Play predominantly roots and fifths; 3) Some improvisation is possible in the final one or two bars of a chord progression.

TONE: Clean. **Bass flat to +6 dB, Mids -3 to +3 dB, Treble -3 to +3 dB.**

GEAR: Electric bass exclusively.

TECHNIQUE: Finger style. Both staccato and legato.

PROGRESSIONS: Progressions tend to be on the simple side.

  1) I7 - I7 - I7 - I7 - IV7 - IV7 - I7 - I7 - V7 - IV7 - I7 - I7
  2) I - I - IV - IV - V - V - I - I
  3) I - I - IV - V - V7 - I - V7 - I
  4) I - I - IV - I - I - IV - V7 - I
  5) V - I - VI - I - VI - I - V - I
  6) I - I - IV - V - IV - V - I - I

QUARTER NOTE = 58 – 184 BPM (ballads on the slow end)

COUNTRY ROCK EXAMPLE 1 (CD 1 TRACK 82)

COUNTRY ROCK EXAMPLE 1 VARIATION 1 (CD 1 TRACK 83, DVD TRACK 42)

COUNTRY ROCK EXAMPLE 1 VARIATION 1 (CD 1 TRACK 84, DVD TRACK 43)

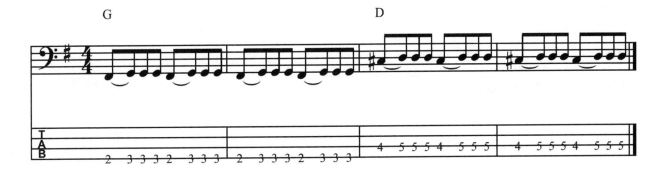

COUNTRY ROCK EXAMPLE 1 VARIATION 3

COUNTRY ROCK BALLAD EXAMPLE 1

In contrast to the normally swung Country Ballad, Country Rock Ballads are always played straight.

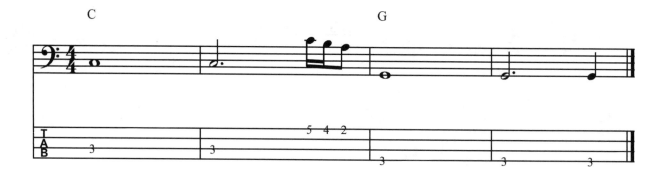

COUNTRY ROCK ROCK BALLAD EXAMPLE 1 VARIATION 1

HALF-TIME COUNTRY ROCK BALLAD EXAMPLE 1

Because of the extremely slow tempo (quarter note = 50 – 80) half-time Country Rock Ballad bass lines may use busier patterns, including sixteenth notes, than you'd find in faster tunes.

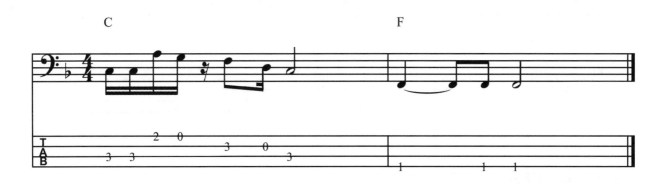

COUNTRY BALLAD

ONE OF THE MOST PROMINENT FORMS in Country music is the slow ballad. The first four grooves are used in many Country Ballads, including Willie Nelson's hits "Night Life" and "Crazy."

Country Ballads are normally swung but written in 4/4. There are, however, occasional Country Ballads played in straight time, a good example being Mickey Gilley's "A Headache Tomorrow or a Heartache Tonight." The primary example and variation 4 will fit such a straight-time ballad. (All other examples and variations should be swung.)

COUNTRY BALLAD CHARACTERISTICS

BASS GROOVES: Play half-note, quarter-note, and eighth-note roots and fifths.

QUARTER NOTE = 50 – 80 BPM (Because Country Ballads are normally swung, despite being written in 4/4, the actual tempo range is **DOTTED QUARTER NOTE = 50 – 80 BPM.**)

COUNTRY BALLAD EXAMPLE 1 (CD 1 TRACK 85)

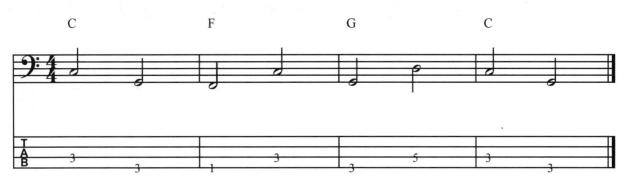

COUNTRY BALLAD EXAMPLE 1 VARIATION 1

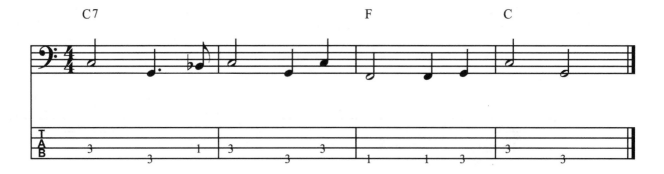

COUNTRY BALLAD EXAMPLE 1 VARIATION 2

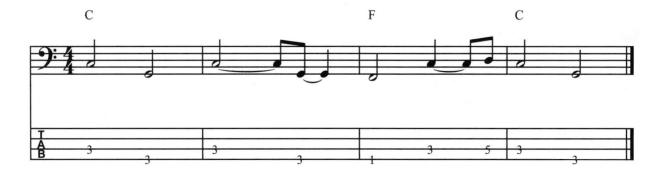

COUNTRY BALLAD EXAMPLE 1 VARIATION 3

The following variation is written in 12/8, because it's easier to read in 12/8 than in 4/4. (The above variations are written in 4/4, with the understanding that the bass player will swing them.)

The following example is written in 4/4 and is played straight, that is, played as written rather than swung.

 ## COUNTRY WALTZ

The Country Waltz spans the history and range of styles within Country music: Bluegrass, Traditional Country, Country Rock, and Modern Day Country. In contrast to Jazz and Cajun/Zydeco waltzes, Country waltzes tend to have less busy/driving bass lines and simpler drumming patterns (e.g., the snare drum is rarely played on beat 2). The Country Waltz is normally used in slower songs or Country Ballads. (See also the Bluegrass section of this chapter.)

COUNTRY WALTZ CHARACTERISTICS

BASS GROOVES: 1) Play dotted half notes, half notes and quarter notes; 2) Play roots, fifths, triads, and walking lines.

TECHNIQUE: Finger style. Play both staccato and legato.

QUARTER NOTE = 76 – 116 BPM

COUNTRY WALTZ EXAMPLE 1

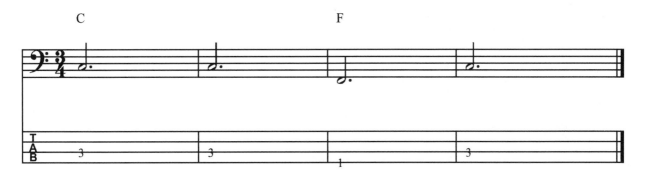

COUNTRY WALTZ EXAMPLE 1 VARIATION 1

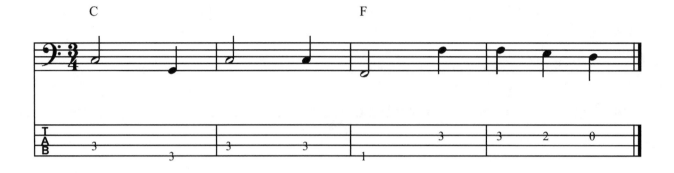

COUNTRY WALTZ EXAMPLE 1 VARIATION 2

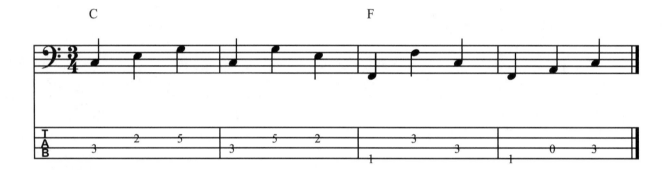

9 DISCO

WHEN LIVE MUSIC was effectively banned in France during WWII, underground clubs sprang up playing records, primarily American Jazz. These new clubs became known as *Discotheques* (which translates as "record libraries"). From there, somehow, the word migrated to the other side of the Atlantic, where three decades later it again referred to a dance club playing canned music—but this time in a very different style.

Disco incorporates stylistic elements of Rock, Funk and the Motown sound, while also drawing from Swing, Soca, Merengue, and Afro-Cuban styles. It is above all else beat-driven dance music. Consequently, the role of the drummer is to make the beat prominent and unwavering at all times. Bassists often create relatively interesting lines to contrast with the incessant "four-on-the-floor" drum patterns.

Although some elements of Disco appeared in the music of Funk groups such as Sly and the Family Stone, the style really began to develop in the early to mid-1970s when dance clubs ("discotheques"), such as the Peppermint Lounge and Studio 54 in New York City, became popular. Major record labels began sup-plying these clubs with dance music on the first known pressings of 12" promo vinyl records (developed by music promoter Tom Moulton), which offered longer "re-mixes" of three-minute standard pop songs.

Disco emerged on the radio with a series of early hit singles including "The Hustle" (Van McCoy & the Soul City Symphony), "Love to Love You Baby" (Donna Summer), "Rock The Boat" (Hues Corporation), "Never Can Say Goodbye" (performed by Gloria Gaynor, written originally by the Jackson Five), and "Le Freak" (Chic). The genre reached its greatest popularity in the years 1977–1978, culminating with the movie *Saturday Night Fever* (featuring the Bee Gees), which pushed Disco high onto the music charts and into major concert venues, and greatly contributed to popularizing Disco's fashion and culture. The movie's soundtrack arguably stands as the most thorough compilation of Disco music. The genre began to fade toward the end of the decade, only to return in the mid-1990s with a trendy "retro revival" in dance clubs, samplings of it in popular songs, and through live Disco/party cover bands.

DISCO CHARACTERISTICS

BASS GROOVES: Bass lines often feature offbeat eighth notes and syncopated eighth and/or sixteenth notes, offsetting the repetitive drum grooves

TONE: Bass +6 to +9 dB, Mids -6 dB @ 500 Hz, Treble +3dB. Flange and chorus are common.

GEAR: Any electric bass can be used. Not much fun for upright players.

PROGRESSIONS: Unlike chord progressions in most genres of American music, Blues-based progressions are seemingly entirely absent in Disco. Stepwise motion is common, especially the i - bVII progression.

1) i7 - i7 - bVII - bVII - i7 - i7 - bVII - bVII - IV - IV - IV - IV

2) I - V - IV - I - vi - I - IV - V

3) IV/V - Imaj7 - Imaj7 - Imaj7 - IV/V - V - V - Imaj7

4) I - IV - I - bVII/I

5) i7 - bVII - bVI - iv

6) i - iv - i - bVI - v - bVI - bVII - i

QUARTER NOTE = 108 – 120 BPM

DISCO EXAMPLE 1 (CD 1 TRACK 86)

DISCO FILL 1 (CD 1 Track 87, DVD Track 44)

It's common in disco bass lines to fill in the last measure of a pattern, or to connect sections of a song, with a chromatic ascending phrase in octaves.

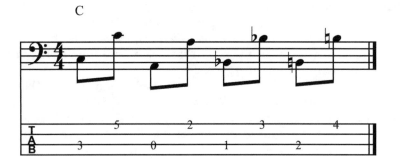

DISCO EXAMPLE 2 (CD 1 Track 88,)

DISCO EXAMPLE 3

DISCO FILL 2

Sixteenth-note fills are common in Disco bass playing.

DISCO EXAMPLE 4

DISCO EXAMPLE 5

10 JUNGLE DRUM N' BASS

THE HISTORY OF DRUM AND BASS/JUNGLE music is relatively short. It is, however, immensely popular within a musical subculture. Jungle was the first of the two styles, emerging around the early 1990s and influenced by the UK hardcore Techno dance scene (specifically the Breakbeat style). Jungle borrowed the frantic, up-tempo, electronic rhythms of Techno, while mixing in Reggae bass lines and Raggamuffin-style vocals (rapping with a Reggae accent and rhythm). In addition, the growing popularity of programmed Hip Hop beats and rhythms had a profound effect on Jungle music.

Many of the compositions in D&B/Jungle and Hip Hop are based on a 1969 B-Side titled "Amen Brother" (by The Winstons). A six-second sample of a drum solo from this track became known as "The Amen Break." This sample has been used on literally hundreds of Drum & Bass, Techno, and Jungle recordings.

Toward the middle of the 1990s, Jungle DJs and composers began experimenting with longer songs with fewer vocals, more synthesizer ambience, Jazz and Funk influence, and live drums, eventually leading to the creation of Drum and Bass (often written as "Drum n' Bass" or "D&B").

There are a lot of subgenres and derivatives, such as Dubstep—slowed down D&B which features a "wobble bass" sound. Others include Drumstep (Dubstep at D&B tempos), Techstep, and Neurofunk. Bands such as Biodiesel and Disco Biscuits play a newer form, Livetronica, a sub-genre of the jam band movement, which fuses electronic tracks and live musicians.

Notable artists include DJ Dara, Dieselboy (Damian Higgins), Aphrodite (Gavin King), Roni Size (Ryan Williams), LTJ Bukem (Danny Williamson), Marcus Intalex (Marcus Kaye), Fabio (Fitzroy Heslop) and Grooverider (Raymond Bingham), Goldie Clifford (Joseph Price), Andy C (Andrew Clark), Dom & Roland (Dominic Angas), AK1200 (Dave Minner), DJ Rap (Charissa Saverio), John B. Craze, and Danny tha Wildchild. Bill Laswell, a U.S. bassist, plays live shows has released several albums in the D&B style beginning in the mid 1990s, and has collaborated with D&B artists and producers worldwide.

The primary difference between Drum and Bass and Jungle is the influence of Reggae in Jungle, as opposed to the influence of Jazz and Acid Jazz in Drum and Bass.

"AMEN BREAK"

This drum pattern (mentioned above) is undoubtedly the most heavily sampled Jungle / Drum n' Bass drum track. A bassist playing in either style should be familiar with it.

Drum n' Bass / Jungle Characteristics

Bass Grooves: Ironically, a live bassist (or drummer) is not always required in Jungle/Drum n' Bass, due to the heavy influence of sampled/sequenced/electronic music. Nevertheless, it can be quite challenging to perform as a live musician on the electric bass. This is largely due to the difficulty of duplicating the mechanical sound and feel of an electronic groove produced by a computer or sequencer. The sometimes very brisk tempos only make the task harder.

The variety of patterns is virtually endless. The appeal of this style musically, for a bassist, is that the bass is out front. In almost all other styles the bass remains in the background, at least most of the time, but in Drum & Bass it's featured prominently (although the drums tend to be more active than the bass).

A bassist will normally follow the kick drum pattern (sometimes without playing beat one, as in Dub and Reggae). Triplet-based lines used in Dub, Dancehall and Reggae are common. One common variation is to take a kick drum pattern and create a bass line from an arpeggiated chord. It's common to use ascending or descending patterns in minor scales or the blues scale.

A consistent repetitive pattern (often referred to as a "loop") is common in almost all Jungle / Drum n' Bass grooves. Even though establishment and maintenance of a groove is crucial, it's possible to improvise. But if the drums are very active, play fewer notes.

If you follow these guidelines, your Jungle / Drum n' Bass patterns should sound authentic: 1) Follow kick drum patterns; 2) With active drums, play sparsely, and use long notes; 3) With less active drums (Dancehall, Reggae) use funky syncopated patterns and consider dropping beat one; 4) Play roots unless playing a syncopated line; 5) Use other chord tones as pedal tones to change the tonal center.

Tone: Dry. Generally, use as little treble as possible. Boost the bass and roll off everything above 100 Hz. Tone is vital. **Bass +9 to +15 dB, Mids -15 dB @ 500 Hz, Treble -15 dB.** In order to reproduce the sounds of Drum n' Bass's programmed grooves, you can also use effects patches that sound synthetic and robotic, but it is important to stay away from anything that has a lot of treble.

Gear: Bass lines are mostly computer samples or synthesizer and sequencer based. But some upright bassists play this style, as do some electric bassists and electric upright bassists. Effects are often used, including low pass filter, ring modulator, heavy compression, and octave boxes. MIDI pickups on an electric bass could be employed to trigger synthesizers or samplers.

Technique: Primarily finger style. You can mute with your palm or your left hand. A piece of foam under the bridge to mute the strings might also prove effective. You can emulate the large amounts of compression and gated sounds that are sometimes used in D & B by muting with your left hand (releasing the fretted note).

Progressions: Progressions tend to be simple but can vary widely.

1) I - I - II - III
2) i - i - iv - iv/v
3) i - i - vi - vi
4) i/biii - iv/v
5) I - I - bIII - bVII
6) I - VII - I - VII
7) i7 - i7 - i7 - i7
8) I - I - I - I

Quarter Note = 144 – 192 bpm

JUNGLE / DRUM & BASS EXAMPLE 1 (CD 1 TRACK 89, DVD TRACK 45)

This minimalistic line is appropriate with an active drum pattern.

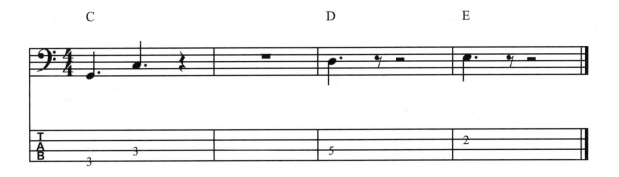

JUNGLE / DRUM & BASS EXAMPLE 1 VARIATION 1 (CD 1 TRACK 90)

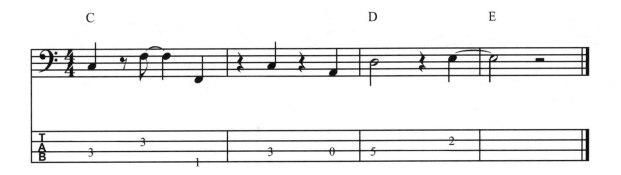

JUNGLE / DRUM & BASS EXAMPLE 2

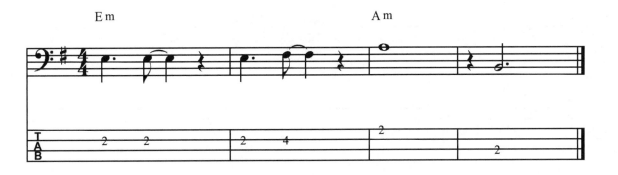

Jungle / Drum & Bass Example 3 (CD 1 Track 91)

Jungle / Drum & Bass Example 4

Jungle / Drum & Bass Example 5 (CD 1 Track 92, DVD Track 46)

JUNGLE / DRUM & BASS EXAMPLE 6 (CD 1 TRACK 93, DVD TRACK 47)

For a Dancehall/Reggae sound, drop beat one and come in on the "and" of beat two.

11 FLAMENCO

FLAMENCO IS A MUSIC AND DANCE FORM that originated over 500 years ago in Andalucia in southern Spain. Early Flamenco blended influences from European and Middle Eastern cultures (Gypsies, Jews, Moors/Arabs, native Andalucians), including Hindu dances mixed with emotional Greek and Roman poems and songs. Flamenco music comes in many feels (3/4, 4/4, 6/8, "12 count," etc.). The most practical traditional forms incorporating the bass are Rumba (Rumba Gitena and Catalana, not to be confused with the Cuban style of Rumba) and Tangos (not to be confused with the Argentine Tango), both in 4/4.

Traditional Flamenco instrumentation includes classical guitar, singing, vocal chanting, the percussive sounds of staccato hand clapping, castanets, and the stomping of the dancers' heels—all to an unwavering, steady pulse. Although its development took many centuries, it wasn't until the early 1900s that Flamenco reached its greatest popularity. Today, artists such as the Gipsy Kings with bassist Gerard Prevost have become popular worldwide (while modernizing the style of Rumba Catalana), and traditional Flamenco continues to be performed throughout the world and in annual festivals, notably in Andalucia.

Other notable Flamenco bassists include Carles Benevent, who plays with Chick Corea and Paco de Lucia, Javier Colina, Dominique Di Piazza, Abraham Laboriel, and Stanley Clarke. Flamenco can even be played on bass as a solo instrument, as exemplified by Victor Wooten's "The Lesson."

Nuevo Flamenco ("New Flamenco") is a modern hybrid of Flamenco, Jazz, Afro-Cuban, Brazilian, and other styles. Bass lines in it often come from these styles rather than traditional Flamenco. Notable Nuevo Flamenco artists include Paco de Lucia, Pata Negra, and Ketama.

FLAMENCO CHARACTERISTICS

BASS GROOVES: Flamenco bass patterns are dance oriented, resembling Soca grooves. (See Caribbean chapter.) Nuevo Flamenco bass lines, however, often borrow grooves from Afro-Cuban, Brazilian, and other styles.

Occasionally Flamenco bassists will play complicated solos at the beginnings of songs, but basic Flamenco bass patterns tend to be simple and relatively unsyncopated. The bass sometimes drops out for entire sections of songs, especially during solos.

TONE: Bass flat to +3 dB, Mids flat to +3 dB @ 500–700 Hz, Treble flat. Effects such as chorus or flange can be used. A little natural (overdriven) distortion can creep in on vigorous, up-tempo tunes.

GEAR: The bass is not normally used in traditional Flamenco. However, in "pop style" or Nuevo Flamenco, any type of bass can be used, including acoustic bass guitar.

TECHNIQUE: Finger style. At times percussive. A bit of slap and pop (see Funk chapter) can be used in solos.

PROGRESSIONS: Chord progressions in Flamenco are usually in minor keys and often use the major chords from their relative major keys plus the dominant (V). (For instance, when the key is Em you could use the major chords from G major — G, C, D — and also the dominant in Em: B). Since guitarists often use the Phrygian scale in Flamenco, some progressions (especially i - bII, and elaborations on it) are derived from that scale.

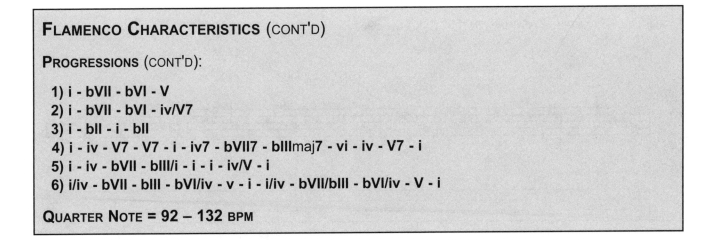

Flamenco Characteristics (CONT'D)

PROGRESSIONS (CONT'D):

1) i - bVII - bVI - V
2) i - bVII - bVI - iv/V7
3) i - bII - i - bII
4) i - iv - V7 - V7 - i - iv7 - bVII7 - bIIImaj7 - vi - iv - V7 - i
5) i - iv - bVII - bIII/i - i - i - iv/V - i
6) i/iv - bVII - bIII - bVI/iv - v - i - i/iv - bVII/bIII - bVI/iv - V - i

QUARTER NOTE = 92 – 132 BPM

FLAMENCO EXAMPLE 1 (CD 1 TRACK 94, DVD TRACK 48)

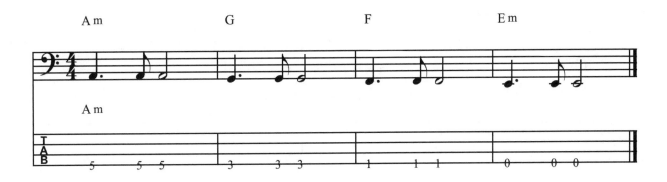

FLAMENCO EXAMPLE 2 (CD 1 TRACK 95, DVD TRACK 49)

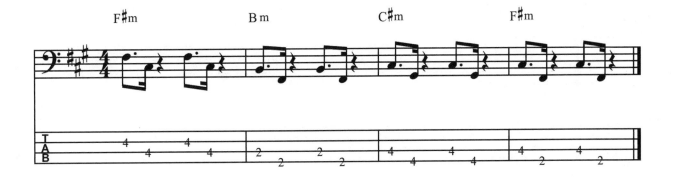

Flamenco Example 2 Variation 1 (CD 1 Track 96)

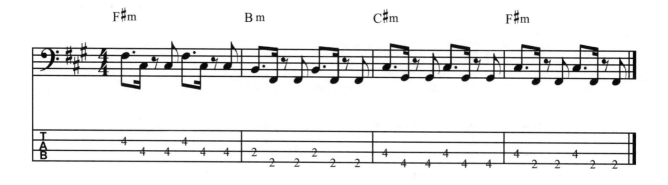

Flamenco Example 3

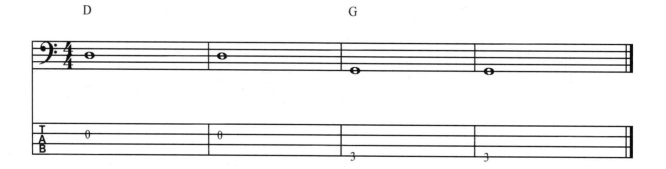

Flamenco Example 3 Variation 1

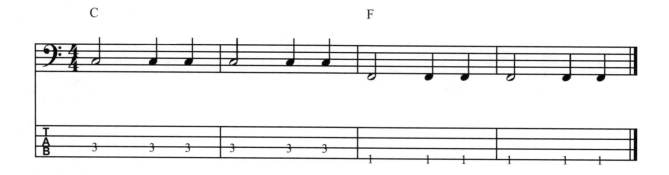

FLAMENCO EXAMPLE 4 (CD 1 TRACK 97)

FLAMENCO EXAMPLE 5

NUEVO FLAMENCO EXAMPLE 1

A simple Samba bass line can work well in Nuevo Flamenco. See the Brazilian chapter for more ideas.

NUEVO FLAMENCO EXAMPLE 2

Playing on the 1 and the "and" of 2 can help develop news ideas. See Afro-Cuban chapter.

12 FUNK

LIKE JAZZ, BE BOP, AND ROCK N' ROLL, Funk acquired its name from a slang expression with sexual connotations. In musical terms, it originally meant anything that was off the traditional path or something that was "funky," especially in the sense of being syncopated. Some of the earliest forms of Funk began in the city that gave birth to Jazz, New Orleans. Along with New Orleans native Fats Domino, one of the most influential musicians to contribute to the genre is piano player Henry Roeland "Roy" Byrd, popularly known as "Professor Longhair." His style combines the sounds of early Rock n' Roll and Blues with Afro-Cuban-influenced New Orleans Second Line.

In the 1950s, another primary precursor of Funk arose—Soul Music. It combined elements of Rock n' Roll and Rhythm & Blues, with Ray Charles being among the first prominent Soul performers.

Near the end of the decade, another artist appeared who would become the driving force of Soul/Funk music for over 40 years: James Brown, "The Godfather of Soul." Brown created driving dance music which combined advanced musicianship with the syncopated and displaced rhythms which have come to characterize Funk. (This refers to "displacing" one of the snare drum strokes on beats 2 and 4 to the "and" of one of those beats.) Brown's prominent bass players include Bernard Odum, William "Bootsy" Collins, Fred Thomas, and Ray Brundridge.

In 1960 in Detroit, Motown Records, founded and run by Berry Gordy, composer of "Money," helped create what is now called "the Motown sound." Prominent bassists who recorded on the Motown label included James Jamerson and Bob Babbitt. They and other session musicians, informally known as the Funk Brothers, played on hundreds of recordings by different artists, without credit and with scanty financial compensation. Jamison, Babbitt and other Motown session musicians performed on more number one hits than the Beatles, Rolling Stones, Beach Boys, and Elvis combined, yet they benefited little from their string of hits.

The other prominent Soul label at the time was Stax, whose recordings often featured bassist Donald "Duck" Dunn. By the mid-1960s, through the influence of James Brown, Stax, and Motown Records, the Soul style had become firmly established. Straight time, syncopated rhythms, conspicuous bass lines (utilizing offbeat eighth and/or sixteenth notes, often made prominent through staccato playing), displaced snare drum notes, percussive horn arrangements, and reliance on the blues scale all emerged as defining sounds of Funk—characteristics that remain to this day.

As the sixties came to a close, several bands latched on to the infectious energy of Funk, with Sly and the Family Stone taking it into the pop mainstream. In addition to Sly Stone's song writing, the group relied on bass lines devised by one of the most important musicians of the Funk style, Larry Graham. Graham almost single handedly changed the way electric bass guitar was played, as his slap and pop technique propelled the bass to the front of Funk ensembles.

By the early 1970s, Funk had become popular around the globe. Along with Graham and Sly and the Family Stone, Dr. John, the Meters, and later the Neville Brothers (with the latter three bands featuring bassist George Porter, Jr.) helped mature the sounds of Funk as it became ever more popular. During the rest of the decade, Funk continued to blossom through the success of artists/groups such as War, Tower of Power, Curtis Mayfield, George Clinton and Funkadelic, Earth, Wind and Fire, The Commodores, The Ohio Players, Stevie Wonder, Barry White, The Brothers Johnson, and The Average White Band.

By the 1980s, Funk's popularity had begun to diminish, even though the grooves of the Funk rhythm section had made their way into pop music through artists such as Prince, Michael Jackson, and Kool and the Gang. Even Rock bands of the past three decades have relied on Funk concepts, Dave Matthews, The Red Hot Chili Peppers, and Primus being prominent examples. Hip Hop and modern R&B have also borrowed heavily from the rhythms and grooves of traditional Funk. Today, the sounds and ideas of Funk pervade all popular music to such an extent that it has become an essential style for the working bassist.

As a bonus to bass players, the bass line is very prominent in Funk and often determines the "hook" of a song (e.g.., M.C. Hammer's "Can't Touch This," which uses the bass line from Rick James' "Superfreak"). This has created the long-awaited opportunity for the bass player to stand out as a leading instrumentalist.

■ NEW ORLEANS FUNK

NEW ORLEANS FUNK bass playing stresses rhythmic accuracy. Although the bassist's notes are sparse, the painstaking accuracy of the notes' placement creates an infectious and conspicuous bottom.

The pioneers in this style include bassists Billy Diamond, Frank Fields, and later Will Harvey, Jr. The current most prominent New Orleans Funk bassist is George Porter, Jr., who is the bassist for the Neville Brothers and The Meters, and who has appeared on recordings with Dr. John, Jimmy Buffet, David Byrne, Robbie Robertson, and Paul McCartney. Other notable musicians in this genre include Professor Longhair and Dr. John.

LEGBA BEAT

The most common rhythm found in New Orleans Funk bass lines is the "Legba beat." (Legba is a spirit in Haitian/Creole culture.) It consists of beat 1, the "and" of beat 2, and beat 4. The Legba beat is identical to the Cuban Tumbao rhythm, except that the "one" is played in Legba, while it is held over from the fourth beat of the previous measure in Tumbao.

However this primary rhythm is not strictly maintained. While it appears as the main groove in songs such as "Brother John," "Fire on the Bayou," and "Hey Pocky A-Way," permutations appear in such classics as "Big Chief" and "Meet the Boys on the Battlefront."

NEW ORLEANS FUNK CHARACTERISTICS

BASS GROOVES: As with all Funk patterns, New Orleans Funk bass patterns are syncopated. The Blues Scale is the norm, and repetitive patterns are prominent. Bass grooves utilizing the Legba beat (beat 1, the "and" of beat 2, and beat 4) are played more staccato than legato. Derivations of the Legba beat are often used as a two-part complementary phrase.

TONE: Bass +3 to +9 dB, Mids flat to +3 dB @ 500 Hz, Treble flat to +3 dB. Effects such as flange and chorus are commonly used.

GEAR: Electric bass is the norm.

TECHNIQUE: Finger style.

PROGRESSIONS: Progressions normally center on the I, IV and V or i, iv and v, but often stray somewhat.

1) I7 - I7 - I7 - I7- IV7 - IV7 - I7 - I7 - V7 - IV7 - I7 - I7
2) I - I - IV - IV - V7 - V7 - I - I
3) I - I - I - V7 (bridge) bIII - bIII - bIII - bIII
4) i - i - i - i - VI - iv - VI - iv
5) IV - V - I - I - I - I - IV - vi - IV - IV - V - I
6) i7 - i7 - v7 - iv7 - v7 - i7 - i7
7) I - i - V - iii/V7
8) i - bIII - bVI7 - V7 - IV - bIII - bVI7 - V7/i

QUARTER NOTE = 70 – 104 BPM

LEGBA BEAT EXAMPLE 1 (CD 2 TRACK 1, DVD TRACK 50)

LEGBA BEAT EXAMPLE 1 VARIATION 1

LEGBA BEAT EXAMPLE 1 VARIATION 2 (CD 2 TRACK 2)

Legba Beat Example 1 Variation 3

New Orleans Funk Example 1 (CD 2 Track 3, DVD Track 51)

New Orleans Funk Example 1 Variation 1

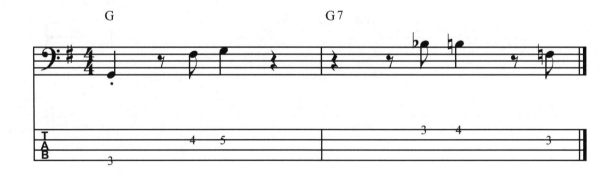

MOTOWN / STAX

MOTOWN, A SUB-GENRE OF FUNK AND SOUL music, is associated with Motown Records, (founded by Berry Gordy in 1960 in Detroit). It was the first label owned by an African-American, and featured artists who crossed over to the pop charts. Artists such as Smokey Robinson and the Miracles, Stevie Wonder, Marvin Gaye, The Supremes, The Four Tops, The Temptations, Jr. Walker and the All Stars, and many more all played and recorded with one bassist: James Jamerson.

As a core member of a group of studio musicians informally called The Funk Brothers, and playing on reportedly 95 percent of Motown recordings between 1962 and 1968, Jamerson was one of the most influential bassists in modern music. His playing expanded the role of the bassist in dance music from playing repetitive patterns to playing melodic, syncopated, and improvisational lines. Jamerson influenced countless bassists not only by the licks he played, but also in the imaginative ways he modified his licks as a song progressed, changing just a few notes or the phrasing to keep the groove interesting yet solid and infectious. (The history of the Funk Brothers is detailed in a 1989 book by Allan Slutsky, *Standing in the Shadows of Motown*, which was turned into a documentary film in 2002.) After Jamerson left Motown, Bob Babbitt suc-

ceeded him in the Funk Brothers. Babbitt's playing tended more toward regular syncopated patterns than Jamerson's. (Motown Example 1 on p. 120 is similar to Babbitt's lines, while Example 2 on page 121 is similar to Jamerson's.)

The main competitors of Motown, Stax, Volt, and Atco records, and their distributor Atlantic Records, produced hits from 1959 through 1968 using their own studio house band, Booker T and the MG's, with bassist Donald "Duck" Dunn. Dunn's lines were somewhat similar to Babbitt's, with perhaps a bit less syncopation than Babbitt employed.

Artists in the Stax roster included Otis Redding, Sam and Dave, Issac Hayes, Albert King, Wilson Pickett, King Curtis, and The Staple Singers. Overall sonically and rhythmically similar to the bass lines in Motown, the bass lines in the Atlantic recordings were derived from R&B.

Since Stax and Motown bass lines are quite similar, they are both included in this section. The primary distinction is that Stax lines are more repetitive than those in Motown, and are built predominantly from the Blues Scale, whereas Motown lines include non-Blues-Scale notes and wander further afield harmonically.

MOTOWN / STAX CHARACTERISTICS

BASS GROOVES:

MOTOWN: Grooves have an eighth-note feel, but utilize syncopation; they use notes from the Blues Scale, but also include non-Blues-Scale notes; and the bassist often establishes a pattern and then embellishes it.

STAX: Grooves have an eighth-note feel, but utilize syncopation; they primarily use notes from the Blues Scale; and they're repetitive.

TONE (MOTOWN): Bass +9 to +12 dB, Mids flat, Treble +3 dB. If you're playing with round wound strings, roll the treble off on your instrument's tone control.

TONE (STAX): Bass +6 to +12 dB, Mids flat to +3 dB @ 350 Hz, Treble +3 dB.

GEAR: Electric bass is the norm.

TECHNIQUE: Finger style for both.

PROGRESSIONS: As well as Blues progressions and variants of them, both Motown and Stax compositions utilize the bVI, bVII, bIII and II chords mixed in with I, IV, and V chords. A lot of songs stay on the I chord during the bridge or chorus sections. Abrupt modulations are also used in some progressions, most commonly moving the key up a full step at the beginning of a new verse (as from C to D). There are many unique progressions, though not many formulas.

1) I7 - I7 - I7 - I7 - IV7 - IV7 - I7 - I7 - V7 - IV7 - I7 - I7
2) i7 - i7 - i7 - i7 - iv7 - iv7 - i7 - i7 - v7 - iv7 - i7 - i7
3) I - I - I - I - IV - IV - IV - IV - I - bIII - IV - I
4) I - I/IV - I - I/IV - I - I/IV - I/V - I
5) I - I - V - V - IV - IV - V - V
6) bVII - V - IV - bIII - I7 - IV7 - I7 - IV7 - I7 - IV7 - I7 - IV7
7) iv - v - i - i - iv - v - bVI - bVII - bIII - bIII - bIII - bIII
8) I - IV - bVI/bVII - I
9) I7 - I7 - I7 - I7 - IV7 - IV7 - IV7 - IV7 - I - bIII - IV - I
10) i - i - V7 - IV - vi - IV - i - IV
11) i - i/bVII - bVImaj7 - V7sus4/V7
12) I - ii7 - IV - V

QUARTER NOTE = 100 – 140 BPM

MOTOWN EXAMPLE 1 (CD 2 TRACK 5, DVD TRACK 52)

MOTOWN EXAMPLE 2 (CD 2 TRACK 6)

Though impossible to fully demonstrate in only four bars, this example shows how James Jamerson might have improvised on a theme. The first bar is the original line and the next three bars vary the line. See the excellent book *Standing in the Shadows of Motown* for more in-depth information.

STAX EXAMPLE 1 (CD 2 TRACK 7, DVD TRACK 53)

STAX EXAMPLE 2 (CD 2 TRACK 8)

EARLY FUNK

"THE GODFATHER OF SOUL," James Brown, for all intents and purposes *was* Funk for most of the 1960s. He was largely responsible for both the name Funk and its popularity in that decade. (Some attribute the name to drummer Earl Palmer.) Although Brown was already developing his unique style in the late 1950s, while moving away from straight R&B, it wasn't until 1963 that the first arguably Funk hit album landed on the charts: "James Brown Live at the Apollo."

The hallmarks of Brown's new style were use of Blues and R&B progressions, extensive syncopation, especially "displaced" drum beats which strayed from the snare drum's traditional backbeats on "2" and "4," and extensive use of horns in a percussive manner ("horn punches"). All of this lent itself to the descriptive term, "funky."

Early Funk basically covers the period between its origination by James Brown in the late 1950s and early 1960s and his stylistic shift away from progression-oriented songs and into one-and-two-chord vamp-oriented songs (Later Funk) in the late 1960s. "Cold Sweat" (1967) and "Say It Loud, I'm Black and I'm Proud" (1968), are landmarks in Brown's shift in styles.

EARLY FUNK CHARACTERISTICS

BASS GROOVES: Early Funk makes use of syncopation, but with a more driving feel than that of the laid back New Orleans groove. Just as in New Orleans Funk, Early Funk grooves may be felt over one or two measures, although two-measure grooves are common. When two-bar phrases are used, the second bar is often more syncopated than the first.

Early Funk grooves utilize notes from the Blues Scale (plus, of course, the major third), and syncopated eighth notes are prominent. (The use of syncopated sixteenth notes is much more prevalent in Later Funk.)

TONE: Bass +3 to +6 dB, Mids flat to +3 dB, Treble flat to +3 dB. Just a hair of natural distortion.

GEAR: Electric bass.

TECHNIQUE: Finger style.

PROGRESSIONS: In contrast with those in Later Funk, Early Funk progressions were often built on standard Blues and R&B progressions (e.g., "Papa's Got A Brand New Bag," "I Feel Good," "Night Train"), although other types of progressions, even Doo Wop progressions ("Try Me"), were employed. There were also repetitious two-chord patterns (e.g., "Tighten Up," by Archie Bell and the Drells, and the body of James Brown's "Think") that foreshadowed to some extent what was to come in Later Funk: endless one-and-two-chord vamps.

1) I7 - I7 - I7 - I7 - IV7 - IV7 - I7 - I7 - V7 - IV7 - I7 - I7
(with or without a bridge — here's a sample bridge progression) IV7 - IV7 - I7 - I7 - IV7 - IV7 - V7 - V7
2) I7 - IV9 - I7 - IV9 - I7 - I7 - V7 - V7 - IV9 - IV9 - I7 - I7/V7#9
3) I7 - I7 - I7 - I7 - I7 - I7 - I7 - I7 - V7 - V7 - V7 - V7 - V7 - V7 - V7 - V7
4) I - bVII - I - bVII
5) I - vi - IV - V
6) Imaj7 - Imaj7 - iim9 - iim9 - Imaj7 - Imaj7 - iim9 - iim9

QUARTER NOTE = 100 – 140 BPM

EARLY FUNK EXAMPLE 1 (CD 2 TRACK 9)

EARLY FUNK EXAMPLE 1 VARIATION 1 (CD 2 TRACK 10, DVD TRACK 54)

EARLY FUNK EXAMPLE 2 (CD 2 TRACK 11)

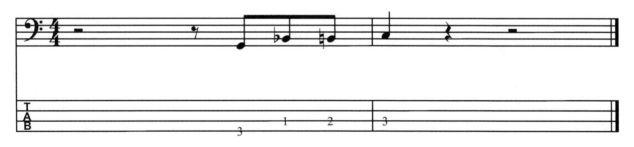

EARLY FUNK EXAMPLE 2 VARIATION 1 (CD 2 TRACK 12)

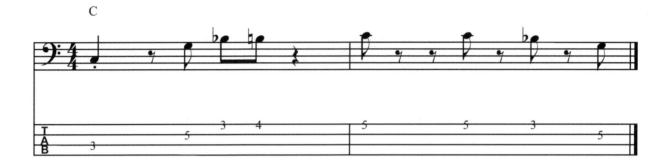

EARLY FUNK EXAMPLE 2 VARIATION 2

EARLY FUNK EXAMPLE 3

■ LATER FUNK

LATER FUNK CAME IN on James Brown's coattails in the late 1960s and early 1970s. In that period, as rhythm became an even more important component of Funk, songs often used only one chord. Eliminating chord changes enabled Funk musicians to use more syncopation, often in the familiar two-part pattern. In this period, syncopation expanded from eighth-note syncopation to sixteenth-note syncopation. In addition, the tempo was often slower than in Early Funk.

All of these factors contributed to bass lines emerging as the "hooks" of songs. Tunes such as "People Say"

by the Meters, "Chameleon," (written by bassist Paul Jackson, Bennie Maupin, Harvey Mason and Herbie Hancock), and "Cold Sweat" by James Brown, emphasize offbeat eighth and sixteenth notes. Generally, the faster the song, the more the bass groove relied on eighth notes, while the slower the song, the more the bass groove relied on sixteenth notes. Whereas New Orleans Funk and Early Funk can be felt in eighth notes over two-measure patterns, Later (more syncopated) Funk is more easily felt in one-measure patterns.

LATER FUNK CHARACTERISTICS

BASS GROOVES: Sixteenth-note syncopation is common, as is use of notes from the Blues Scale. Bass lines are comprised of a repetitive, complementary two-part (two-measure) pattern, with the second measure contrasting with the first, and often feature large interval leaps of an octave or more.

As Funk became more syncopated, an emphasis on beat 1 became less necessary; instead, a bassist can anticipate it by playing ahead of the downbeat, often tying the note over to beat 1. Both playing beat 1 or anticipating beat 1 are effective in Funk — it's simply a matter of choice.

The bassist often plays the "hook" and stands out much more than in other genres.

TONE: Bass +3 to +6 dB, Mids flat to +6 dB @ 500 Hz, Treble +3 to +6 dB. Slight overdrive is normal. (Paul Jackson [Headhunters] sets his amp's tone controls at Bass +3 to +9 dB, Mids -2 to -4 dB between 330 and 475 Hz, Treble +3 to +6 dB. He sets his bass's tone controls flat.)

GEAR: Electric bass. Any bass with active electronics is recommended, as are punchy amps with good definition. Effects commonly used are distortion, flange, chorus, and auto-wah. Mutron stomp boxes provide a classic sound.

TECHNIQUE: Finger style, featuring slapping and popping.

PROGRESSIONS: It's common for Later Funk tunes to stay in the tonic (often on a 9th chord scratched on guitar, "Sex Machine" being a good example) with an unwavering bass line, with perhaps a "bridge" of a IV9 or V9 chord (e.g., "Cold Sweat," whose body consists of dozens of I9 chords and whose bridge consists entirely of IV9 chords, and "Super Bad," whose body consists of endless bars of the I9 chord [literally about three minutes worth] and whose bridge consists of endless bars of IV9 followed by just two bars of V7). Many Later Funk songs went even further and had no progression at all — just an endless bass lick in the tonic, with vocal and instrumental vamping on top of it.

1) **I9 - I9 - I9 - I9** (etc.)   (bridge) **IV9 - IV9 - IV9 - IV9** (etc.)
2) **bVII9 - I9 - bVII9 - I9** (bridge) **bIII9 - IV9 - bIII9 - IV9**
3) **I9 - bVII9 - I9 - bVII9** (etc.)
4) **I9 - I9 - I9 - I9** (etc.)   (bridge) **bVII9 - bIII9 - bVII9 - bIII9** (etc.)

QUARTER NOTE = 80 – 120 BPM

LATER FUNK EXAMPLE 1 (CD 2 TRACK 13)

LATER FUNK EXAMPLE 1 VARIATION 1

LATER FUNK EXAMPLE 2 (CD 2 TRACK 14)

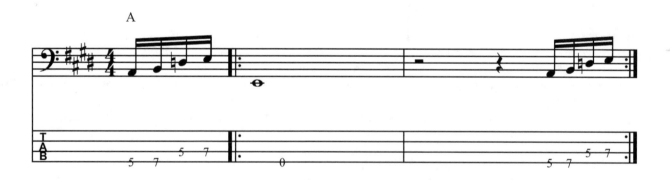

NOTE: Anticipating beat 1 will tend to pull the music forward. The challenge lies in doing this while holding the tempo back. It is also important to keep track of beat 1 even as you are anticipating it, or simply not playing it. Example 1, Example 1 Variation 1, and Example 2 all provide good illustrations of anticipation.

LATER FUNK EXAMPLE 3 (CD 2 TRACK 15, DVD TRACK 55)

LATER FUNK EXAMPLE 3 VARIATION 1

LATER FUNK EXAMPLE 3 VARIATION 2 (CD 2 TRACK 16)

LATER FUNK EXAMPLE 4

LATER FUNK EXAMPLE 5

"HAMBONE" EXAMPLE

Thanks to Paul Jackson for this rhythm, which pops up all over the place in Funk patterns. Think of it as the clave of Funk. Like Afro-Cuban clave rhythms, it can be reversed. Experiment, and have fun, with it.

FUNK ROCK

THOUGH NOT TECHNICALLY an established style, the term "Funk Rock" describes music that can be classified as Rock, but that incorporates elements from Funk, such as syncopated rhythms and percussive horn lines. Bands and artists such as Earth, Wind and Fire, the Commodores, Michael Jackson, the Red Hot Chili Peppers, and Sly and the Family Stone fall into both the Funk and Rock genres. As opposed to those in the other Funk styles, Funk Rock bass lines usually have fewer syncopated notes and place more emphasis on the beat. What distinguishes Funk Rock from Rock is that is still maintains a certain amount of syncopation characteristic of Funk music.

FUNK ROCK CHARACTERISTICS

BASS GROOVES: Bass lines are more on the beat (have less syncopation), are slightly less active, and have a narrower range than in standard Funk. Also, two-part patterns are less common than in standard Funk. But as in standard Funk the bass lines in Funk Rock are repetitive and use notes from the Blues Scale.

TONE: Bass +3 to +9 dB, Mids +3 to +6 dB @ 500 Hz, Treble +3 to +6 dB.

GEAR: Electric bass. Any bass with active electronics is recommended, as are punchy amps with good definition. Effects commonly used are distortion, flange, chorus, and auto-wah.

TECHNIQUE: Finger style, featuring slapping and popping (if called for).

PROGRESSIONS: Funk Rock progressions tend toward the simple side and sometimes repeat the same relatively short progression over and over.

1) **I9 - I9 - I9 - I9** (etc.)   (bridge) **IV7 - bVII9 - bIII7 - bVI9**
2) **i - iii7 - ii7 - V9sus4**
3) **I - V - III - III**
4) **I - vi - I - vi - IV - V - I - vi**
5) **i - bIII - iv - i - bVI - bVII - i - i**
6) **i7 - ii7/v7 - i7 - ii7/v7**
7) **I - I - IV - I**
8) **I - IV - I - bVII - VI - II - VI - V**

QUARTER NOTE = 80 – 120 BPM

Funk Rock Example 1

Funk Rock Example 1 Variation 1

Funk Rock Example 2 (CD 2 Track 17, DVD Track 56)

130

FUNK ROCK EXAMPLE 3 (CD 2 TRACK 18)

FUNK ROCK EXAMPLE 3 VARIATION 1

HALF-TIME FUNK ROCK EXAMPLE 1

C

■ SLAP AND POP

SLAP AND POP IS NOT A STYLE. It's a technique—but an important one. Larry Graham, bassist of Sly and the Family Stone, is generally credited with the invention of slap and pop (which he refers to as "thumpin' and pluckin'"). Graham originally developed this technique while he was playing bass as a youngster with his piano-player mother in a lounge act, The Del Graham Trio. Later, in the Family Stone, he employed it to provide a percussive pulse. His slap and pop technique revolutionized bass expression.

Slap and pop is actually two techniques: striking the thumb on the lower-pitched strings against the fretboard (slap) while plucking the upper (higher-pitched) strings so that they bounce (pop) off the fretboard. Although you can slap or pop on any string, it is more difficult to slap on the D and G strings, so it's more common to slap on E and A. The result is a unique percussive sound. These techniques are applicable only to electric bass; they are very difficult on upright, and upright slapping is a different technique.

A bassist may combine slaps and pops with hammer-ons and hammer-offs, tapping, bending notes, playing harmonics, and other techniques traditionally used by guitarists. Pioneer bassists using this technique include Louis Johnson (The Brothers Johnson), Bootsy Collins (James Brown, Parliament, Funkadelic). Stanley Clarke (Return to Forever), Victor Wooten (Bella Fleck and the Flecktones, Chick Corea), and Marcus Miller (Miles Davis), all of whom incorporated these and other Funk techniques into Jazz. Les Claypool (Primus), Mark King (Level 42), Flea (Red Hot Chili Peppers), and P-Nut (311) brought the technique into Rock. Finally, John Norwood Fisher (Fishbone) incorporated this Funk technique into Ska.

(For spectacular examples of Slap and Pop playing, check out the band SMV, which includes master bassists Stanley Clark, Marcus Miller, and Victor Wooten.)

SLAP AND POP TECHNIQUES

1) **Slap**. Use the side of the thumb in a percussive manner (generally on the lower strings), striking the string against the fretboard.

2) **Pop**. Pull an upper string up off the fretboard with your index or middle finger and release the string so that it rebounds off the fretboard.

3) **Play dead notes**. Mute a string with your fretting hand by touching a string without actually pressing it down on the fret and slap or pop (or pluck conventionally) with the other hand. Take care not to play harmonics (if your intention is to produce a dead note).

4) **Bend notes**. Push or pull a string horizontally on the fretboard with a finger on your fretting hand as the note rings. (It's easier to pull than to push and to use the middle finger rather than any of the others.)

5) **Play hammer-ons**. While slapping or popping play a note and, while the string is still vibrating, hammer the tip of a finger down on a fret higher up on the fretboard in a percussive manner.

6) **Play hammer-offs**. After you play a hammer-on, pull the finger on the upper fret off the fretboard using the same finger to pluck the string as you pull it off.

7) **Play harmonics**. The normal way to do this is to pluck a note while touching the same string (without depressing it) at the 12th, 7th, or 5th frets. It's easiest to produce harmonics at the 12th fret, noticeably harder at the 7th fret, and (especially on cheaper instruments) difficult at the 5th fret. Many other fret positions can produce harmonics, but with increasing difficulty. It's also possible to produce "artificial harmonics" by fretting a note and then stretching your hand and touching a string above a fret with your little finger—experiment with it. (For a classic example of harmonic-playing on bass, listen to "Portrait of Tracy," by Jaco Pastorius.)

SLAP AND POP EXAMPLE 1 (CD 2 TRACK 20, DVD TRACK 57)

One way to learn this style is to work with octaves. Slap (thump: T) on the root and pop (pluck: P) on the octave.

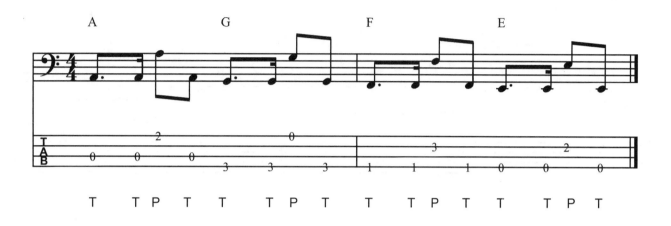

SLAP AND POP EXAMPLE 1 VARIATION 1

Playing triplets also gives you the opportunity to pop twice or "double pop" with the index (P1) and middle (P2) fingers.

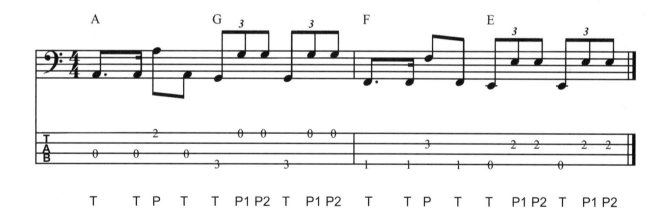

SLAP AND POP EXAMPLE 2 (CD 2 TRACK 21)

Thanks to Alex Szotak for this example and its recording. The "x" note heads denote ghost notes.

13 GOSPEL

GOSPEL MUSIC BROUGHT BLUES into the African-American Baptist Church. Gospel Music (originally called "Gospel Songs") became prominent in the early 20th century through the efforts of a single individual, Thomas A. Dorsey. Born in Villa Rica, Georgia in 1899, Dorsey learned to play piano as a youth in the Baptist Church. An accompanist for such famed Blues singers as Ma Rainey and Bessie Smith, Dorsey decided to compose church music with a Blues influence. One of his primary inspirations was witnessing Charles A. Tindley (1851–1933) perform at the National Baptist Convention. (A Methodist minister who composed and published early African-American religious music, Tindley wrote "I'll Overcome Someday" in 1900, which evolved into the celebrated anthem of the 1960's Civil Rights movement, "We Shall Overcome.") Although these new sounds were initially rejected by the Baptist establishment, Dorsey assiduously promoted his music.

After several years of Dorsey's struggling to win Gospel Music's acceptance by the church, other singers/musicians, such as Mother Willie Mae Ford and Lucy Campbell, began to promote it. This, along with Dorsey's persistent efforts, finally led to Gospel Music's acceptance. By 1932, Dorsey had established The National Convention of Gospel Choirs and Choruses, an institution which still flourishes today. By the time of his death in 1993, Dorsey had written over 800 songs, spanning the near-century of Gospel Music's existence.

Originally sung by large choirs, Gospel was primarily vocal music with no bass instruments, though it did have compelling rhythms produced by hand-clapping, foot-stomping, and the use of drums, cymbals, and tambourines. In the 1930s, Gospel Music began to branch out from its traditional choir arrangements to emphasize solo vocalists. Inspired by Sister Rosetta Tharpe (with George "Pops" Foster on bass), Gospel singer Clara Ward mixed Jazz and Blues with Gospel.

Ward, who sang Gospel Music in nightclubs, reached a wider audience than traditional Gospel singers and soon signed a recording contract. Her 1950s hit, "Surely God Is Able," is believed to be Gospel Music's first million-selling record. In the same decade, several Gospel singers, such as Mahalia Jackson and James Cleveland, emerged as national stars along with such notable Gospel groups as The Caravans and The Soul Stirrers, with founding singer and manager Jesse Farley. Farley then broke more new ground by hiring one of Gospel's first electric bassists, Benny Turner (younger brother of blues guitarist Freddie King).

As the use of instruments increased in Gospel, the acoustic bass and electric bass replaced bass vocalists. Musician/composers such as Ray Charles, Little Richard, and later musicians like Aretha Franklin, Wilson Pickett (The Violinairs) and Ashford and Simpson (The Followers) all created music with strong Gospel overtones and prominent electric bass lines. Other artists, such as The Staple Singers, followed using more R&B and Soul sounds in their primarily Gospel music. Some songs even crossed over into both the R&B/Soul and Gospel genres, with "Oh Happy Day" being the first. The 1980s even saw the rise to "Rap Gospel," a reaction to the Rap music sweeping urban African-American communities.

In the first quarter of the 21st century, Gospel continued to thrive in both the secular and sacred worlds, particularly in large ensembles and choirs within the Baptist Church.

Contemporary Gospel artists include Sweet Honey in the Rock, The Blind Boys of Alabama, Al Green, Shirley Caesar, Marion Williams, and Yolanda Adams along with Christian pop recording star Michael W. Smith. Current Gospel bassists include Tracy Pierce, Andrew Gouche, Joel Smith, Maurice Fitzgerald, and Charles "Volley" Craig, all of whom step outside the traditional Gospel forms.

Gospel Characteristics

Bass Grooves: Bass lines in Gospel tend to be straightforward, without much use of syncopation. In Contemporary Gospel, the bass is sometimes a featured instrument. Although a Gospel bassist's usual task is to support the vocalist(s), his or her role can still be complex. Often playing 5- or 6-string basses with altered tunings, Gospel bassists may use passing tones, hammer ons and offs, slides, vibrato, and fills common to Jazz and R&B. It is important to remember, however, that no matter how complex the embellishments, the main task of the Gospel bassist continues to be laying down a solid groove and supporting the other players and singers.

There are six prominent grooves in Gospel: Polka; Rock; 12/8 Slow Blues; Shuffle; Waltz; and, less commonly, Bossa Nova (in Contemporary Gospel).

Tone:

Early Gospel: Bass +3 to +9 dB, Mids flat, Treble -6 dB. Emulates upright.

Later Gospel: Bass +3 to +6 dB, Mids flat, Treble flat.

Contemporary: Bass +3 to +9 dB, Mid flat to +6 dB @ 500 Hz, Treble flat to +6dB. Tone is similar to Later Gospel or may emulate Funk. (See Funk chapter.) Effects can be used.

Gear:

Early and Later Gospel: Upright was originally used, but today any type of bass can be used.

Contemporary Gospel: With electric basses, active electronics help emphasize midrange and treble. Effects such as flange and chorus are sometimes used, as are 5- and 6-string basses. Upright, however, can be—and still is—used.

Technique:

Early Gospel: Finger Style.

Later Gospel: Finger style, but a pick can be used.

Contemporary Gospel: Finger style. Similar to Later Gospel, or may emulate funk, including slap and pop, hammer-ons/offs, and tapping.

Progressions: The range of styles and progressions used in Gospel has been steadily expanding since its inception. Early Gospel songs tended to use simple chord progressions in major keys, often employing only the I, IV, and/or V. As Gospel developed, one of the signature Gospel patterns, I-IV-I, became common, as did "Shouts," and in Contemporary Gospel almost anything goes, including traditional Gospel tunes, Bossa Novas, II/V patterns from Jazz, and adapted (by, among others, The Blind Boys of Alabama) Rock tunes.

1) I - I - IV - I - I - I - V7 - I
2) I - V7 - V7 - I7 - I7 - V7 - V7 - I
3) I - I - V7 - V7 - V7 - V7 - I - I
4) I - I - I - I - V - V - I - I - ii - V7 - I - I
5) I - I - IV - IV - I - I - V7/II7 - V7
6) I - I - IV - IV - I - V7 - I/IV - I
7) I - IV - I - I - II - V7 - I - V7
8) I - IV - I - I - IV - vi/II - V7 - I
9) III - VI - II/V7 - I
10) I - IV - IV - I - V - V - I - I - IV - IV - I - vi - ii - V - I - I

TURNAROUNDS: Gospel has many characteristics in common with Blues, among them the use of turnarounds.

1) I7/IV7 - I7/V7
2) I7 - I7/V7
3) I7/vi7 - ii7/V7

FALSE ENDINGS: It's common to play the end of a song three times in Gospel (which is also fairly common in Blues). However, all musicians, including the bassist, should be prepared to resume playing yet again. This occurs upon cue, after an apparent (but actually false) ending.

QUARTER NOTE = 100 – 120 BPM
This is the range for traditional Gospel. When playing Gospel tunes using other styles (Rock, Bossa Nova, Jazz, Blues, Polka beat, etc.), see the relevant chapters for normal tempos.

GOSPEL POLKA EXAMPLE 1 (CD 2 TRACK 22, DVD TRACK 58)

The first example is a standard Polka bass line or Two-Step pattern written in 4/4. (Two-four feels are at times written in 4/4.) It is prominent in Early Gospel, and only has two beats per measure, with the beats coming on the first and third quarter notes.

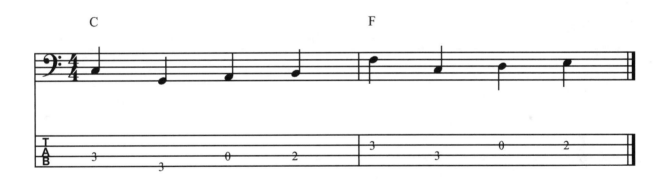

This is the same example written in 2/4.

GOSPEL POLKA EXAMPLE 1 VARIATION 1

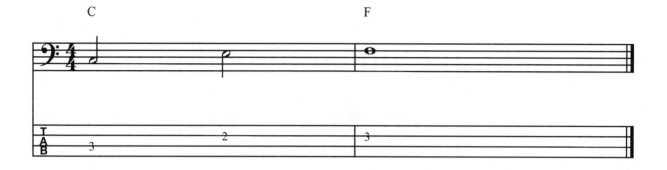

GOSPEL POLKA EXAMPLE 1 VARIATION 2

GOSPEL ROCK EXAMPLE 1 (CD 2 TRACK 23, DVD TRACK 59)

GOSPEL ROCK EXAMPLE 1 VARIATION 1

GOSPEL ROCK EXAMPLE 1 VARIATION 2

GOSPEL 12/8 SLOW BLUES EXAMPLE 1 (CD 2 TRACK 24, DVD TRACK 60)

GOSPEL 12/8 SLOW BLUES EXAMPLE 2 (CD 1 TRACK 38)

GOSPEL 12/8 SLOW BLUES EXAMPLE 2 VARIATION 1 (CD 1 TRACK 39)

GOSPEL SHUFFLE EXAMPLE 1

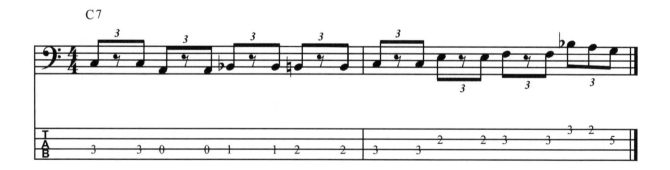

GOSPEL SHUFFLE EXAMPLE 2 (CD 1 TRACK 35, DVD TRACK 14)

GOSPEL SHUFFLE EXAMPLE 3 (CD 1 TRACK 36, DVD TRACK 15)

GOSPEL WALTZ EXAMPLE 1 (CD 2 TRACK 25)

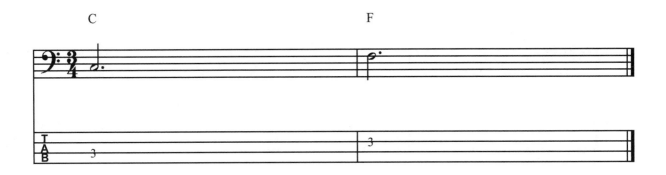

GOSPEL WALTZ EXAMPLE 1 VARIATION 1 (CD 2 TRACK 26)

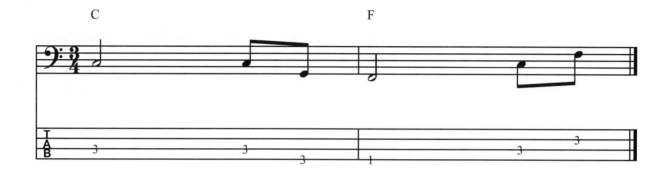

GOSPEL WALTZ EXAMPLE 1 VARIATION 2

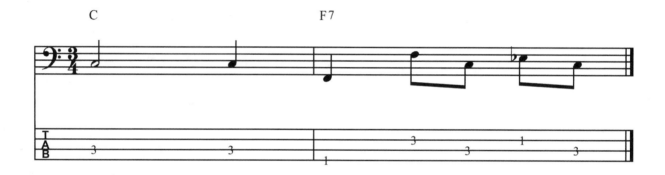

GOSPEL BOSSA NOVA EXAMPLE 1 (CD 1 TRACK 53, DVD TRACK 23)

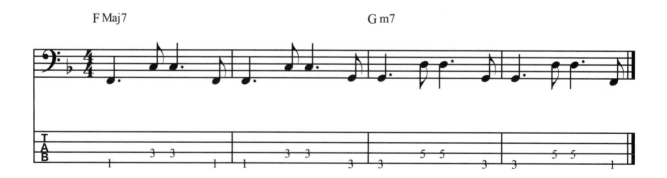

SHOUTS

"Shouts" occur spontaneously in Gospel music, upon the ensemble's inspiration. The feel is identical to that of a Polka. A reliable formula for creating shout bass lines is to employ chromatic intervals within the line, or to utilize the root, 5th and 7th of the chord, as in the examples below. (Unlike Polka, the example and variations below are written in 4/4, with the snare drum/backbeat played on the "ands.") **QUARTER NOTE = 100 – 120 BPM**

GOSPEL SHOUT EXAMPLE (CD 2 TRACK 27, DVD TRACK 61)

GOSPEL SHOUT EXAMPLE VARIATION 1

GOSPEL SHOUT EXAMPLE VARIATION 2

14 HIP HOP / RAP

THE POPULARITY OF RAP MUSIC and the Hip Hop culture has increased immensely over the past 30 years. Its roots extend all the way back to the earliest forms of African call-and-response vocalizings, which are a direct ancestor of Hip Hop/Rap's rhyming spoken lyrics (and to Blues and Funk). At the same time that its roots lie deep in history, Hip Hop, in common with Techno, uses the advanced, modern technology of electronic sampling and sequencing.

One of the most prominent recorded early examples of spoken word technique (in a call-and-response format) in a popular song is the chant "Hi-de-hi-de-hi-de-ho" from Cab Calloway's "Minnie the Moocher" in 1931. By the 1950s, early forms of Rock n' Roll and Doo Wop utilized spoken word in sections of songs (e.g., "Little Darlin'," written by Maurice Williams). Within the next few decades, popular songs such as "Alice's Restaurant," by Arlo Guthrie and "The Devil Went Down to Georgia," by The Charlie Daniels Band, not to mention countless Country songs, had lyrics primarily in spoken word format; and Country artist Red Sovine made a career of recording songs entirely in spoken-word format, such as "Phantom 309" and "Giddy Up Go."

In the 1970s, African-American musicians coupled the spoken word format with the sounds of Funk to produce the earliest easily recognizable antecedents of Rap music. Artists such as Lou Rawls, Barry White, James Brown, The Brothers Johnson, and Isaac Hayes were the pioneers.

At the same time, Jamaican DJs in New York City began to improvise rhymes over Reggae music and rhythms, using the tradition of "toasting" found in Jamaica, where recitation of poetry or sayings over music was common. By 1979, the style began to find a wider audience through its first recordings, most notably "Rapper's Delight" by the Sugar Hill Gang. At the close of the decade, drum machines such as the Linn Drum and slightly later the TR-808 appeared and helped create the first significant electronic grooves to accompany the Rap style.

The success of MTV in the early 1980s exposed Rap to a worldwide audience through artists such as Grandmaster Flash, Blondie (with her top ten hit "Rapture," though she's not considered an essential Rap artist), and the immensely popular Run DMC. As well, Rap culture began creating new styles of clothing, images, and dance ("break dancing") to accompany this rising new musical style. By the middle of the decade, the first forms of sampling appeared, a process incorporating a previously recorded piece of music into a remixed form, often creating a loop.

With the huge success of the collaboration between Run DMC and Aerosmith, with their revised/sampled version of "Walk This Way" in 1986, Run DMC blazed the path which Rap music would follow. The popularity of other sampled songs such as "Wild Thing," by Tone Loc (borrowed from Van Halen's "Jamie's Cryin'") and "Can't Touch This," by MC Hammer (borrowed from Rick James' "Superfreak") produced Rap music's first superstars. Later sensations such as Public Enemy and LL Cool J helped elevate Rap to its place as a dominant style in the music industry. The popularity of Rap became so great that by the end of the decade MTV established a program dedicated solely to the style entitled "Yo MTV Raps."

Also in the 1980s, a new derivative style called Hip Hop made it to film, with the release of "Wild Style," "Beat Street," "Breakin'," and "Krush Groove." The films gave the new style exposure outside of New York, where it developed. The new Hip Hop artists also explored creating rhythms directly from the human body, using vocal "percussion" (imitating instruments), and even turntable "scratching."

In the early years of the 1990s, the term Hip Hop began to replace the more traditional term Rap, as a subculture developed around Rap/Hip Hop. By this time, the music had acquired a darker edge, incorporating more political, social, and angry (and sometimes misogynistic and scatological) lyrics. Ice T, Body Count, and NWA are among the prominent artists associated with the style commonly referred to as "Gangsta Rap." This tougher, more aggressive style continued to evolve through the 1990s with artists such as Snoop Doggy Dog, Tupac Shakur, and Dr. Dre, many of whom recorded on the hugely successful recording label Death Row Records, owned by Marion "Suge" Knight. Other artists such as The Fugees, began to have a more positive message in their music, and espoused political awareness and equality.

As live musicians began to accompany Hip Hop artists on stage and in the studio, the popularity of sampling and sequencing began to diminish. Artists such as The Beastie Boys, Meshell Ndegeocello (herself a bassist), and especially R&B singer D'Angelo often use live musicians. Other artists include Eminem, Busta Rhymes, E-40, Jay-Z, Lil Kim, Nas, RJD2, Ludacris, Usher, 50 Cents, Rhianna, Wu-Tang Clan, T.Pain, and Wycleff Jean (originally from the Fugees).

Hip Hop is evolving so quickly that some relatively new substyles are already considered dated. Little Wayne does "freestylin'" and LSOB (Lighter Shade of Brown) is all about Mexican-American Hip Hop. There are also Electro-rap, Emo Rap (T-Man, Gym Class Heroes) and many other substyles.

HIP HOP CHARACTERISTICS

BASS GROOVES: Hip Hop bass is minimalistic. Fills are very uncommon, and lines are sparse with a lot of rests. It's common to play whole notes and/or half notes, and to lay out (rest) for several measures in a row. The use of syncopated lines (often sampled) is common, as is the use of sequenced or loop-sounding lines. The variations available in this genre are virtually endless. Consequently, there is no standard Hip Hop/Rap bass line. However, there are common elements.

As vocals dominate in Hip Hop even more than in other pop styles, the music is relatively unimportant and the bassist usually stays in the background. As well, the rhythm of the bass line is more important than its harmonic role.

When bass lines are complicated, they've usually been sampled from Funk, Jazz, Rock, R&B or other genres. (See the relevant chapters for bass lines.)

TONE:

FUNK-LIKE: Bass +3 to +9 dB, Mids +3 to +6 dB @ 500 Hz, Treble +3 to +6 dB.

DUB-LIKE: Bass +9 to +12 dB, Mids from flat to -15 dB @500 Hz, Treble -6 to -12 dB.

STANDUP-LIKE: Bass +3 to +9dB, Mids flat, Treble -3 to -6 dB.

GEAR: Most bass lines in Hip Hop are computer based (sampled). When live musicians are used, both electric and upright bass are common. Synth Bass can be employed as can electric upright bass.

TECHNIQUE: Finger style.

PROGRESSIONS: Hip Hop progressions are simple, and the progressions in many songs are dependent on sampled bass lines. There are infinite variations; these are just a few examples.

  1) i - i - i - i
  2) I - bii
  3) v/i - v/iv
  4) I - v - bVI - bIII
  5) i - bvi - bvii - bvi
  6) i - bIII - bVII - IV

QUARTER NOTE = 60 – 108 BPM (Standard Hip Hop)

QUARTER NOTE = 132 – 172 BPM (Half-Time)

HIP HOP EXAMPLE 1 (CD 2 TRACK 28, DVD TRACK 62)

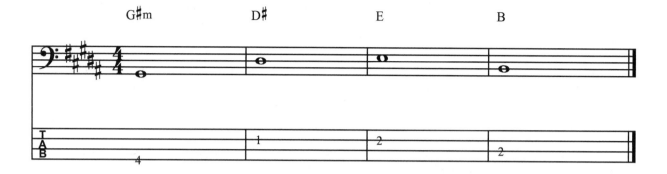

HIP HOP EXAMPLE 2 (CD 2 TRACK 95)

This Disco/House groove from the Techno chapter is effective in up-tempo tunes, especially if you use a deep synth sound and a gate to scale down the attack.

HIP HOP EXAMPLE 2 VARIATION 1

Hɪᴘ Hᴏᴘ Exᴀᴍᴘʟᴇ 2 Vᴀʀɪᴀᴛɪᴏɴ 2

This groove is normally played at a very slow tempo (around 85 bpm). The notes on beats one, "and" of two, and four show an Afro-Cuban/New Orleans influence. This groove can also be used at a much faster tempo (around 160 bpm).

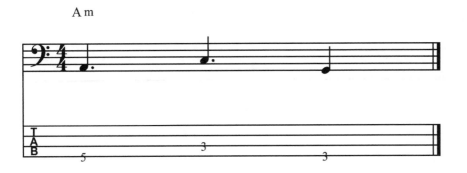

Hɪᴘ Hᴏᴘ Exᴀᴍᴘʟᴇ 2 Vᴀʀɪᴀᴛɪᴏɴ 3

Hɪᴘ Hᴏᴘ Exᴀᴍᴘʟᴇ 3 (CD 2 Tʀᴀᴄᴋ 29, DVD Tʀᴀᴄᴋ 62)

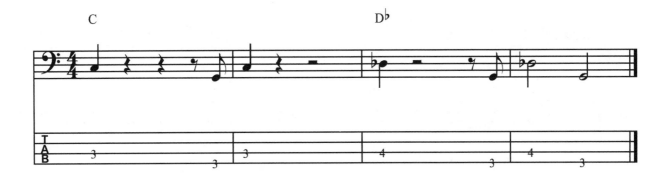

HIP HOP EXAMPLE 4 (CD 2 TRACK 30, DVD TRACK 63)

HIP HOP EXAMPLE 5 (CD 2 TRACK 31, DVD TRACK 64)

HIP HOP EXAMPLE 6 (CD 2 TRACK 32)

Due to the sparseness of Hip Hop bass lines (other than sampled lines), it's possible to play two notes at once ("double stops"). It's an unusual effect and worth experimenting with.

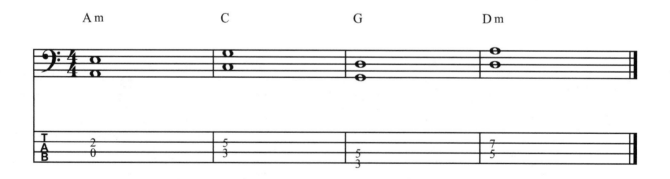

15 JAZZ

■ NEW ORLEANS SECOND LINE

SITUATED AT THE MOUTH OF THE MISSISSIPPI, New Orleans has been a major port for nearly three centuries. It's a melting pot of cultures: African, Cuban, South American, European, Caribbean, and many others. The fusion of all these cultures created a new style of music, laying the foundation for all the varieties of Jazz that followed.

The end of slavery was a catalyst for a specifically New Orleans-type of music, especially what is known as New Orleans Second Line. In the latter part of the 19th century, funeral and parade bands consisting of former slaves and their descendants became an important musical/cultural institution.

The "first line" of the funeral consisted of the hearse and funeral procession, while the "second line" was composed of musicians, dancers, and friends of the deceased—hence the name associated with this style. The makeup of these parade bands in New Orleans was similar to the marching or parade bands that we are familiar with today, consisting of horns with a marching percussion section.

The bass parts were normally played on a tuba, sometimes referred to as "brass bass," which was the dominant bass instrument in Second Line until the late 1920s. Even today, bassists who specialize in Second Line often play the tuba for variety and to make some songs sound more authentic.

THE "BIG FOUR"

THE DRUMMING FEEL is neither triple nor duple; it is played "in the crack" (a feel halfway between straight and swung). In addition to playing "in the crack," drummers do not play an obvious "one" on every measure. Rather, they play the "Big Four," a bass drum accent on beat four of the second measure of a two-bar pattern that acts as a rhythmic "kick" which pushes the music ahead to the next measure. This is key to playing a Second Line song authentically.

For the bass player in particular, knowing where beat one is, while not stressing it, is essential. A Second Line bass player needs to "own" the one, rather than relying on the drummer, but should not audibly emphasize it; rather, the bassist needs to emphasize the "Big Four" audibly, and hear beat one in his head. Sometimes to emphasize the "Big Four," the bassist can simply de-emphasize beat one—that is, play it more quietly than the other notes. However, the drummer may put enough emphasis on the "Big Four" that the bassist need not stress it.

SECOND LINE CHARACTERISTICS

BASS GROOVES: Second Line bass grooves are written in a two-measure pattern to correspond to the differences in measures (the "Big Four" being the last note of the second measure). The whole trick is to feel the emphasis, while not speeding up.

TONE: Bass flat to +6 dB, Mids flat to -6 dB, Treble flat to -6 dB. To replicate the sound of the tuba, limit the sustain of the notes played. Use moderate bass—not too deep.

SECOND LINE EXAMPLE 1 (CD 2 TRACK 33)

SECOND LINE EXAMPLE 1 VARIATION 1 (CD 2 TRACK 34)

Although the second measure of this variation uses all four quarter notes, it should not be thought of as walking, as the quarter-note rhythm serves primarily as a fill that propels the bass line toward the "Big Four."

SECOND LINE EXAMPLE 1 VARIATION 2 (CD 2 TRACK 35)

SECOND LINE EXAMPLE 1 VARIATION 3 (CD 2 TRACK 36, DVD TRACK 65)

SECOND LINE EXAMPLE 1 VARIATION 4

SECOND LINE EXAMPLE 1 VARIATION 5

SECOND LINE EXAMPLE 1 VARIATION 6

SECOND LINE FILL EXAMPLE

NOTE: Bass players often fill in weaker measures of a song to "fatten" the feel. Fills usually occur on bar 4, bar 8, bar 12, or bar 16 in 16-bar songs. It's also possible to play two-bar fills, usually in bars 3 & 4, 7 & 8, etc. (Please note that, as in the rest of Jazz, patterns typically run from 12 bars to 32 bars.) Additional fills can be created from the second measures in the preceding "Big Four" patterns. The above example is a common fill.

DIXIELAND

DIXIELAND GAVE BIRTH TO TRADITIONAL JAZZ, and served as a bridge between New Orleans music and the Swing/Big Band era. Dixieland bass playing is simpler than that of Second Line. In addition, Dixieland has more of a traditional swing feel rather than the "in the crack" feel of Second Line.

The term "Dixieland" refers to the music that flourished in the Storyville (red light) District of New Orleans between approximately 1900 and 1917. Musicians responsible for creating Dixieland include New Orleans natives Buddy Bolden, Ferdinand "Jelly Roll" Morton, Joe "King" Oliver, and Louis Armstrong.

Due to the shutdown of Storyville during World War I, Jazz musicians migrated north on the Mississippi River and ultimately ended up in Chicago in speakeasies. Dixieland continued to thrive throughout the 1920s as the defining sound of the "Jazz Age." With the legalization of alcohol in 1933, Jazz began to appear in more respectable establishments, giving rise to the Big Band era. This coincided with a diminishment of Dixieland's popularity. But the style has continued to thrive in traditional festivals and Dixieland venues throughout the world, as well as in the cities where it developed and became popular.

As bands moved from marching and playing Second Line to Dixieland, string bassists became more common as the "brass bass" (tuba) was no longer necessary in bands that performed in fixed (non-marching) venues. An early type of string bass was the wash tub bass, played in street corner Blues groups. It was made of a cord, a broom handle, and an inverted wash tub. The cord was fastened to the top of the broom handle and to the inverted tub, while the broom stick's bottom rested on the inverted tub. Slapping or plucking the string produced a tone while increasing or decreasing the tension on the stick (and consequently the string) by moving it up or down changed the pitch. Early versions of the wash tub bass can be traced to the West Indies and West and Central Africa, where it was developed from hunting snares and bows. A primitive version was composed of a bow with a hole in the ground used as a resonating chamber. Later variations used a wooden box for resonance, while in Haiti, a bucket or can was used instead of a box. All of these primitive instruments were played in the same style, primarily slapping with fingers.

But by the 1920s, bassists were moving away from both tuba and washtub bass. Having played both tuba and string bass, George "Pops" Foster, a New Orleans native who played with Louis Armstrong, has been credited for the transition to the string bass. One possible reason for his use of the upright bass was that he recognized its timekeeping quality, and made use of it. Foster used all three techniques: plucking, slapping, and bowing, sometimes within a single song, which can be heard on several recordings. (See listening appendix.) He also played with more pressure on the neck than was customary, resulting in longer sustains, with more harmonic content than was typical of his period. His playing with Luis Russell's Louisiana Swing Orchestra in New York in 1929 was so percussive, and his time so precise, that a number of other band leaders began suggesting to their tuba players that they learn to play string bass. Thus by 1930 tubas were used less and less.

In the 1920s and 1930s, bassists also began to play more dynamically with soloists, changing from two-beat feels to four-beat feels, while at times even playing whole notes to change the mood, all of which was easier on string bass than tuba.

DIXIELAND CHARACTERISTICS

BASS GROOVES: Dixieland bass lines are even simpler than Second Line grooves, consisting primarily of quarter-note and half-note roots and fifths. In Dixieland, the bassist sometimes plays four quarter notes per measure, but doesn't walk.

TONE: Bass +3 dB, Mids flat to -12dB, Treble -6 dB (if using electric bass).

GEAR: Tuba or upright bass is most authentic. Under some circumstances (such as a restaurant gig with a small trio) it's probably better to use an upright. Electric can be used, but it should emulate an upright, as per the above tone settings.

DIXIELAND CHARACTERISTICS (CONT'D)

TECHNIQUE: Finger style, percussive, played staccato. If emulating tuba on electric, play short, muted notes. If emulating upright on electric, play similarly, but with a little more sustain.

PROGRESSIONS: Dixieland progressions range from the simple, built on the I, IV and V, to the complex, sometimes utilizing more than one chord per measure. (See also Second Line progressions.)

  1) I7 - I7 - I7 - I7 - IV7 - IV7 - I7 - I7 - V7 - IV7 - I7 - I7
  2) i - i - V7 - V7 - V7 - V7 - V7 - i
  3) I - I - I - I - I - I - II - II
  4) IV - iv - I - I - VII/bVII - VI - ii - V - I/vi - ii/V
  5) I - I - I - I - I - I - V7 - V7 - I - I7- IV - IV - I - I - V7 - I

TURNAROUNDS: Dixieland utilizes one primary turnaround: I/vi - ii/V. The bass normally plays the roots of all four chords.

QUARTER NOTE = 160 – 264 BPM

DIXIELAND EXAMPLE 1 (CD 2 TRACK 37, DVD TRACK 66)

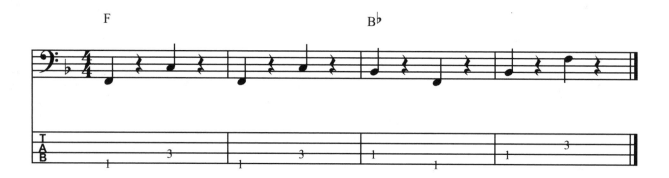

DIXIELAND EXAMPLE 1 VARIATION 1

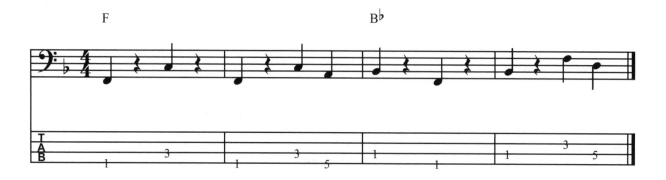

DIXIELAND EXAMPLE 1 VARIATION 2

DIXIELAND EXAMPLE 2

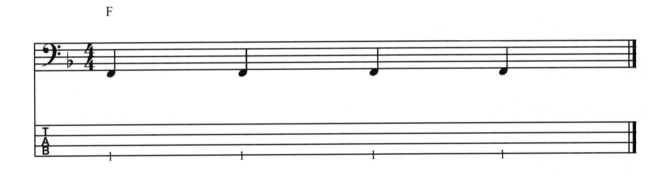

DIXIELAND EXAMPLE 2 VARIATION 1

■ BIG BAND

THE BIG BAND STYLE developed in the 1920s, with Fletcher Henderson being one of the first famous Big Band leaders. In the 1930s and 1940s, Big Band dominated popular music in recordings, radio, and live settings. Prominent band leaders included Duke Ellington, Count Basie, Glenn Miller, and Benny Goodman.

In the 1930s, Big Band bass playing was characterized by a steady, walking, four-to-the-bar pattern. (Walter Page, one of Count Basie's bassists, provides a good example of this kind of playing.) Bassists filled a supporting role, letting other instruments provide the excitement, with the bass holding down the low end rhythmically and harmonically.

Unlike Walter Page, Jimmy Blanton, with Duke Ellington, emulated horn players by playing a lot of eighth, dotted-eighth, and sixteenth notes. He pushed the bass into the spotlight using pizzicato and arco techniques, as well as syncopation. At about the same time, Leroy Eliot "Slam" Stewart developed a unique style, playing arco and singing or humming the same part an octave above. He played with Art Tatum, Benny Goodman, and Dizzy Gillespie.

While it remained popular through the 1940s, by 1950 Big Band music had begun to lose its popularity. Although it never regained the prominence it enjoyed in the 1930s and the World War II years, it continued to have a strong audience through the 1970s and the 1980s, with the Buddy Rich Big Band, Maynard Ferguson, Woody Herman, and the Tonight Show Band, directed by Doc Severinson, being its most prominent performers. Big Band had a brief resurgence of popularity in the mid 1990s through the Jump/Swing revival, most notably in the music of the Brian Setzer Orchestra.

■ WALKING

WALKING IS THE NORM IN BIG BAND, and is used in many other styles of music, especially Blues, Western Swing, Rockabilly, and Small Band Jazz. The predominant characteristic of all styles of walking bass is a consistent quarter note pulse.

The idea behind walking is to provide the foundation for the chord structure with an ever-changing bass line. The root is always played at chord changes. The inexperienced player may get by with quarter notes on roots, fifths, and octaves, but such lines tend to be uninteresting. Further choices include the notes of the chord currently being played, a diatonic note of the chord's scale, or the use of target and approach notes. Diminished chords, augmented chords, and other chords may require an altered (sharp or flat) fifth. (A little traditional chord theory will help immensely.)

TARGET AND APPROACH NOTES

Target notes are the strongest notes in a walking bass line (usually on beat one and sometimes on beat three—if there's a chord change on beat three). The most common target note is the root, and the second most common is the fifth. Approach notes immediately precede target notes, and are always a half-step or a whole step above or below the target note. In sum, a song's chord changes determine the target and approach notes.

WALKING GUIDELINES

1. Play quarter notes on every beat. (Use rhythmic variations sparingly, if at all.)

2. Normally play the root on the first beat of a measure. (You can occasionally play the third or the fifth on the first beat.)

3. Play the root on the first beat on which a new chord appears.

4. Play other notes from the current chord.

5. Play notes from the scale of the current chord, avoiding the fourth.

6. Play notes from the scale of the key as passing tones on the 2nd and 4th beats.

7. To set up a chord change, on the preceding beat play a note from the current chord, a note common to both chords, or use an approach note.

8. To avoid redundancy when playing the same chord for more than a measure, use approach notes (which, of course, lead to target notes).

9. Play evenly—emphasize notes subtly, if at all.

LEAD SHEETS AND CHORD CHARTS

OFTEN IN JAZZ, especially Big Band, the bassist plays from a lead sheet or chord chart, at times with the bass line written out. But often the bassist must create his or her own walking bass line.

In charts without written bass lines, this is normally indicated by the instruction "walk" followed by measures with slash marks and chord symbols above them. For these measures, simply create a four-quarter-note-per-measure walking line with roots beneath every chord symbol (as seen in Example 1).

A lead sheet always appears in treble clef, as the staff is used for the melody only, not the bass line. Again, the bassist will have to create his or her own walking pattern based on the chord progression.

BIG BAND CHORD CHART EXAMPLE

BIG BAND LEAD SHEET EXAMPLE

The notes shown are the melody line, not the bass line.

BIG BAND CHARACTERISTICS

BASS GROOVES: Walking is the norm. Given Big Band's rigid arrangements, there tends to be less improvisation than in other styles of Jazz. It's limited strictly to solos in prescribed places.

TONE: Bass flat to +6 dB, Mids flat, Treble flat to -6 dB. An upright sound is common, although possibly with a little more sustain than you'd get with an actual upright.

GEAR: Big Band was developed on upright, which is still to be preferred; but any bass can be used.

TECHNIQUE: Finger style, relaxed sound; notes can be more legato than those of Dixieland and Second Line.

BIG BAND CHARACTERISTICS (CONT'D)

PROGRESSIONS: Big Band progressions can be quite complex. While some are built on Blues progressions, many feature cycle of fifths movement and chromaticism (movement by half a step). Besides those based on Blues, the most common chord changes in Big Band Jazz are based on the George Gershwin classic song "I Got Rhythm." This progression is so common that it has its own nickname: "Rhythm Changes." There are myriad variations. (The one recorded on CD2 Track 40 is one of the most common.)

1) ii7/V7 - ii7/V7 - iii7/VI7 - iii7/VI7 - vi7b5/II7 - bvi7/bII7 - I - ii7b5/Vi7b9
2) Imaj7 - Imaj7/bii7 - II7 - II7 - ii7 - V7 - Imaj7 - bVI7#5/V7
3) I - I - II7b5 - II7b5 - ii7 - V7 - I - I
4) ii7/V7 - iv7/bVII7 - bvii7 - bIII7 - bVI7 - ii7/V7 - Imaj7 - Imaj7
5) I7/V7#9 - bVII7/bIIImaj7 - bVI7b9/II7 - V7b9/i7 - i7/IV7#5 - v7/I7#11 - i7/IV7#5 - bVIImaj7/V7#5
6) I/vi7 - ii7/V9 - I/vi7 - ii7/V9 - I/vi7 - ii7/V9 - I/VI7 - II9/V7
7) bvidim/V7 - bvidim/V7 - bvidim/V7 - bvidim/V7 - bvidim/V7 - bvidim/V7 - bvidim/V7 - i13

TURNAROUNDS: Big Band (and Small Band) Jazz utilize many turnarounds in the final two bars of a song. While the basic patterns are the same as with turnarounds in Blues, in Jazz the chord extensions vary so much with all of the following turnarounds that we're only listing the basic chords. Check out the final two bars of the above sample chord progressions and also the progressions listed later in the Small Band section for examples of the great diversity of chord forms found in Jazz turnarounds.

1) I/vi - ii/V
2) I - I/V
3) I/IV - I/V
4) I/bIII - II/bII
5) I/bVI - V/bV (in this one, the bVI, V and bV chords are normally 9th chords)

QUARTER NOTE = 60 – 255 BPM

BIG BAND EXAMPLE 1 (CD 2 TRACK 38)

CONTINUED ON FOLLOWING PAGE

BIG BAND EXAMPLE 1 (CONT'D)

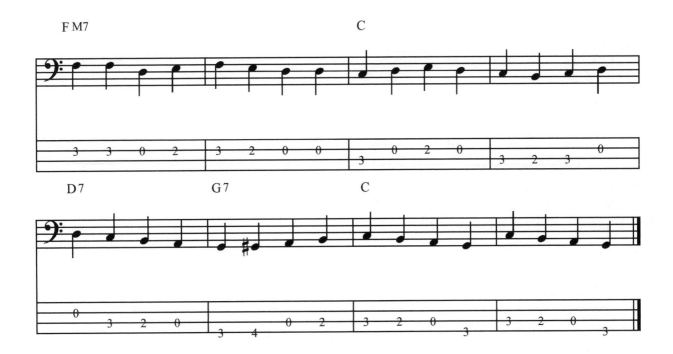

BIG BAND EXAMPLE 1 VARIATION 1 (CD 2 TRACK 39, DVD TRACK 67)

CONTINUED ON FOLLOWING PAGE

Big Band Example 1 Variation 1 (CONT'D)

Big Band Example 1 Variation 2

Big Band Example 1 Variation 3

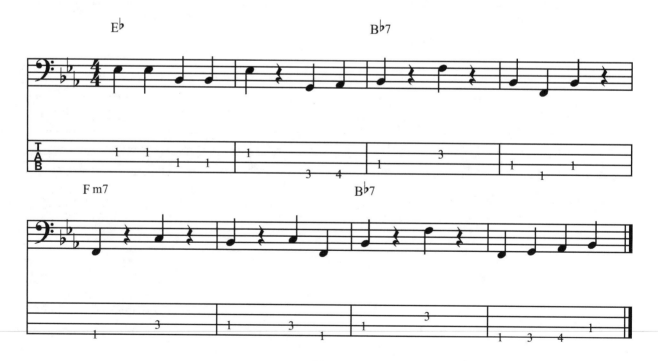

Big Band "Rhythm Changes" Example (CD 2 Track 40)

Thanks to Brandon Essex for writing and recording this bass line.

■ SMALL BAND JAZZ (BE BOP, COOL JAZZ, AVANT GARDE)

FOLLOWING THE SWING ERA, the size of Jazz groups decreased from large Big Band orchestras to much smaller bands. This trend began in the early 1940s and became increasingly pronounced in the late 1940s and early 1950s. Jazz terminology reflected this shift: terms such as "trio," "quartet," and "quintet," and styles like Be Bop, Cool Jazz, and Avant Garde all suggest a small band. (Later styles include Hard Bop, a more intense form of Be Bop, and Soul Jazz, which is influenced by Blues and Funk.) Small bands of the time usually consisted of a lead horn player along with a full rhythm section (drums, bass, and piano). One of the biggest changes in the music was in the approach to improvisation. Although there is improvisation in Big Band music (horn solos or even drum solos in prescribed places), the Big Band genre is based on highly organized, charted arrangements. A small band, however, tends to follow the form of a song rather than a chart, which leaves a lot of room to stretch.

It's important to learn the characteristics of Jazz form when studying the small band format. Every song has a melody (the "head") normally played by a horn player and supported by chords on the piano and a walking bass line. After the melody is played, members of the band solo or improvise over the chord progression/song form that underlies the original melody. One common form of improvisation is "trading fours," with soloists playing alternating four-bar phrases. Following the solo sections of the song, the melody is normally played again, with the tune usually coming to an end following the final statement of the melody.

The driving force behind the development of the small band ensemble was the team of saxophonist Charlie Parker and trumpeter Dizzie Gillespie, who focused on improvisation by all instruments. The hallmarks of this new style, known as Be Bop, were very fast tempos, very fast, complicated harmonic changes, and the use of complex altered chords (with sharp or flat fifths, ninths, etc.) and extensions (9ths, 11ths, etc.).

In the 1940s, as bands became smaller, bassists increasingly focused on timekeeping. As bass drum patterns became more varied, a walking bass line became more important. Tone became cleaner, as epitomized by Ray Brown and Oscar Pettiford, in contrast with the harsher slapping "Pops" Foster had used.

By the mid-1950s, musician/composer Miles Davis had created Cool Jazz, a more relaxed form of Jazz featuring slower tempos, fewer chord changes, and extended solos. His early bassist, Paul Chambers, a master at walking, had precise time, intonation, and great improvisational skill. He sometimes played arco solos and made use of harmonics. (Chambers was featured on the Miles Davis classic "So What," which in turn features the bass line as the melody.)

Ron Carter, one of Miles' later bassists, is one of the most important Jazz bassists, and continues to be so more than five decades after he began performing. He has appeared on over 2500 recordings, and has played with innumerable prominent musicians, including Thelonious Monk, Wes Montgomery, Archie Shepp, McCoy Tyner, Wayne Shorter, Aretha Franklin, and Antonio Carlos Jobim.

Bassist/composer/band leader Charles Mingus, who played with Louis Armstrong and Lionel Hampton in the late 1940s, also played with Red Norvo, Charlie Parker, Bud Powell, Dizzie Gillespie, and Max Roach in the 1950s. He then formed his own band, advancing bass playing not only with new techniques such as bowed harmonics, double stops, and solos above a drone, but also intricate counter melodies to horn solos. His music is often extremely fast, but played with great technical accuracy; and he also experimented with tempo acceleration and deceleration. Fronting his own band, with his harmonically rich compositions, he encouraged collective improvisation, creating material that was very complex and different with every performance. To retain artistic and economic control over their records, he and Max Roach even co-founded their own record label, "Debut Records."

In the early 1960s, bassist Scotty LaFaro developed a contrapuntal soloing style, producing a conversational dynamic with Bill Evans (piano) and Paul Motian (drums). His use of high positions on the neck produced a muted but pure tone.

Both Mingus and LaFaro inspired bassists to participate in ensembles more melodically (more as equals in their bands), while still fulfilling their role as low-end rhythm masters. As techniques evolved, more bassists took advantage of the range of sounds and techniques available to them. In the early 1960s, two of these pioneering bassists were Charlie Haden (playing with Ornette Coleman) and Jimmy Garrison (with John Coltrane); they were among the first who used the chordal strumming technique.

Also in the early 1960s, saxophonists John Coltrane, Sonny Rollins, and Ornette Coleman contributed to the improvisation-based Avant Garde movement which featured famed drummers Elvin Jones, Roy Haynes and Billy Higgins. The emphasis in Avant Garde was mostly on improvisation, and the "songs" played by Avant Garde groups were often improvised on the spot. Though Avant Garde utilizes the ideas of other Jazz styles, it requires more technically advanced musicianship, with the time pattern usually less apparent and sometimes even deliberately obscured or omitted entirely (as with much of the music of Cecil Taylor). As well, tempos may exceed even those of Be Bop. Avant Garde musicians often used polyrhythmic figures, and sometimes abandoned the form of a song entirely—if there was a form to begin with (that is, if the playing wasn't based on pure improvisation).

Following Avant Garde, Jazz fell under the influence of (Jazz/Rock) Fusion and embraced straight feels as well as swung feels (e.g., Herbie Hancock's "Maiden Voyage"). In the late 1960s, Miles Davis began using electric instruments after witnessing the popularity of Sly and the Family Stone and other rockers. This led to a host of Jazz-Rock-Latin fusion bands, such as Weather Report, Return to Forever, and Mahavishnu Orchestra. Stanley Clarke, who played with Pharoah Sanders, Gato Barbieri, and Return to Forever, and Jaco Pastorius, who played with Weather Report, moved bassists from the back of the stage to being full-fledged front men. Both bassists laid down deep grooves, while playing anywhere on the neck with extreme speed and accuracy, and employed electronic effects and extremes in tone. Both became composers and band leaders, and led other bassists even further away from playing roots, fifths, triads, and walking on quarter notes.

Current bassists, such as Victor Wooten, Philip Bailey, Marcus Miller, Oteil Burbridge, John Patitucci, and Jeff Berlin, are blurring the lines between Jazz, Rock, Latin, Funk and World Music. They play basses with five, six, and more strings, use digital effects, and even have second bassists to propel the rhythm section behind them.

As a result of all of these innovations, a Jazz bassist today may utilize any of the styles and ideas of earlier decades.

SMALL BAND CHARACTERISTICS

BASS GROOVES: The role of the bassist in Small Band ensembles varies tremendously, from providing simple support for the band through walking bass, to the most complex soloing. Unlike Big Band, which tends to restrict individual players, the walking bass lines in Small Band have greater rhythmic variety.

TONE: Bass +3 to +6 dB, Mids flat to -3dB, Treble -3 to -6 dB. Emulates upright in traditional Small Band styles. In Fusion almost anything goes. See Funk chapter for tonal ideas.

GEAR: Upright is still the most authentic and under certain circumstances (such as a restaurant gig with a small trio) the best choice, though Small Band Jazz can be played with any type of bass, especially fretless or electric upright bass.

TECHNIQUE: Finger style, with a relaxed sound.

PROGRESSIONS: In Small Band styles, chord progressions vary considerably more than in Big Band (where they usually have a strong cycle-of-fifths component). Be Bop progressions are sometimes even more complex than in Big Band (while retaining the strong cycle-of-fifths tendency), while Cool Jazz progressions are often minimalistic and/or based on Blues patterns, and in the case of Avant Garde Jazz they sometimes verge on the nonexistent. Consequently, bassists must be adaptable.

1) i7 - IV7 - i7 - IV7b9 - IVmaj7 - i7/IV7 - IVmaj7/i7 - ii7/V7

2) i - i - v7 - I7 - IVmaj7 - IVmaj7 - iv7 - bVII - bIIImaj7 - biii7/bVI7 - bIImaj7 - ii7b5/V7b9

3) ii7/V7 - iv7/bVII7 - bvii7 - bIII7 - bVI7 - ii7/V7 - Imaj7 - Imaj7

4) ii7/iii7 - IVmaj7/iii7 - ii7/iii7 - IVmaj7/iii7 - ii7/iii7 - IVmaj7/iii7 - ii7/bII7 - I

5) Imaj7 - IV7 - III7 - VI7 - II7 - V7 - I/vi7 - II7/V7

6) Imaj7 - Imaj7 - i7/IV7 - i7/IV7 - bVIImaj7 - bVIImaj7 - bvii7 - bIII7 - bVI7 - V7 - i - iv7b5/V7

7) I7 - I7 - I7 - I7 - IV7 - IV7 - I7 - bIII7 - bVI7 - V7#9 - I7 - I7

8) I7 - I7 - I7 - I7 - IV7 - IV7 - I7 - I7 - V7#9 - bVI7#9/V7#9 - I7 - I7

9) Imaj7/VI7 - ii7/V7 - Imaj7/VI7 - ii7/V7 - I/iiidim - IV7/bvdim - Imaj7/VI7 - ii7/V7

SMALL BAND EXAMPLE 1 (CD 2 TRACK 41, DVD TRACK 68)

SMALL BAND EXAMPLE 1 VARIATION 1

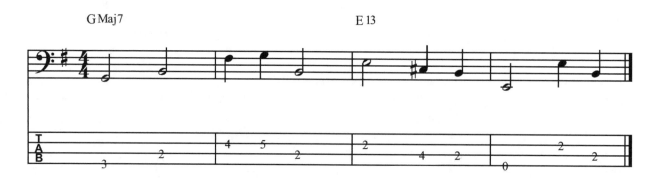

SMALL BAND EXAMPLE 1 VARIATION 2 (CD 2 TRACK 42)

JAZZ WALTZ

NOTE: The primary musical characteristic of the Jazz Waltz is the 3/4 time signature, though drummers play it swung, giving it a 9/8 feel. Bassists, however, simply play quarter notes and sometimes half notes. The Jazz Waltz is found in both Big Band and Small Band Jazz. **QUARTER NOTE = 100 – 208 BPM**

JAZZ WALTZ EXAMPLE 1 (CD 2 TRACK 43, DVD TRACK 69)

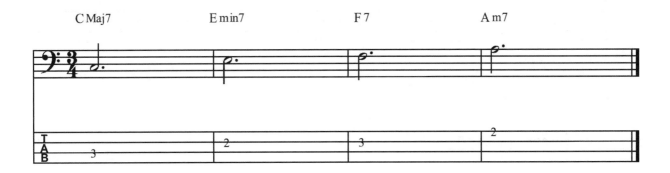

JAZZ WALTZ EXAMPLE 1 VARIATION 1 (CD 2 TRACK 44, DVD TRACK 70)

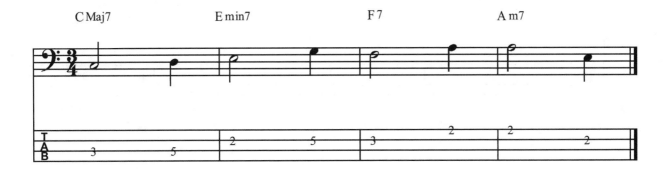

Jazz Waltz Example 1 Variation 2

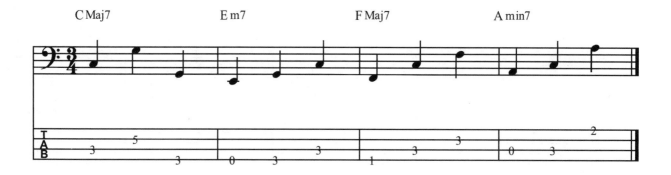

Jazz Waltz Example 1 Variation 3

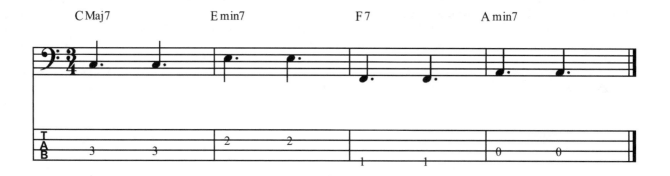

Jazz Waltz Example 1 Variation 4

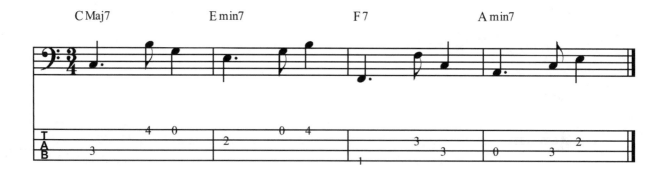

JAZZ BALLAD

NOTE: Most Jazz Ballads are swung, but some are played straight. In line with the slow relaxed feel of ballads, bassists usually stick with quarter notes and half notes. Walking is generally more appropriate in slower tunes. When Jazz Ballads are swung, bassists do not shuffle notes. **QUARTER NOTE = 50 – 80 BPM**

JAZZ BALLAD EXAMPLE 1 (CD 2 TRACK 45)

JAZZ BALLAD EXAMPLE 1 VARIATION 1 (CD 2 TRACK 46)

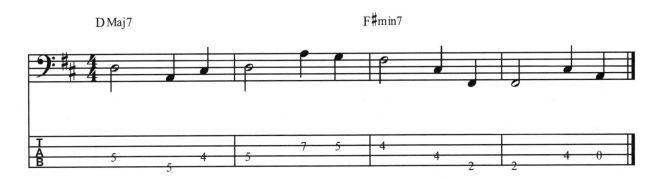

JAZZ BALLAD EXAMPLE 1 VARIATION 2

16 KLEZMER

THE TERM KLEZMER comes from the Hebrew words, "kley" and "zemer," meaning "vessel of music" and by extension musical instrument. The first written documentation for Klezmer dates from the 16th century, although its roots lie deeper in the past. Klezmer's creation and development stems from the Central European Jewish population exiled to Poland, Romania, Ukraine, Belarus, and Lithuania ("the Pale of Settlement," much of which was under Ottoman Turkish rule).

So, Klezmer was (and is) a syncretic music combining many musical styles and traditions: Ashkenazi (European Jewish) music mixed with Ottoman court music, Turkish, Greek, Armenian, and Middle Eastern styles. Early Klezmer was characterized by: 1) an extremely high level of musicianship; 2) unique instrumentation; 3) Middle Eastern polyrhythms.

Many medieval European governments and societies restricted Jewish musicians to specific instruments (e.g., flutes and stringed instruments) and music itself was one of the few occupations Jewish people were allowed to practice. Thus, every major European city possessed highly skilled, professional Jewish bands. These bands, along with Rom (Gypsy) bands, traveled in order to earn a living.

Initially restricted to the quieter instruments, especially violin and tsimbl (the Jewish cimbalom or hammered dulcimer), Klezmer musicians adeptly explored their musical capabilities, developing an emotional depth and expression patterned after the human singing voice (a prominent characteristic still inherent in Klezmer today). In the 18th century, as Jews who had served in the Tsarist army brought in more military-oriented instruments, (trumpets, trombones, convert snare or "little" drums ["tshekal"], bass drums with mounted cymbals ["puk" aka "poik" or "baraban"], cymbals ["tats"] and tambourines), the sounds of modern Klezmer began to emerge.

When 19th-century European governments imposed yet even more hardships upon the Pale of Settlement, emigration to the United States became the logical choice for much of the Jewish population. During the years 1880–1924, Jewish immigration to America (primarily to New York City) exceeded more than two million people; the musicians among them brought Klezmer to the New World, and especially New York. Some of the more respected Klezmer musicians of the period were clarinetists Naftule Brandwein and Dave Tarras. Band leaders such as Harry Kandel produced a wealth of Klezmer recordings, making Klezmer accessible to future generations.

Since the 1920s, Klezmer's popularity has fluctuated, though it has been routinely performed at wedding ceremonies, parties, and in theater productions. After the founding of the Israeli state in 1948, the younger generation felt the need to modernize Jewish culture, causing Klezmer's popularity to diminish.

However, a resurgence began in the latter part of the 20th century in Europe and the United States, with the pioneering ensembles Klezmorim (Yiddish for "musicians") from Berkeley, California and Kapelye (meaning "band") from New York City leading the way. As the number of young European musicians eager to learn the style grew, one of Klezmer's primary markets became, of all places, Germany. Musicians from the United States (many with Rock n' Roll experience) found excited students and audiences in Europe, with bassists Stuart Brottman (of Brave Old World, Veretski Pass, Canned Heat, and Kaleidoscope), Paul Morissett (The Klezmatics), and Jim Guttman (The Klezmer Conservatory Band) teaching a new generation of mostly non-Jewish Klezmer musicians. Continually evolving, contemporary Klezmer music has incorporated the drum set, upright bass, and electric bass.

Finally, special thanks to Stuart Brotman for writing and playing all of the Klezmer examples.

KLEZMER CHARACTERISTICS

BASS GROOVES: The bassist provides a solid harmonic foundation by playing the root on the first beat and establishing the time and feel. This function is obviously in the forefront in ensembles lacking a drum set. Note that while the melodic instruments play Middle Eastern-sounding scales (Freygish: E F G# A B C D E and Dorish: D E F G# A B C D), the bass sticks to playing notes of the chord and passing tones on (normally but not always) the offbeats. A peculiarity of Klezmer bass patterns is that in 2/4 tunes (Bulgars, Freylakhs and Khosidls) the bass will sometimes play the third (of the chord) on the second beat, rather than the fifth as in most other 2/4 styles such as Polka.

TONE: Bass +6 to +9 dB, Mids flat, Treble -6 dB Emulates upright.

GEAR: The upright bass produces the most authentic Klezmer sound. Electric bass can be used in the upright's place, played pizzicato with a pick. EUBs can also be used.

TECHNIQUE: As with other Old World upright bass styles, Klezmer was traditionally played with a bow. It can, of course, be played pizzicato or on electric bass. Bulgars, Freylacks, Khosodils and Horas are often played arco; Terkishers are more likely candidates for pizzicato. When repeated or played as medleys, Bulgar, Freylekhs and Khosidl may accelerate to a frantic climax; Terkisher usually does not accelerate.

PROGRESSIONS: Chords in Klezmer progressions often move a whole step up or down, while changing from major to minor, or minor to major, as in the first sample progression.

1) I - I - bvii - I - I - I - bvii - I
2) V - V / I - V - I - V - V/I - V/IV - V
3) III - VII - VII/VII7 - III/V7 - I - V - V - I/VII
4) i - i - bvii - i
5) V - i - V - i - V - i - V - iv
6) V - i - V - i - V - i - V - bVII
7) bIII - bVII - bVII/V - i - V - V - i - i

KLEZMER DANCES

BULGAR, written and played in 2/4, originated in Bessarabia (present day Moldova) and is quite similar to the Israeli Hora (a dance performed in a circle, in line, or in couples—not to be confused with the Klezmer Hora found below). Bulgar music's form may be divided into many parts, while a two-part arrangement is the most common form. **QUARTER NOTE = 112 – 152 BPM**

FREYLAKHS (pronounced Fray-locks), written and played in 2/4, is similar to Bulgar and is another Jewish circle dance, this one originating in Romania, with a two-step feel. It differs from the Bulgar in its slightly more syncopated drum rhythm, and does not include two primary sections as does the Bulgar. All bass lines of Bulgar can be used in Freylakhs. **QUARTER NOTE = 112 – 152 BPM**

KHOSIDL is a Hasidic folk dance written in duple meter which usually speeds up to a frantic climax. **QUARTER NOTE = 120 BPM**

TERKISHER, written and played in 4/4, also of Romanian origin, is a march-like rhythm with similarities to a Greek "Sirtop" rhythm (both similar to that of a Tango—see Wedding Dance chapter). **QUARTER NOTE = 108–168**

HORA (from Romania and Moldavian cultures, not to be confused with the Jewish Hora danced to "Hava Nagila"; see Wedding Dances chapter) is a circle dance usually written in 3/8 meter as a reminder to avoid phrasing it like a waltz, with the most important characteristic being a de-emphasis of beat 2. However, its melodic phrasing can range from straight to a "2 against 3" polyrhythm, and it can have an "in the crack" quality. **EIGHTH NOTE = 112 – 184 BPM**

BULGAR, FREYLAKHS, KHOSIDL EXAMPLE 1 (CD 2 Track 47)

Please note that the Example 1 and Example 2 are played sequentially on the same CD track.

BULGAR, FREYLAKHS, KHOSIDL EXAMPLE 2 (CD 2 Track 47)

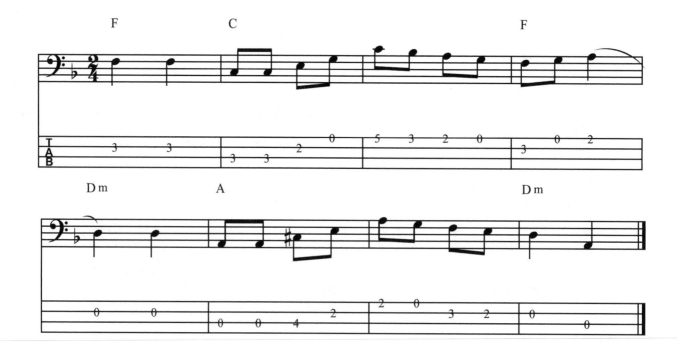

Bulgar, Freylakhs, Khosidl Example 3

Terkisher Example 1 (CD 2 Track 48)

Terkisher Example 2 (CD 2 Track 49)

TERKISHER EXAMPLE 3 (CD 2 Track 49)

Please note that Terkisher Examples 2, 3, and 4 are played sequentially on the same CD track.

TERKISHER EXAMPLE 4 (CD 2 Track 49)

TERKISHER EXAMPLE 5

HORA EXAMPLE 1

Dm

HORA EXAMPLE 2 (CD 2 Track 50)

Dm

HORA EXAMPLE 3 (CD 2 Track 51)

Hora "In the Crack" Example

 ## Fanfares

Fanfare Example

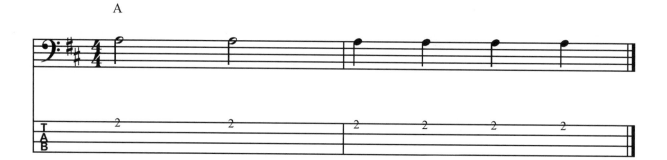

NOTE: Melodies that have a fanfare built in are usually at the beginning of a B or C part of a song. They may be part of a longer sixteen-bar phrase with a repeat. They can occur in every substyle except Hora.

17 LATIN ROCK

LATIN ROCK incorporates elements from Afro-Cuban and Brazilian music into a Rock format, while often utilizing percussion instruments from all three styles. Bassists employ techniques from not only those styles, but also Blues and Jazz. Although the Afro-Cuban and Brazilian chapters contain grooves that can be used in early Latin Rock songs such as "Tequila" (by The Champs), Latin Rock normally features less authentic and often simplified bass patterns.

The late 1960s saw the emergence of Carlos Santana, whose band used Afro-Cuban percussion instruments in a Rock music setting. Still going strong, Santana remains a popular musical figure world wide. Other Latin Rock artists include El Chicano, Malo, Jonny Chingas, Ozomatli, Los Lobos, and Miami Sound Machine, featuring Gloria Estefan, as well as more recent artists such as Ricky Martin, Marc Anthony, Los Hermanos, Los Tres, Mana, Shakira, and Juanes.

LATIN ROCK CHARACTERISTICS

BASS GROOVES: Latin Rock bass lines are often similar to Afro-Cuban Tumbao bass lines, but they emphasize the first beat instead of the "and" of beat 2 and beat 4. The style is played in both one-bar and two-bar phrases, though much of the phrasing retains the basic sense of the 2-bar clave. (See the Afro-Cuban chapter.) In all Latin Rock styles, bassists use the Blues Scale (primarily) and play repetitive patterns. Beyond that, grooves vary with the style.

CHA CHA: Bass grooves in Latin Rock Cha Chas are very different from those in the Afro-Cuban Cha Cha. (See Afro-Cuban chapter.) In Latin Rock Cha Chas, the bassist emphasizes beat 1 and the "and" of beat 2, while often leaving beat 4 unplayed. Syncopated eighth notes are a hallmark of Latin Rock Cha Chas. Also, the notes in Latin Rock Cha Cha tend to be more staccato than in the legato Afro-Cuban Tumbao Mambo pattern.

MAMBO: Latin Rock Mambo bass lines are almost the same as Afro-Cuban Mambo Tumbao bass lines, except that in Latin Rock Mambo lines you play beat 1. (See Afro-Cuban chapter.) In Latin Rock, the rhythmic pattern is simply beat 1, the "and" of beat 2, and beat 4.

AFRO-CUBAN 6/8: An uncommon groove in this style, Latin Rock 6/8 bass lines are the same as Afro-Cuban 6/8 bass lines. (See Afro-Cuban chapter for more extensive treatment of this groove.)

BAIAO: Baiao bass lines have a nondeviating, specific rhythm. It features consistent syncopation, and is usually written over two measures. (See Brazilian chapter.)

RUMBA: Rumba bass lines can be highly syncopated or very straight. (See Afro-Cuban and Blues chapters,)

BOSSA NOVA: Bossa Nova bass lines are either unsyncopated or tend to have a specific, repetitive, lightly syncopated pattern: beat 1, the "and" of beat 2, beat 3, and the "and" of beat 4. This has the effect of emphasizing beats 1 and 3. (See Brazilian chapter.)

TONE: Bass +3 to +9 dB, Mids +3 to +6 dB @ 500 Hz, Treble flat to +6 dB. There is also normally a little natural distortion due to high volume. Effects such as chorus and flange can be used.

LATIN ROCK CHARACTERISTICS (CONT'D)

GEAR: Upright is used occasionally on recorded tracks, but Latin Rock is primarily an electric bass genre. High volume is normal. Choose gear accordingly.

TECHNIQUE: Finger style. Staccato/percussive lines are appropriate for faster grooves, while slower grooves tend to be more legato.

PROGRESSIONS: Latin Rock progressions can be as simple as two chords or as complex as those in Jazz.

1) i7 - V - i7 - V
2) i - i - i - V7 - i - i - i - bVI7/V7 - i
3) i7 - i7 - i7 - i7 - iv7 - iv7 - i7 - i7 - v7 - iv7 - i7 - i7/V7#9
4) I - IV - V - IV
5) i7 - ii7 - i7 - i7 - i7 - ii7 - i7 - i7 - i7 - ii7 - bIII - IV - i7 - ii7 - bIII - V
6) i7 - bVII7 - bVI7 - V7
7) i7 - IV9/bVII7 - i7 - bVI/V - i7 - IV9/bVII7 - i7 - bVI/V
   (bridge) bIII - bIII - bVII - bVII - iv7 - iv7 - V7 - V7

QUARTER NOTE = 90 – 120 BPM (CHA CHA, RUMBA)
90 – 130 BPM (BOSSA NOVA)
180 – 220 BPM (MAMBO, BAIAO)

DOTTED QUARTER = 90 – 110 BPM (AFRO-CUBAN 6/8)

LATIN ROCK CHA CHA EXAMPLE 1 (CD 2 Track 52, DVD Track 71)

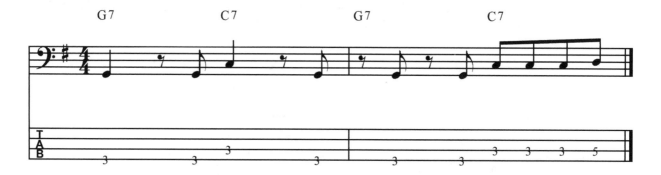

LATIN ROCK CHA CHA EXAMPLE 1 VARIATION 1 (CD 2 Track 53, DVD Track 72)

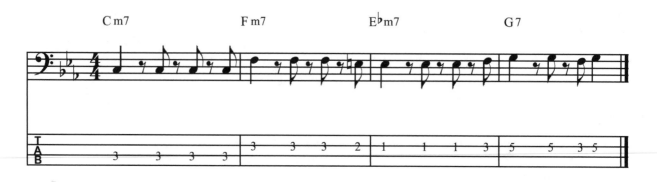

LATIN ROCK CHA CHA EXAMPLE 1 VARIATION 2

LATIN ROCK CHA CHA EXAMPLE 1 VARIATION 3

LATIN ROCK MAMBO EXAMPLE 1 (CD 1 Track 13)

LATIN ROCK MAMBO EXAMPLE 1 VARIATION 1 (CD 1 Track 14)

LATIN ROCK 6/8 EXAMPLE 1 (CD 1 Track 31)

LATIN ROCK BAIAO EXAMPLE 1

LATIN ROCK BAIAO EXAMPLE 1 VARIATION 1

LATIN ROCK BAIAO EXAMPLE 1 VARIATION 2 (CD 2 Track 54, DVD Track 73)

LATIN ROCK BAIAO EXAMPLE 1 VARIATION 3

LATIN ROCK RUMBA EXAMPLE 1

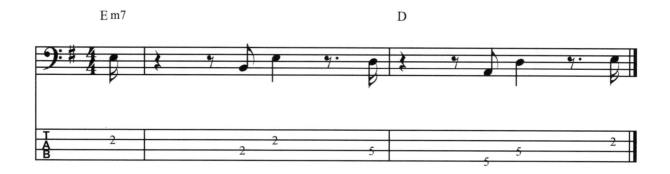

LATIN ROCK RUMBA EXAMPLE 2 (CD 2 Track 55, DVD Track 74)

LATIN ROCK RUMBA EXAMPLE 2 VARIATION 1

LATIN ROCK BOSSA NOVA EXAMPLE 1

A m7

LATIN ROCK BOSSA NOVA EXAMPLE 2 (CD 1 TRACK 53)

F m7   G m7

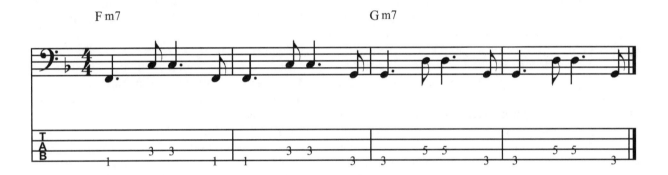

18 METAL

METAL MUSIC HAS BEEN A DRIVING FORCE in Rock for over 40 years. Originally called Heavy Metal, the style developed in the late 1960s/early 1970s through classic Hard Rock and the louder Blues Rock bands, such as The Who (John Entwistle, bass), Jimi Hendrix (Noel Redding, bass), Blue Cheer (Dickie Peterson, bass), Led Zeppelin (John Paul Jones, bass), Deep Purple (Roger Glover, bass), Black Sabbath (Geezer Butler, bass), and solo artist Alice Cooper. Since then, it has evolved into a style featuring exceptionally fast, technically challenging rhythms (always straight, never swung) and heavy bass lines, frequently accompanied by growling vocals and heavily distorted, overdriven guitar tones. The style requires an exceptional amount of endurance from the musicians playing it.

Ever since its inception, Metal has featured louder, harsher guitar, more active bass and drum parts, and darker lyrics than in standard Rock. Another feature of Metal is that many of its artists (e.g., Kiss) put on live concerts involving elaborate stage sets, intricate light shows, pyrotechnics, and outrageous costumes. The Metal sound initially relied on high-tenor singers, such as Led Zeppelin's Robert Plant, but has since embraced lower-range, roaring vocals, with Motorhead (Ian Fraser Kilmister ["Lemmy"], bass), being one of the first exemplifying this trend.

Over the past quarter century, Metal bands such as Venom, Napalm Death, Carcass, Cannibal Corpse, and Slayer set the standard for Metal intensity. This paved the way for newer Metal acts such as Meshuggah, Emperor, Alver, Tchort (aka Terje Schei), GWAR. and Slipknot. Terms associated with contemporary Metal are "Death Metal," "Goth Metal," "Black Metal," "Speed Metal," and "Thrash," which all suggest its sound.

Metal Bassists are as aggressive as the other instrumentalists in the genre. Sometimes bassists, such as Metallica's Cliff Burton, who plays finger style, are featured as lead instrumentalists. Other finger style players include Alex Webster, Eric Langlois, Derek Boyer, Sean Malone, Stefan Fimmers, and Steve Digiorgio, who often follow guitar lines instead of playing roots, while Bart Williams (The Black Dahlia Murder) plays slower half or quarter time, in support of the other players, rather than merely displaying his virtuosity.

Be forewarned: hearing loss may result from playing this music, so ear protection is essential.

METAL CHARACTERISTICS

BASS GROOVES: Metal bassists hold down the bottom, often overstating the root. The bass often plays in unison with (although an octave below) intricate guitar lines. It's also common for the bass to play pedal points on open strings, often against dissonant chords or melodies.

Early Metal tended to be slow, while Metal of the late 1970s through today tends to be faster. At its extreme, it incorporates the infamous blast beat (with the bass drum playing sixteenth notes at 200 bpm), with the bass playing matching, locked-in, sixteenth-note patterns. The bass in slow ballads usually uses longer notes such as dotted quarters or even whole notes.

TONE: Bass +6 to +9 dB, Mids +3 to +6 dB @ 500k, Treble +3 to +6 dB. Derived from John Entwistle (The Who), Metal bass tone is normally dirty and heavy on both bass and mids, with heavy distortion produced by the extreme volume at which Metal is routinely played.

Metal Characteristics (cont'd)

GEAR: Electric exclusively. Almost any gear used in rock can be used in Metal. Given the extreme volume of the guitar(s), any mid-power to high-power basic amp with at least one 4x10, 2x12, 1x15, or 1x18 speaker cabinet is about the least you can get away with. Marshalls stacks and Ampeg SVTs with 8x10 cabinets are typical, but in smaller venues may not be appropriate if you want to be booked again. Another approach is to use a smaller, cleaner amp and produce distortion with a pedal rather than with volume, and to run the bass through the p.a. system. (And, yeah, we know. We don't expect anyone to actually do this, but it is a good idea.)

Instruments include four-string basses, while Death Metal may use five- or six-string instruments or a detuned bass with an extended lower range. Metal bassists often use round wound strings, which help in getting a near-piano sound—another innovation pioneered by John Entwistle.

TECHNIQUE: Picking is more common than finger style, as Metal music requires clear articulation at fast tempos, while emphasizing attack, clarity, and accuracy. Bassists that play finger style often use three or four fingers, as some lines include extended 64th-note passages. Detuning (that is, tuning the bass to lower than standard EADG tuning) often helps players attain the necessary blistering speed. Other techniques used by Metal bassists include tapping and slapping.

TUNING: Metal bassists often use alternative tunings, generally tuning down from standard EADG tuning. Care should be taken with alternate tunings. A bass tuned lower than standard may have problems due to the difference in tension in the neck. Heavier gauge strings help reduce fret buzz when a bass is tuned down. Some popular tunings are:

DROP D = DADG
D STANDARD = DGCF
DROP C = CGCF

PROGRESSIONS: Many Metal songs are based on a main, mode-based groove of short, two- or three-note rhythmic figures comprised of eighth or sixteenth notes. Chord movement of a tritone (augmented fourth, as from IV to VII) is fairly common, as is chromaticism. Most progressions are based on the notes of the Aeolian mode (ABCDEFGA) or the Phrygian mode (EFGABCDE). Power chords (using only the root and the fifth) are quite common in Metal.

Aeolian Progressions
Note: In the Aeolian mode (ABCDEFGA) the III, VI and VII chords are major, but power chords are often used in place of triads.

1) i - VI - VII
2) i - VII - VI
3) i - VI - IV

Phrygian Progressions
Note: In the Phrygian mode (EFGABCDE), the II, III, and VI chords are major, and there's only a half-step from the i to the II. Power chords are often used in place of triads.

1) i - II - i
2) i - II - III
3) i - II - vii
4) i - iv - vii

QUARTER NOTE = 60 – 350 BPM

METAL EXAMPLE 1 (CD 2 TRACK 56, DVD TRACK 75)

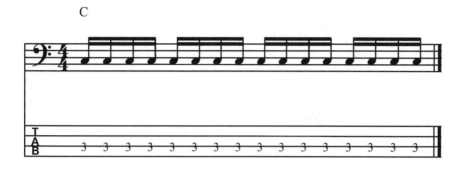

METAL EXAMPLE 1 VARIATION 1 (CD2 TRACK 57, DVD TRACK 76)

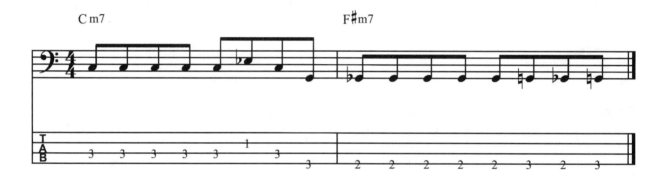

METAL (BLAST BEAT) EXAMPLE 1 VARIATION 2

Metal (Blast Beat) Example 1 Variation 3

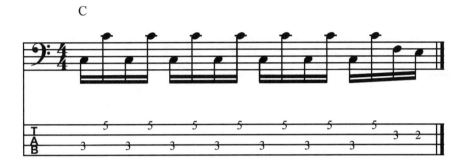

Metal (Blast Beat) Example 1 Variation 4

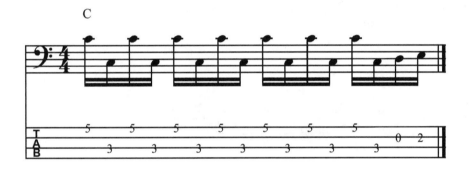

Metal Example 2 (CD 2 Track 58)

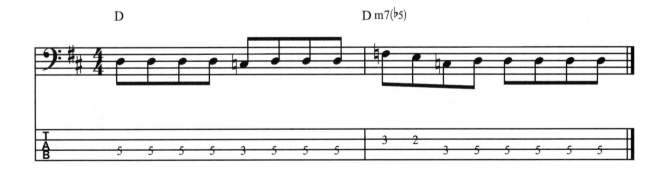

METAL EXAMPLE 2 VARIATION 1 (CD 2 TRACK 59)

METAL EXAMPLE 2 VARIATION 2

Accents can make a simple eighth-note groove much more interesting.

METAL EXAMPLE 2 VARIATION 3 (CD 2 TRACK 60, DVD TRACK 77)

19 MIDDLE EASTERN

THE MUSIC OF THE MIDDLE EAST/ARABIC nations dates back thousands of years, and has influenced countless other musical traditions. Contemporary Middle Eastern music combines the traits of traditional Eastern folk music with the popular and (to a slight extent) classical music of the Western world. Middle Eastern music is not monolithic: Ghazal, Qawali, Maghrebi, Kahleeji and Arabic Pop are just a few of the numerous musical styles emanating from Egypt, Morocco, Algeria, Tunisia, Saudi Arabia, Turkey, and the Persian Gulf.

In the music's early modern forms, Middle Eastern composers integrated folk materials with Western-influenced orchestras, though currently the trend has been toward smaller ensembles. (Pre-Western Middle Eastern music also utilized smaller ensembles.)

Instruments such as the oud (a pear-shaped, stringed instrument), Persian tars (a plucked/strummed instrument, similar to an oud, with a soundboard of stretched skin rather than wood), neys (wind instrument), qanouns (horizontal instrument with many strings, resembling a dulcimer) and kamenches & rebabas (both fiddle-like, bowed instruments) still characterize this musical genre. Notable Arabic musicians include Kazem el-Saher (Majid Yihia, bass), Nawal Al Zoghbi, Najwa Karam, Assi el-Hillani, George Wassouf, Amr Diab (Yerhia Ghannam, bass), Nancy Ajram, Ramy Ayach, Kadim al-Sahir, Hatem al-Iraqi, Lara Iskander, Haifa Wehbe, and Hamza El Din.

Middle Eastern percussion rhythms were originally played on frame drums, the Arabian tabla, the doumbek, the darabuka, finger cymbals, and other traditional percussion instruments. Although an authentic Middle Eastern ensemble still contains such instruments, the drum set is often used in modern-day Middle Eastern ensembles.

MIDDLE EASTERN CHARACTERISTICS

BASS GROOVES: Drones and ostinatos are common features in Middle Eastern music. (Drones are simply sustained tones held for at least several measures—sometimes throughout an entire song. Ostinatos are repeated patterns.) Ostinatos often mimic the lowest drum tone in a song. Bass drones and ostinatos are usually played on the tonic to allow soloists harmonic flexibility. Arco drones should be bowed smoothly. Pizzicato ostinatos can be slow and relaxed or fast and tense tremolos, but in either case they should be smooth and at low volume.

In contrast to the melodic instruments and vocals, the bass in Middle Eastern pop music sticks pretty closely to standard major and minor scales, with a heavy emphasis on the root, some use of the fifth and seventh, and occasional use of approach notes. It is possible, of course, to use "Middle Eastern-sounding" scales with the bass, but it's normally not done.

Syncopation is common in Middle Eastern grooves.

TONE:

TRADITIONAL: Bass +3 to +9 dB, Mids flat, Treble flat to -6 dB. Emulates upright.

MODERN: Bass +3 to +9 dB, Mids +3 to +6 dB @ 500 Hz, Treble +3 to +6 dB. Funk-like tone.

MIDDLE EASTERN CHARACTERISTICS (CONT'D)

GEAR: In traditional (pre-Western-influence) Middle Eastern/Arabic ensembles, the bass was absent, its place largely taken by drums tuned to different tonal centers. In early Middle Eastern Western-influenced (orchestral) music, the upright was used. In modern Middle Eastern/Arabic pop, electric bass is the norm.

TECHNIQUE: All playing techniques can be used: picks, finger style, and arco (on upright).

SCALES: Typically, scales used in Middle Eastern music contain both minor seconds and augmented seconds. However, such scales are used almost exclusively by vocalists and melodic instrument players. Likewise, the quarter tones commonly found in Middle Eastern music are typically used in vocals and in lines played by melodic string and wind instruments. In contrast, the bass sticks closely to standard major and minor scales.

PROGRESSIONS:

1) i - i - vii - i
2) I - I - vii - i
3) iv - III - bII - i
4) I - V - I - V
5) I - I - I - I

QUARTER NOTE = 100 – 132 BPM (On average, but will vary considerably with different rhythmic patterns. The following tempo indications are typical of what we found; they are not definitive.)

QUARTER NOTE = 200 BPM (SAUDI RYHTHM)

QUARTER NOTE = 120 BPM (SAYYIDI RHYTHM)

EIGHTH NOTE = 192 – 320 BPM (LAZ & KARSILAMA RHYTHMS)

OSTINATO EXAMPLE 1

OSTINATO EXAMPLE 1 VARIATION 1

D

OSTINATO EXAMPLE 1 VARIATION 2

G

OSTINATO EXAMPLE 1 VARIATION 3

C

OSTINATO EXAMPLE 1 VARIATION 4

E

OSTINATO EXAMPLE 1 VARIATION 5

E

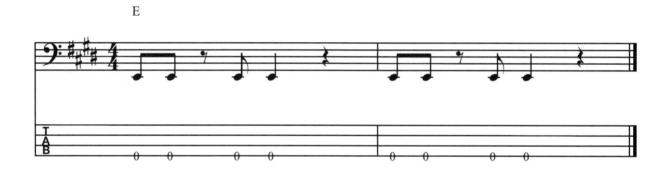

OSTINATO EXAMPLE 1 VARIATION 6

D

SAUDI CHARACTERISTICS

Traditional Middle Eastern rhythms cover a wide array of odd-time and compound signatures. However, as a result of Western music's influence, a large portion of contemporary Middle Eastern music is written in 4/4. Here, 4/4 is broken up into 3 + 3 + 2. (For a clear example of this rhythm—for those who can read piano music—see the sixth Dance in Bulgarian Rhythm in Book 6 of Bela Bartok's "Mikrokosmos" piano series.)

QUARTER NOTE = 200 BPM

SAUDI RHYTHM EXAMPLE 1 (CD 2 TRACK 61)

SAUDI RHYTHM EXAMPLE 2

SAUDI RHYTHM EXAMPLE 3

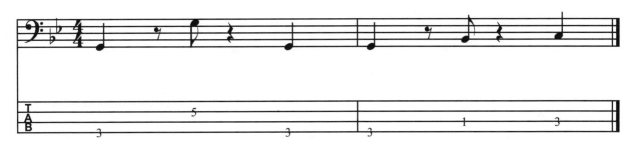

SAUDI RHYTHM EXAMPLE 4

SAYYIDI CHARACTERISTICS

The rhythm in this pattern is a Sayyidi rhythm, from the Maqsuum family. It is the most common rhythm found in popular contemporary Middle Eastern music.

QUARTER NOTE = 120 BPM

SAYYIDI RHYTHM EXAMPLE 1 (CD 2 TRACK 62, DVD TRACK 79)

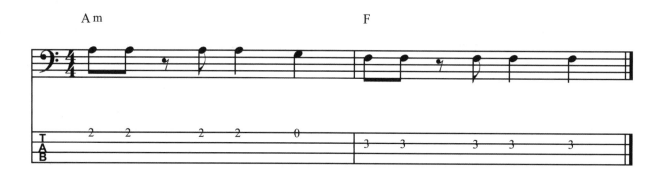

SAYYIDI RHYTHM EXAMPLE 1 VARIATION 1

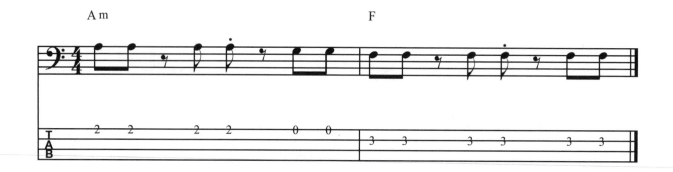

SAYYIDI RHYTHM EXAMPLE 1 VARIATION 2

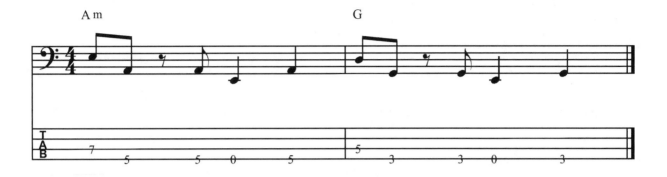

SAYYIDI RHYTHM EXAMPLE 2 (CD 2 TRACK 63)

SAYYIDI RHYTHM EXAMPLE 2 VARIATION 1

LAZ CHARACTERISTICS

This is a standard grouping of 2 + 2 + 3 in a 7/8 time signature. It's of Turkish/Arabic origin and is used in Greek folk songs as well as Middle Eastern music.

EIGHTH NOTE = 192 – 320 BPM

LAZ RHYTHM EXAMPLE (CD 2 TRACK 64, DVD TRACK 80)

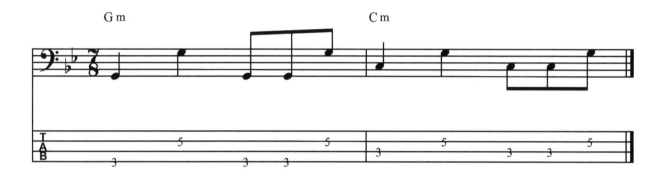

KARSILAMA CHARACTERISTICS

This is a common 2 + 2 + 2 + 3 breakdown of a 9/8 meter. It is of Turkish origin, and from a large family of 9/8 rhythms known as Aqsaaq rhythms. The best known example of this rhythm in Western music is Dave Brubeck's "Blue Rondo a la Turk."

EIGHTH NOTE = 192 – 320 BPM

KARSILAMA 9/8 RHYTHM EXAMPLE (CD 2 TRACK 65, DVD TRACK 81)

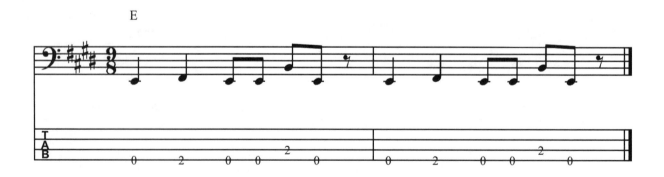

RAI

Rai developed in Algeria, primarily in the port city of Oran. Its roots go back to the early 1900s when the folk music of nomadic North African tribes was combined with romantic Arabic poetry. As 20th-century popular music spread, Western Algerian culture incorporated pop sounds and ideas into its indigenous music. Rai is influenced by such diverse styles as Funk, Rock, Ska, Reggae, Jazz, Hip Hop, Techno/House, and Afro-Cuban.

Prominent Rai musicians include Bellemou Messaoud ("the Father of Rai," a trumpet player who also played bass), Belkachem Bouteldja, Khaled Hadj Brahim ("the King of Rai"), Cheb Mami ("the Prince of Rai"), Chaba Fadela, and Cheb Khaled (whose "Kutche" album,

with Jazz musician Safy Boutella brought Rai international recognition). In the late 1980s and early 1990s female Rai singers such as Cheba Zahouania rose to stardom despite the pressures of living in a patriarchal culture.

Since Rai music draws from many genres, the grooves for the styles mentioned in the first paragraph can be (and are) used in Rai. But idiomatic Rai grooves are more common.

While Rai is a northern African style, it's covered here because it has more in common with Middle Eastern styles—Arabic-language vocals, quarter-tone scales, highly syncopated, percussive bass lines—than with the sub-Saharan African styles covered in Chapter 2.

RAI CHARACTERISTICS

BASS GROOVES: Rai patterns are usually, but not always, highly syncopated and performed in an ostinato-like manner. They often consist of just the root, although they sometimes use the flat seventh, fifth, and occasionally the flat third, especially toward the end of a bar, driving the pattern toward the next bar.

TONE: Bass +3 to +9 dB, Mids flat to +3 dB @ 500 Hz, Treble flat to +3 dB. Effects can be used, such as a small amount of flange or chorus.

GEAR: The plentiful use of percussion presents volume problems to upright bassists and makes electric bass more appropriate in Rai, although electronic upright bass can be used.

CHORD PROGRESSIONS: Rai progressions are predominantly in the minor keys. Unlike minor progressions in Blues and Rock, which center on the i, iv and v chords, minor progressions in Rai usually center on the tonic minor (i), the dominant (V) and the major chords of the relative major key. (For instance, the relative major of A minor is C major; its major chords, C, F, and G, correspond to the bIII, bVI, and bVII in A minor). So, the most common chords in Rai seem to be the i, V, bVII, bVI, and bIII. For example, in the key of Cm chords in a Rai progression could include C minor, Bb major, Ab major, Eb major, and G major.

RAI CHARACTERISTICS (CONT'D)

1) i7 - i7 - bVII - bVII - i7 - i7 - bVII - bVII
2) i7 - i7 - i7 - i7 - bVII - bVII - i7 - i7
3) i7 - bVII - bVI - V7
4) i7 - bvii7 - bvi7 - v7
5) i7 - i7- bVII - bVII - bVI - bVI - V7 - V7
6) I7 - I7 - V7- V7
7) i7 - bVII - i7 - bVII
8) bVII - bVI - V - bVII - bVI - V - bVI - V - i7 - bVII - bVI - V
9) i7 - i7 - IV7 - IV7 - V7 - V7 - V7 - V7 - i7 - i7
10) i7 - i7 - bVII - bVII - bVI - bVI - V - V - bVI - V - bVI - V
11) i7 - bVI - V7 - i7 - V7 - bVI - bVII - bIII - i7 - bVI - V7 - i7
12) i7 - i7 - bIII - bIII

QUARTER NOTE = 100 – 132 BPM

RAI EXAMPLE 1 (CD 1 TRACK 1, DVD TRACK 78)

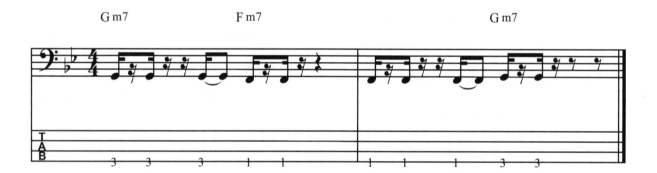

RAI EXAMPLE 1 VARIATION 1

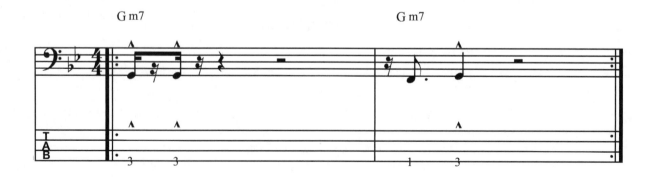

Rai Example 2 (CD 1 Track 2)

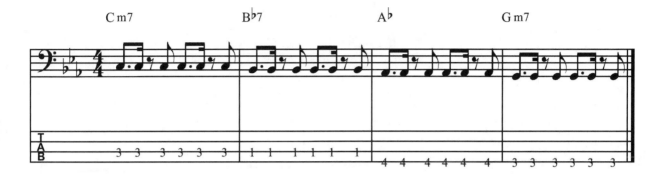

Rai Example 2 Variation 1 (CD 1 Track 3)

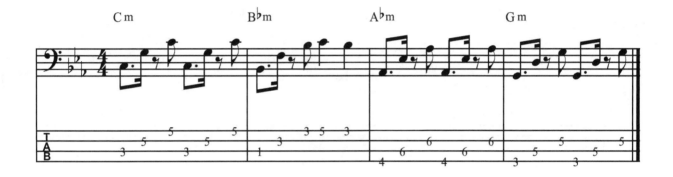

Rai Example 3

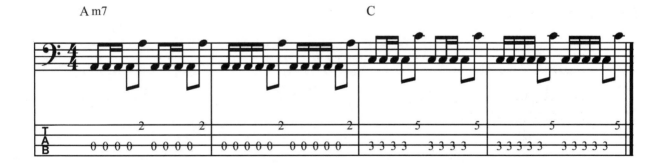

Rai Example 4

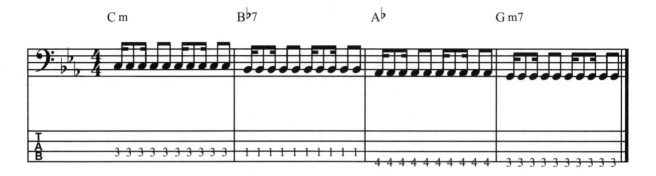

Rai Example 5

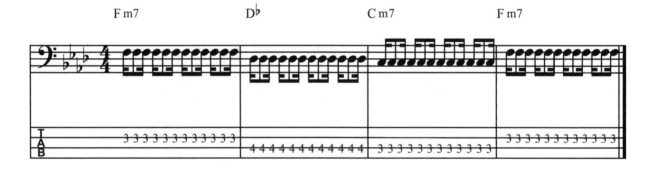

Rai Example 6

Dm7

20 POLKA

POLKA MUSIC ORIGINATED IN THE EARLY 1800s in what is now the Czech Republic. The term probably stems from the word "pulka," which refers to the short half-steps integrated into the dance. Toward the middle of the 19th century, the style spread to other European countries, including France, Germany, Austria, and especially Poland. Primarily composed and felt in 2/4, Polka is an upbeat, celebratory music traditionally played on accordion, concertina, and fiddle accompanied by a rhythm section. Currently the instrumentation often includes clarinet, trumpet, tuba, and saxophone. Artists such as the late Frankie Yankovic and Lawrence Welk, and the contemporary Texas-based Brave Combo, are a testimony to Polka's enduring popularity.

Most traditional Polka forms are Czech, with the two other primary forms being Polish and Slovenian. (Others include Scandinavian, German, Dutch, and French.) Polka bands use the term "Polka" to also refer to other forms of dance-style music, including the Waltz Schottische and the waltz-like Oberek.

The primary instrument in Polka is the accordion (button box and concertina). The newest forms blend modern electric instruments (including electric bass) and styles such as Rock with traditional forms to create variations such as Texas Polka, as played by The Texas Tornados and The Brave Combo, and Punk Polka, as played by San Francisco's Polkacide and Chicago's Polkaholics.

In the Western Hemisphere, the Polka rhythm appears in many other genres of music, including Country, Rock n' Roll, Gospel, Metal, and Punk. As well, a large number of show tunes utilize the Polka rhythm (commonly referred to in charts as a "Two Beat").

Polka's influence is particularly strong in the Southswest, where it can also be found in Tejano, Tex-Mex, Conjunto, and the Southwestern U.S./Northern Mexican Norteña style, which blends Polka with Ranchera; it has its roots in the Mexican states of Chihuahua and Durango, and in Texas via the many German immigrant colonies established during the 19th century. An even further afield Polka variant is found in Southern Arizona, where Tohono O'odham musicians play a variety of Norteña called "Chicken Scratch," which is characterized by the use of Rock instrumentation (trap set, electric bass, electric guitar) plus accordion and sometimes saxophone.

Innovative Polka bassists who expand the style beyond the basic root-fifth pattern include Cenobio "Bubba" Hernandez, Dave "Nigel" Kurdziel, Eddie Blazonczyk, Church Srnick, Tony Vadnal, Hernan Hernandez, Lou Kershishnik, and Anne Marie Harrop.

POLKA CHARACTERISTICS

BASS GROOVES: Polka grooves are based around root-fifth-root-fifth movement, as shown in the first two examples, which typify the classic Polka groove. Each of the three major ethnic styles has unique characteristic bass lines, and the bassist has an integral part in defining the variations between these styles.

TONE: Bass +3 dB, Mids flat to -3 dB @ 350 to 500 Hz, Treble -3 dB. The tone emulates the sound of the tuba. Use of flat wound strings is common, as is playing without sustain.

GEAR: Modern bands mostly use electric bass, although upright is still sometimes used. Fretless electric can also be used.

BASIC POLKA DRUM PATTERN

NOTE: Polka is normally written and is always felt in 2/4. Even when written in 4/4, it's played exactly the same as if it were written in 2/4 (with two beats per measure).

The following three examples can be used in all Polka styles. Root-fifth movement is the most common pattern, but root-third movement, as in Example 2, is also practical.

POLKA EXAMPLE 1 (CD 2 TRACK 67)

Polka Example 1 Variation 1

Polka Example 2

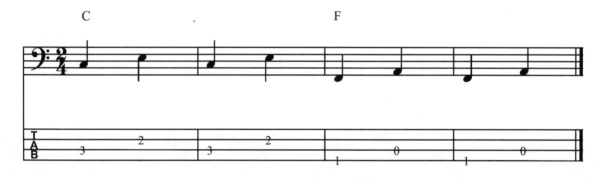

CZECH POLKA

Czech Polka is the most traditional style of Polka, and is closest to what is played in Europe. It is similar to the music played in Germany during Oktoberfest, but is not the same.

The Czech style is "straighter" than the other Polka styles played in America, as it is influenced less by other cultures. Two dance grooves other than Polka are typically played by Czech-American bands are the Schottische and the Waltz. The bass lines are tuba-like in tone, playing style, and musical lines.

Czech-American Polka bands. include Ernie Kucera, Harold Schultz Orchestra, the Greiner Brothers Orchestra, the Czechlander's Orchestra of Nebraska, Al Grebnik and more recently Czech And Then Some.

Czech Polka Example 1

C

Czech Polka Example 1 Variation 1

C

Czech Polka Example 2

C

9

G

CZECH POLKA EXAMPLE 3

POLISH POLKA

The Polish style, which has roots in Chicago, originated in family-oriented bars where immigrant communities kept alive cultural ties with their families in Europe. Each new community added its own influence. Lawrence Welk is a good example of this hybrid style, though technically his music is the German-American Polka.

Two sub-styles of Chicago Polka, whose influences are still felt, are "Chicago Honky" and "Chicago Push." "Chicago Honky" uses clarinet and trumpet, is often more improvisational than arranged, and has somewhat slower tempos than "Chicago Push." "Chicago Push" is differentiated largely by its faster

tempos, '50s Rock and Roll influence, and its use of different combinations of instruments in different bands, including accordions, concertinas, trumpets, electric bass, upright bass and trap set. Chicago-style Polka bands include Crusade. the Versatones, the Dynatones, and Marion Lush.

The other major Polish substyle is "Eastern," whose influences lie in the Big Band era. Eastern style bands include Jimmy Sturr, Frank Wojnarowski, and Bernie Witowski.

Contemporary Polish bass lines include chords, pedal tones, and rhythmic variations beyond the basic quarter-note pulse.

POLISH POLKA EXAMPLE 1 (CD 2 TRACK 68, DVD TRACK 82)

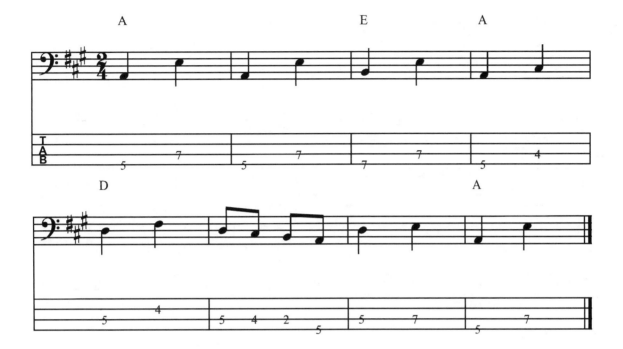

POLISH POLKA EXAMPLE 2

In this example the bassist doubles the lead (accordion, horn, or reed) line in measures 6, 9, 10, and 14.

Measures 5 and 6 are part of a call and response with the vocals.

SLOVENIAN POLKA

Also known as the "Cleveland Style," Slovenian Polka is an American style influenced by Slovenian folk songs. Instruments include the keyboard (chromatic) accordion, the diatonic button accordion (button box), saxophone, clarinet, drums, bass, guitar, and banjo.

Johnny Pecon, his son Jeff Pecon (Ralph Delligatti, Bass), Johnny Vadnal (Tony Vadnal, Bass), and Lou Trebar expanded the style through use of blue notes and elements of Jazz, such as substitutions and altered chords. In line with this, Slovenian Polka has a relatively jazzy, walking bass style.

Slovenian Polka songs may change keys several times since a full sized chromatic accordion is commonly used.

Frankie Yankovic's music provides a good example of this style.

SLOVENIAN POLKA EXAMPLE 1 (CD 2 TRACK 70, DVD TRACK 83)

SLOVENIAN POLKA EXAMPLE 1 VARIATION 1 (CD 2 TRACK 69)

The combination of the traditional root-fifth-root-fifth Polka bass pattern with walking lines is characteristic of Slovenian Polka bass lines.

21 PUNK

THE PUNK ATTITUDE/MUSICAL APPROACH surfaced in the mid to late 1960s in, arguably, UK Rock n' Roll groups such as The Rolling Stones, The Who, and The Kinks. In the United States, around the same time, proto-Punk groups included The MC5, The Stooges (fronted by Iggy Pop), and the lesser known The Count Five. Other less directly related U.S. groups of the time included The Seeds, the Velvet Underground, and Blue Cheer. In the early 1970s, The New York Dolls of the short-lived "Glam" Punk movement continued the trend. By the mid-1970s, the Ramones were playing high energy music which concentrated on rebellious posturing, both musically and lyrically.

In 1977, the British group The Sex Pistols won worldwide recognition with their pivotal album, "Never Mind the Bollocks Here's the Sex Pistols." This album firmly established the Punk genre and—hearkening back to The MC5—brought to it overt political content. At the same time, the even more political The Clash debuted with their influential, eponymous "garage-sound" album, "The Clash."

The rebellious style of the Sex Pistols and The Clash gave rise to countless other UK and North American groups in the next wave of Punk known as "Hardcore," with bands such as the very political (anarchist) Dead Kennedys, MDC, The Germs, Circle Jerks, and Black Flag leading the pack.

In the 1980s, Punk entered the mainstream through groups like Generation X and the still active, more polished-sounding The Clash. Perhaps, paradoxically, because of this mainstream acceptance the musical momentum of Punk soon dissipated, despite the 1984 hit movie *Repo Man* and its popular, all-Punk soundtrack. In spite of its musical eclipse in the mid-1980s, the Punk subculture continued to flourish throughout the decade, providing Punk bands with a supportive (in spirit, if not financially) audience.

Punk music and spirit had a great resurgence in the early and mid 1990s with "Grunge" music and the success of the Seattle sensation, Nirvana. Grunge is to be (slightly) distinguished from Punk in that Grunge bands sometimes employ quiet acoustic passages interspersed with loud, Punk-style sections in their songs, often in a formulaic manner (brilliantly parodied by the Austin Lounge Lizards in their "Grunge Song"). Punk music thrives today through popular bands such as Green Day and Blink 182. A more recent Punk trend is "Garage," with the most prominent bands being The Hives, The Vines, The Strokes, and the White Stripes (unique in this genre, as they have no bassist). Other notable modern Punk bands include Social Distortion, Jimmy Eat World, Rise Against, Voodoo Glow Skulls, My Chemical Romance, NOFX, Yellow Card, Bad Religion, Fall Out Boy, Alkaline Trio, and You Me At Six.

Musically, Punk is a relatively simple style featuring stripped-down instrumentation — generally bass, drums, one or two overdriven electric guitars, and a lead singer (almost always with no back-up vocals) — and rhythmically and harmonically simple songs which are generally played fast and at ear-splitting volume. (The dynamic range in Punk songs varies normally, if it varies at all, from very loud to unbearably loud.) As defiance is its defining attitude, Punk lyrics usually deal with despair, anger, teenage angst, aggression, and politics. When they are employed, background vocals are often sung in unison with the lead vocal or limited to shouting.

As Punk music and culture had little or no initial support (and outright resistance from) the music industry, Punk musicians developed a do-it-yourself approach, which manifested itself in "indie" record companies, fanzines, self-promotions, tours set up by the bands themselves, and mail-order record sales (the latter as early as 1979).

In keeping with this approach, Punk musicians, bassists included, typically avoid and even shun formal musical training (like early Surf bassists), preferring to learn their instruments by playing in a band. As attitude is respected more than technique, Punk bassists are often less familiar with music than either their drummers or guitarists.

Though many abhor technical expertise, most Punk musicians take great pride in their music's execution.

Playing bass in this aggressive, loud style can take huge amounts of endurance and concentration.

For info on the Punk attitude, see *The Philosophy of Punk*, by Craig O'Hara. The following quotation from Green Day's Billy Joe Armstrong serves as a wonderful example of the Punk attitude: "Punk is not just the sound, the music. Punk is a lifestyle. There are a lot of bands around who claim to be Punk and they only play the music; they have no clue what it's all about. It's a lifestyle I chose for myself."

In the film "Punk Attitude," by Don Letts, Roberta Bailey, CBGB scene photographer, describes the punk scene: "You didn't have to wait to start doing something. If you wanted to do it you could try doing it." Later in the same movie, Chrissie Hynde of the Pretenders describes the beginnings of the English Punk bands: "That was the beauty of that scene. Everyone got a band together. And everyone was in a band."

Discussing the early bands' musical maturation and their breaking away or moving on from Punk, she says: "Punk inherently was going to have a short life-span because the beauty of Punk music, anyway, was that no one could really play very good. And what happens is that if you get into music, and you actually like playing and you want to make music your life . . . if you wanted to pursue that, inevitably you got better at your craft."

Contrary to Hynde's statement, Punk hasn't been short lived.

PUNK CHARACTERISTICS

BASS GROOVES: Punk bass lines are usually very simple and played very fast. The challenges tend to be keeping the groove solid at fast tempos and locking in with the guitarist's chords and riffs in often-unpredictable places.

TONE: Bass +6 to +9 dB, Mids +3 Db @ 350 Hz, Treble flat. An extremely loud, overdriven, and distorted sound.

GEAR: Electric bass. Any type of amp can be used as long as it's loud enough and dirty enough. If you're playing in a smaller hall where the volume might overwhelm the audience (and, more importantly, the bar owner or manager) and prevent you from ever playing there again, an alternative to using one of the usual very powerful amps is to use a smaller amp with a distortion box and to mike the output of that through the p.a. (And, as with Metal gear, yeah, we know. We don't expect anyone to actually do this, but it is a good idea.)

TECHNIQUE: Forceful picking is the norm.

PROGRESSIONS: Songs are often constructed with just two to four chords, sometimes in patterns as simple as I-IV-I-IV or iii-V-iii-V-I, endlessly repeated without bridges or turnarounds. Occasionally, though, progressions are moderately complex.

The chords are often open-fifth "power chords" (root and 5th only), consequently not major or minor (as they don't have thirds). Bassists typically play the roots of these chords, but occasionally will play a distinctive pattern or riff for a particular song.

1) I - IV - V
2) I - bIII - IV - V
3) I - V - I - V
4) vi - I - IV - V - vi
5) I - IV - II - V
6) I - I - IV - V - I - I - IV - V (chorus) ii - VI - IV - V - ii - VI - IV - V
7) I - bVII - bIII - I (chorus) bIII/IV - I - I - bIII/IV - I - bVII - bIII - I
8) V/IV - I/V - V - I/ii - V - ii/V - V - ii/V (chorus) I - bVII - V - V

QUARTER NOTE = 120 – 270 BPM (but tends toward the faster tempos)

PUNK EXAMPLE 1 (CD 2 TRACK 71, DVD TRACK 84)

PUNK EXAMPLE 1 VARIATION 1 (CD 2 TRACK 72, DVD TRACK 85)

PUNK EXAMPLE 1 VARIATION 2

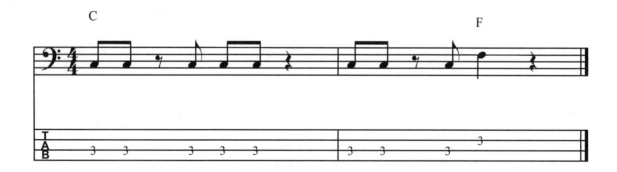

PUNK EXAMPLE 2 (CD 2 TRACK 73)

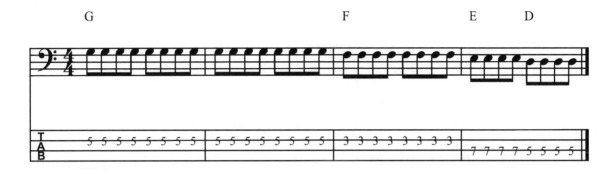

PUNK EXAMPLE 3

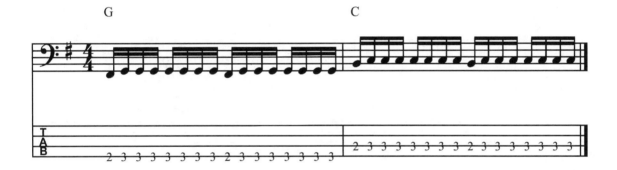

PUNK EXAMPLE 4 (CD 2 TRACK 74)

This example creates a three against two feel through the use of accents.

PUNK EXAMPLE 5

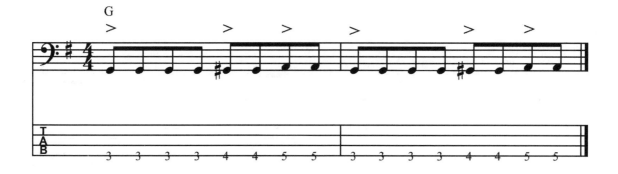

EXAMPLE 6

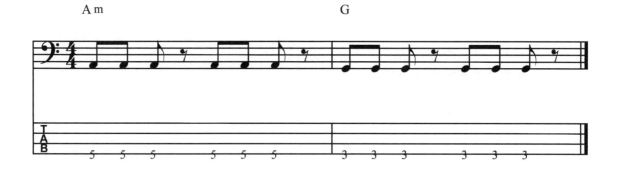

EXAMPLE 7

22 ROCK

ROCK MUSIC IN ALL ITS VARIATIONS is arguably the most popular, identifiable, and universal style of music throughout the world. Due to the enormous number of Rock n' Roll songwriters, musicians, and bands, it is impossible to cite every major influence in the genre within the confines of this chapter. The ones we cover are merely among the most prominent.

In the early 1950s, as Jazz became more of a listening music played by small ensembles, audiences sought music which provided an unwavering and obvious pulse for dancing. This factor, as well as the appeal of a lead singer emphasizing lyrics and the advancing development and use of electric instruments (guitar, bass, etc.) played with high energy, and with a heavy drumming backbeat, all contributed to the beginnings of Rock n' Roll.

The names of many 20th-century popular music styles were originally slang terms with sexual connotations—e.g., Swing, Jazz, Bop. Rock n' Roll is no exception. Although Alan Freed, an early 1950s disc jockey from Cleveland, Ohio, is often credited with coining the term "Rock n' Roll," it can be traced back much further, at least as far back as the song "Rock and Roll," written by Richard Whiting in 1934.

In the 1950s, a series of early hits, including "Sixty Minute Man," by the Dominoes, and several by Bill Haley and the Comets (especially "Rock Around the Clock"), grabbed the attention of American youth. As the new music gained popularity, musicians such as Antoine "Fats" Domino, Little Richard (Richard Penniman), and Chuck Berry emerged as its stars. And with Elvis Presley's phenomenal rise, Rock n' Roll produced its first superstar. Other 1950s stars included Sam Cooke, originally of the Gospel group The Soul Stirrers, Buddy Holly, Richie Valens, and Carl Perkins.

A lot of early Rock n' Roll, and what was later termed Rockabilly, featured acoustic bass. Having to compete against drums, and with p.a. systems used for vocals only, bassists were often drowned out in the mix. When Leo Fender, who had started making electric solid body guitars in the late 1940s, introduced the Precision Bass in 1951, the music changed radically (over the next decade). The advent of the Precision Bass alone brought bassists to the forefront, at least sonically.

By the early 1960s, Surf music had become very popular, and by the mid-1960s Soul Music, and more especially The Motown Sound, also became popular. These driving forces of early/mid 1960s pop music helped to establish Rock music's signature straight feel, as opposed to the swung feel of the Jazz bands of the 1930s and 1940s, and West Coast and Jump Blues of the 1940s and 1950s.

By the 1960s, Rock n' Roll had also found a large audience in Britain, inspiring the formation of many British bands and the "British Invasion" of the U.S. music scene. Beatlemania and the Beatles' continuing success were perhaps the best indications of Rock n' Roll's universal appeal and lasting popularity. The British Invasion also coincided with an emphasis on bands rather than individual musicians.

But, paradoxically, some of the more famous names in the history of bass rose to prominence in this period: Paul McCartney (The Beatles), Bill Wyman (The Rolling Stones), Pete Quaife (The Kinks), and John Entwistle (The Who). The mid to late 1960s saw a proliferation of Rock bands with prominent bassists, including Cream (Jack Bruce), The Jefferson Airplane (Jack Casady), Jimi Hendrix (Noel Redding, Billy Cox), and The Grateful Dead (Phil Lesh).

Many of the bands of this era began to experiment with improvisation in concert, taking tunes and playing them differently every night. Bassists and guitarists began a pseudo-rivalry in which both instruments could solo simultaneously. At times this led to exotic new textures, while at other times it led to chaos. With the extreme volume of the amplifiers and multiple stacks of speaker cabinets, plus large p.a. systems, it became impossible for bassists to "cut through" sonically. This led to further changes in tone, with many bassists turning to more extreme sounds, adding more mid-range and treble, and experimenting with effects such as distortion, reverb, flange, and chorus to distinguish themselves in the mix.

By the beginning of the 1970s, several bands had become well established—Led Zeppelin, Deep Purple, and Black Sabbath—that are considered founders of the Heavy Metal style. (See Metal chapter.) Another category that had become widely popular by the early 1970s was Progressive Rock, a style of music characterized by lengthy compositions, odd time signatures, and a high level of musicianship. Frank Zappa and the Mothers of Invention, Emerson, Lake & Palmer, Genesis, King Crimson, Kansas, Yes, Jethro Tull, and Rush all contributed to the development of this style that has influenced countless bassists and other musicians for over 40 years.

The success of Progressive Rock mixed with the instrumental improvisation of Jazz produced the Fusion style, initially pioneered by Miles Davis, and very soon after further developed by the Mahavishnu Orchestra, Herbie Hancock and the Headhunters, Weather Report, and Chick Corea with Return to Forever. Fusion bassists were (and for the most part still are) among the most notable bassists of any style, mixing a Rock feel with Jazz improvisation. They use alternate scales and modes, take extended solos, and play on the upper frets, often in odd-time signatures.

Other prominent Rock bands and musicians of the early to mid '70s included The Allman Brothers, Lynyrd Skynyrd, Chicago, Steely Dan, Aerosmith, The Eagles, Kiss, Styx, and David Bowie. They all helped create the genre now called Classic Rock—music which has a driving beat in standard time signatures.

In addition, session bassists firmly established themselves at this time, and appeared on numerous famous recordings. Famous session bassists of this and other eras include James Jamerson and Bob Babbit of Motown, Nathan East, Pino Paladino, John Paul Jones, Anthony Jackson, Abe Laboriel, Carol Kaye, Willie Weeks, Dave Hungate, Joe Osborne, Phil Chen, Freddie Washington, Will Lee, and Bill Lee.

By the end of the decade, Punk music (see Punk chapter) was leading Rock music in still another direction—a high-volume, aggressive sound with loud, overdriven instruments, bass included.

With the debut of Music Television (MTV) in August 1981, Rock music rose to even higher levels of popularity. Music videos allowed audiences to not only hear but see popular Rock artists and bands such as Prince, Michael Jackson, The Cars, Talking Heads, The Police, Toto, Bruce Springsteen and the E Street Band, and The Stray Cats.

At the same time, Hard Rock/Heavy Metal had begun to gain wide popularity through groups such as Motley Crue, Def Leppard, Judas Priest, AC/DC, and Van Halen. Hard Rock bass playing retained the force and musicianship of early Heavy Metal (Led Zeppelin, et al.), yet was focused on supporting song structure. By the late 1980s, the division between Hard Rock and Heavy Metal became more apparent, as bands playing the louder, faster, and more aggressive style of Heavy Metal, such as Metallica, Anthrax, Pantera, Iron Maiden, Megadeth, and Slayer, gained tremendous cult followings.

The Hard Rock bands dominating mainstream Rock included Whitesnake, Skid Row, Dokken, Poison, and Guns n' Roses. Many of them set a fashion trend of long hair, makeup, and costume-like clothing. Whereas Hard Rock continued to emphasize short songs with "hooks" and a recognizable drum beat, Heavy Metal emphasized rapid-fire melodic bass lines often played in unison or harmony with the guitar lines, growling or high pitched vocals, and fast tempos.

Early in the 1990s, the Pacific Northwest and especially the city of Seattle gave birth to the "Grunge" or Alternative Rock movement, through bands like Nirvana, Pearl Jam, Soundgarden, and Alice In Chains. All of these bands featured a raw, stripped-down sound and heavy drumming. Bands following the Alternative trend through the middle of the 1990s included The Red Hot Chili Peppers and The Smashing Pumpkins, along with the lighter Counting Crows, Lennie Kravitz, and The Dave Matthews Band.

The latter part of the decade saw a resurgence of the Punk style through bands such as Green Day, and Blink 182. As the decade closed, Metal returned fused with the vocal stylings of Hip Hop in a new "Rap Rock" style performed by Limp Bizkit, Korn, P.O.D., and Incubus.

Starting with The Grateful Dead (and, even though it's not commonly known, The Jefferson Airplane) in the 1960s, jam bands have been an integral part of the Rock scene ever since. More recent jam bands include Col. Bruce Hampton and the Aquarium Rescue Unit, Phish, Left Over Salmon, The String Cheese Incident, and Tea Leaf Green.

The twenty-first century, not surprisingly, has seen an even greater number of bands in the Rock genre. Though there are far too many to list, some of the more prominent recent bands include Linken Park, Death Cab for Cutie, Papa Roach, The Killers, Radiohead, Coldplay, Creed, Nickelback, 3 Doors Down, The Mars Volta, and The Foo Fighters.

A large number of Rock subgenres (Latin Rock, Metal, Punk, Alternative Rock, Rap Rock, Jam, Rockabilly, Surf) continue to be popular well into the current century, with no end in sight.

Rock Bass Guidelines

There are countless possibilities for bass lines in Rock. As in all styles, the lines are derived from two components: rhythm and harmony. The following guidelines provide good building blocks from which to construct Rock bass lines.

1) **Choose notes from the Blues Scale or the diatonic scale of the key of the song.**

2) **If using the Blues Scale, also include the major third for songs in major keys (e.g., G# in the key of E).**

3) **Fills can be used at the 4th, 8th, 12th or 16th bar.**

■ Early Rock

Early Rock Characteristics

Grooves: The bass lines in the Surf chapter and the Blues chapter can also be used in Early Rock. Early Rock uses many drum grooves: Blues Shuffle, Rockabilly, 12/8 Slow Blues, Mersey Beat and, most importantly, the Standard Rock Beat.

Tone: Bass boost +3 to +6 dB, Mids flat, Treble -6 dB. Emulates upright.

Gear: The earliest Rock was played on uprights, but since the late 1950s the electric bass has dominated. The choice of instrument depends on the genre.

Technique: Finger style is most common, but picks are sometimes used.

Progressions: Early Rock progressions are by and large derived from Blues progressions, and rarely stray far from the I7, IV7 and V7. Turnarounds are unusual in Early Rock progressions.

1) I7 - I7 - I7 - I7 - IV7 - IV7 - I7 - I7 - V7 - IV7 - I7 - I7
2) I7 - I7 - I7 - I7 - IV7 - IV7 - I7 - I7 - V7 - V7 - I7 - I7
3) I/IV - V/IV - I/IV - V/IV
4) I - I - vi - vi - I - I - vi - vi - I - V7 - I - IV - I/vi - ii/V7 - I - V7
5) i - i/V - i - i - IV - IV - i - i - V7 - IV7 - i - i/V7
6) I7 - bVI - I7 - bVI - V7 - I7 - I7 - IV7 - V7 - IV7 - I7 - I7
7) I7#9 - I7#9/VII7 - I7#9 - I7#9 - IV7 - IV7 - I7 - I7 - V7/V11 - IV7 - I7#9/IV7 - I7
8) I - vi - IV - V (Doo Wop)
9) I/vi7 - ii7/V7b9 - I/vi7 - ii7/V7b9 - I/vi7 - ii7/V7b9 - I/bII9 - V7
10) I - I - I - I - V - V- I - I

Eight-bar bridges are common, e.g.:

1) IV - IV - I - I - vi - vi - V - V
2) IV - I - II - V - II - II - II - V

Quarter Note = 60 – 200 bpm

STANDARD ROCK DRUM PATTERN

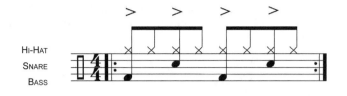

EARLY ROCK EXAMPLE 1 (CD 2 TRACK 75, DVD TRACK 86)

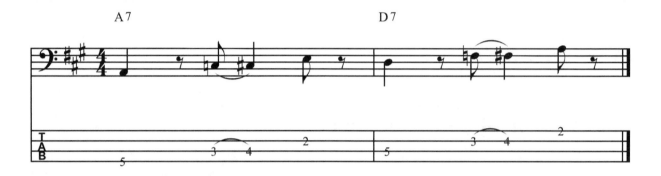

EARLY ROCK EXAMPLE 1 VARIATION 1 (CD 2 TRACK 76)

EARLY ROCK EXAMPLE 1 VARIATION 2

Early Rock Example 1 Variation 3

Early Rock Example 1 Variation 4

Early Rock Example 1 Variation 5

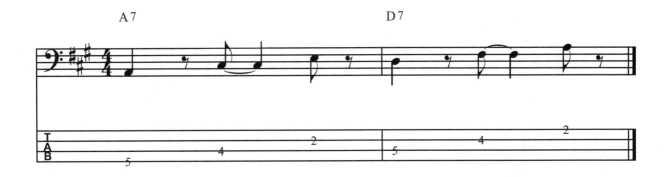

Early Rock Doo Wop Example 1

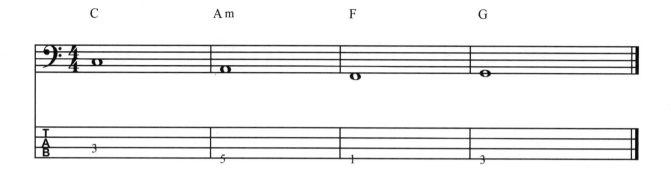

Early Rock Doo Wop Example 1 Variation 1

Early Rock Shuffle Example 1 (CD 2 Track 77, DVD Track 87)

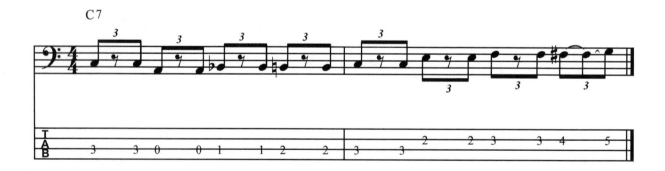

EARLY ROCK SHUFFLE EXAMPLE 2 (CD 2 Track 78, DVD Track 15)

EARLY ROCK SHUFFLE EXAMPLE 3

EARLY ROCK MERSEY BEAT EXAMPLE 1 (CD 2 Track 79)

EARLY ROCK MERSEY BEAT EXAMPLE 2 (CD 2 TRACK 80, DVD TRACK 90)

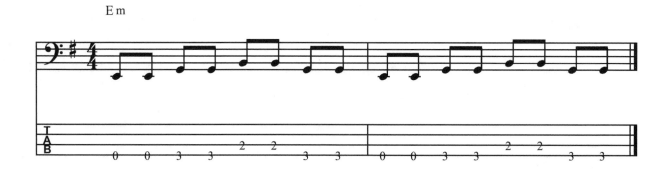

EARLY ROCK MERSEY BEAT EXAMPLE 3 (CD 2 TRACK 81)

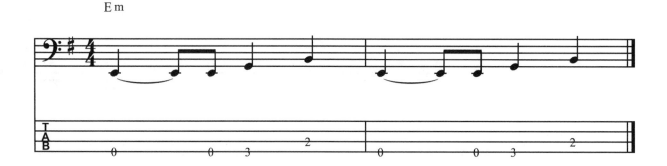

 # ROCKABILLY

One of the first forms of Rock n' Roll, Rockabilly emphasized a strong guitar and piano sound with a heavy backbeat on the snare drum, similar to that of Jump Blues. Prominent creators of the Rockabilly sound were Bill Haley and the Comets, Carl Perkins, Jerry Lee Lewis, and Elvis Presley. Rockabilly's popularity diminished by the early 1960s, but has since rebounded through Dave Edmunds, The Stray Cats in the 1980s, and, more recently, Brian Setzer (former Stray Cats guitarist) and the Reverend Horton Heat.

Finally, a special thanks to Brandon Essex for playing Example 1, Example 1 Variation 1, and Example 2.

ROCKABILLY CHARACTERISTICS

GROOVES: In contrast to other Rock styles, Rockabilly is swung. A walking bass line can be used in most Rockabilly songs, and 12/8 Blues patterns can be used in slower songs. (see Blues chapter.)

TONE: Bass flat to +6dB, Mids flat, Treble flat to -6 dB. If electric bass is used, it emulates standup: prominent and percussive. When electric is used, some natural overdrive is normal.

ROCKABILLY CHARACTERISTICS (CONT'D)

GEAR: Rockabilly was originally played on the upright, which is still the norm, but some contemporary Rockabilly bands use the electric bass. Very loud bands have feedback issues, so electric bass is the instrument of choice when such problems arise. Special, durable strings are required for upright slapping. Some players even use "Weedwacker" strings on upright.

TECHNIQUE: Finger style, employing slapping on an upright. Rockabilly slapping is only done correctly on upright. (Rockabilly slapping is very different from Funk slapping and popping. In Rockabilly, you slap with the fingers. In Funk, you slap with the thumb.)

PROGRESSIONS: Rockabilly progressions are derived from basic Blues progressions and rarely stray far from them.

1) I7 - I7 - I7 - I7 - IV7 - IV7 - I7 - I7 - V7 - IV7 - I7 - I7
2) I7 - I7 - IV7 - I7 - V7 - IV7 - I7 - V7
3) I - I - I7 - I7 - IV7 - IV7 - I - I - V7 - IV7 - I - I
4) I7 - I7 - IV7 - IV7 - V7 - IV7 - I7 - I7
5) I - I - I - I/I7 - IV - IV - I - I - V - IV - I - I
6) I - I - I - I - IV7 - IV7 - I - I - V7 - V7 - I - I
7) I7 - I7 - IV7 - IV7 - V7 - V7 - I7 - I7
8) I - I7 - IV - I - I - I7 - V - V7 - I - I7 - IV - I - I - V - I - IV/I

QUARTER NOTE = 120 – 240 BPM

ROCKABILLY EXAMPLE 1 (CD 2 TRACK 82)

ROCKABILLY EXAMPLE 1 VARIATION 1 (CD 2 TRACK 83)

ROCKABILLY EXAMPLE 2 (CD 2 TRACK 84)

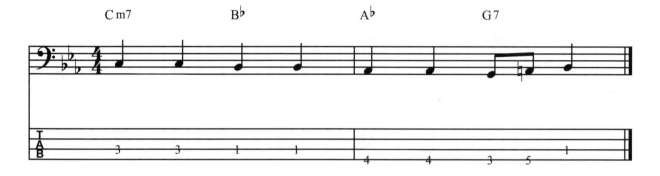

ROCKABILLY EXAMPLE 3 (CD 1 TRACK 38)

ROCKABILLY EXAMPLE 4 (CD 1 TRACK 39)

■ STANDARD ROCK

STANDARD ROCK CHARACTERISTICS

TONE: Varies greatly, depending on the style, from the clean bass sound of The Beatles and Yes to the overdriven, distorted sound of The Who, Jimi Hendrix, and Red Hot Chile Peppers.

GEAR: Electric. There are volume issues with standup instruments. Rock bass gear varies as greatly as the styles of Rock bands. Effects are often employed, again depending on the style.

TECHNIQUE: Both finger style and picking.

PROGRESSIONS: Many Rock progressions are based on Blues progressions. But Rock progressions vary greatly, from the ultra-simple to the extremely complex. The following relatively simple samples only scratch the surface.

1) I7 - I7 - I7 - I7 - IV7 - IV7 - I7 - I7 - V7 - IV7 - I7 - I7
2) I7 - I7 - IV7 - I7 - V7 - IV7 - I7 - I
3) I/IV - I/IV - I/IV - I/IV - I/IV - I/IV - I - bIII - IV - bVII - I/IV - I/IV
4) I/IV - V/IV - I/IV - V/IV
5) I/I/bVII/IV - I/I/bVII/IV
6) i7 - bVII7 - bVI 7- bVII7
7) i - i - i - i - i - i - i - i - IV9 - IV9 - IV9 - IV9 - V7 - bVI7/V7 - i - i
8) i7 - bVII - i7 - bVII - i7 - bVII - i7 - bVII
9) I7 - I7 - I7 - I7 - V - V - I7 - I7
10) I - I - I - I - bIII/bVII - bVI/V - I - I - V - V
11) i7 - bIII - bVI7/bVII7 - i7 - i7 - bIII - bVI7/bVII7 - i7 (bridge) bIII/bVI7 - i7 - bIII/bVI7 - i7
12) i - i - i - IV - i - i - bIII - IV - i - i - i - v
13) i7 - IV - i7 - IV - bVII - bIII - bVI - V7 - V7 - V7#9 - i7 - IV - i7 - IV - I7 - V7#9
14) i7 - i7 - i7 - V7#9 - i7 - i7 - bVI/V - i

QUARTER NOTE = 60 – 220 BPM

STANDARD ROCK EXAMPLE 1 (CD 1 TRACK 85)

STANDARD ROCK EXAMPLE 2 (CD 1 TRACK 86, DVD TRACK 88)

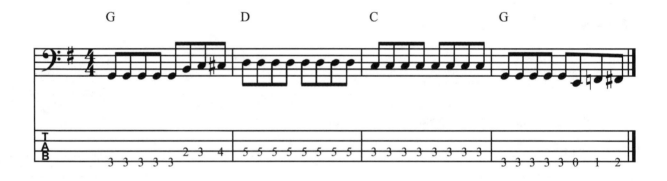

STANDARD ROCK EXAMPLE 3 (CD 1 TRACK 87)

STANDARD ROCK EXAMPLE 4

STANDARD ROCK EXAMPLE 5

Even this syncopated pattern works with the Standard Rock drum pattern.

HALF-TIME STANDARD ROCK EXAMPLE 1 (CD 2 Track 88)

Half-time Rock is played as if it has two beats per measure rather than four, and tends to have a more laid back feel than Standard Rock.

23 SURF

INSPIRED BY 1950s ROCK N' ROLL, Surf music evolved in the early 1960s as an instrumental genre performed by artists such as The Surfaris, The Ventures, and guitarist Dick Dale (who cites, of all things, Greek folk songs as a major influence). Purists consider instrumental Surf the most authentic form of Surf music. It emphasizes drums and guitar, typically very trebly, somewhat overdriven, and with heavy reverb, to evoke the experience of surfing.

When vocal-oriented Surf groups such as Jan and Dean and The Beach Boys arose in the mid-1960s, and featured lyrics (of a teen-jock-oriented type, usually sung in a high tenor—or outright falsetto—voice, with often-extensive vocal harmonies), the style achieved mainstream popularity.

Perhaps the most popular instrumental surfing drum song is "Wipe Out," recorded by the Surfaris in 1963 and further popularized by the Ventures, while the most influential guitar-driven Surf song is probably "Walk Don't Run," by the Ventures, recorded in 1960. Other instrumental Surf hits include "Pipeline," by the Chantays, "Apache," by The Shadows, and "Sleepwalk," by Santo and Johnny. Vocal Surf classics include The Beach Boys' "Surfin' Safari" and "Surfin' U.S.A.," and Jan and Dean's "Surf City."

Surf bands included bassists for both recording and touring. Not necessarily known for their virtuosity, some Surf bassists were initially entirely unskilled on the instrument and learned to play bass by playing in a band (similar to the path taken by many Punk bassists). This lack of formal training, along with the fast and complex guitar riffs endemic to Surf, served to inspire simple bass lines that supported the melody. The most important bassist of Surf's golden age was Carol Kaye, studio bassist and educator.

In the mid-to-late 1960s, Surf's popularity gave way to British Rock (The Beatles, The Rolling Stones, The Who, et al.) and, a bit later, to the Psychedelic Sound (The Doors, Cream, Jimi Hendrix, Pink Floyd, et al.). However, in the mid-1990s, the use of Dick Dale's 1960s-era classic "Miserlou" (originally played in Athens, Greece in 1927 by the Michalis Patrinos Rebetiko band) in the *Pulp Fiction* soundtrack stimulated renewed interest in Surf music.

Modern Surf music is played across the globe. Jack Johnson, son of legendary surfer Jeff Johnson, plays Surf and writes the soundtracks for the Surf films he makes. The Surf tradition is carried on by The Phantom Surfer, The Mermen, The Aqua Velvets, Los Straitjackets, the Russian-American band The Red Elvises, and the Greece-based The Invisible Surfers. Surf has also crossed over into other musical forms including Punk, Orange County's Agent Orange providing an example. And to this day The Ventures remain enormously popular in Japan.

SURF CHARACTERISTICS

TONE: Bass +3 to +9 dB, Mids flat to +3 dB, Treble flat to +3 dB. No distortion, no effects.

TECHNIQUE: Often played with a pick. The bassist plays on top of the beat. Reportedly, Carol Kaye put foam between the strings and played with a pick for recording, muting the strings, and thus making each note sound more "definite." Although this technique is somewhat unorthodox, it records well and remains useful in producing a Surf sound.

SURF CHARACTERISTICS (CONT'D)

PROGRESSIONS: Surf music is melodically driven. Unlike Blues forms that rely heavily on chord progressions, Surf music is often based on the simple i - iv as the primary chord change. From there, a song may include a simple change or two, or modulate abruptly, generally a full step up, at the beginning of a new verse (as in the TV theme song and subsequent Surf hit "Hawaii Five-O"), but the chord changes are less important than the melody. "Pipeline" and "Sleepwalk" are prime examples of this melodic emphasis. But even 12-bar blues ("Barbara Ann") and blues-derived progressions can be found in vocal Surf. Whatever the harmonic structure, the bass patterns in Surf always resolve and repeat so that the bassist, after one pass, has the entire pattern set. Most chords are simple major and minor triads; even 7ths are relatively uncommon.

1) i - iv - V - bVI - V - bVI - V - bVI - iv - iv - i - i
2) I - vi - I - I - I - vi - I - I - IV - ii - bVII - V (vocal Surf)
3) I - IV - ii - V
4) I - IV - I - iii
5) i/bVII - bVI/V - i/bVII - bVI/V - bIII - b III - i - i - bVI - V - i - i
6) i/vi - iv/V7 - i/vi - iv/V7
7) I - I - I - IV/I - I - I - V - II/V - I - IV - II/bVII - V
8) I - I - I - I - IV - IV - I - I - V - IV - I - I (vocal Surf)

QUARTER NOTE = 138 – 184 BPM

MERSEY BEAT DRUM PATTERN

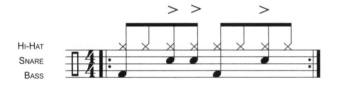

NOTE: The Mersey Beat is the standard beat in instrumental Surf. Vocal Surf uses a normal Rock beat. The following grooves will work with both instrumental and vocal Surf. For more variations for vocal Surf, see the Rock chapter.

INSTRUMENTAL SURF EXAMPLE 1 (CD 2 TRACK 89, DVD TRACK 89)

INSTRUMENTAL SURF EXAMPLE 2 (CD 2 TRACK 80, DVD TRACK 90)

INSTRUMENTAL SURF EXAMPLE 3 (CD 2 TRACK 90)

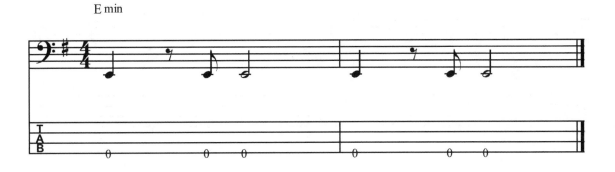

INSTRUMENTAL SURF EXAMPLE 4 (CD 2 TRACK 81)

Instrumental Surf Example 5

Am

Vocal Surf Example 1 (CD 2 Track 91)

Em

Surf Ballad Example 1 (CD 2 Track 92)

Notice the similarity to Baiao bass lines. (See Brazilian chapter.)

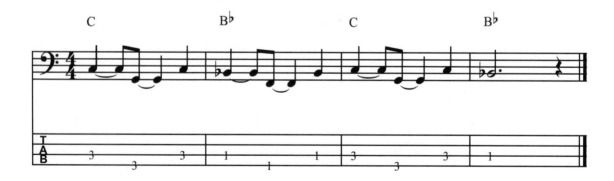

SURF BALLAD EXAMPLE 2

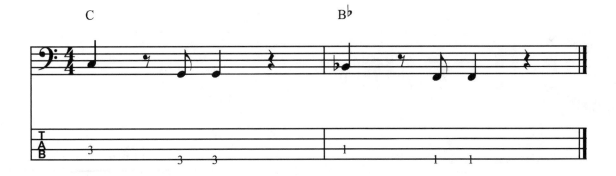

24 TECHNO

THE INVENTION OF THE THERAMIN and Ondes Martinot in the 1920s and 1930s ushered in the era of "electronic music." This new electronic approach remained largely confined to classical composers (e.g., Stockhausen and Messiaen) until the late 1960s and early 1970s, when pop ensembles such as Beaver & Krause in the U.S. and Kraftwerk in Germany began to replace acoustic and electric instruments (guitar, bass, etc.) with electronic instruments (synthesizers) producing "electronic music" (essentially proto-Techno).

Kraftwerk was the most popular and longest lived of these early groups. Formed in 1970, their 1975 hit "Autobahn" gave them a fan base throughout the world. Their 1977 album "Trans-Europe Express" inspired "The Belleview Three"—college students Juan Atkins, Derrick May, and Kevin Saunderson—to begin creating electronic music in Detroit, where it became known as "Techno." The electronic music scene continued to flourish in Detroit in the following years, spawning such works as the 1981 release by Afrika Bambaataa and Soulsonic Force, "Planet Rock."

In the 1980s, Techno's influence reached a mass audience through artists such as Devo, The Buggles, Human League, Yaz, and Erasure, all of whom combined Techno's electronic instrumentation and robotic beats with melodies and (more or less) conventional song forms.

Techno achieved its most widespread popularity in the 1990s (especially in Britain) through hard, "dance driven" music. During this time the term "remix" became associated with Techno. It refers to adding new tracks to a popular song, subtracting original tracks, (especially drums), and then "remixing" the result. This process usually results in a faster feel and a heavy, repetitive drum beat.

Currently, Techno has a large variety of substyles, including House (with a non-deviating "four on the floor" beat), Trance (emphasizing dramatic crescendos and use of dynamics, breakdowns and buildups, and sometimes sampled vocals), and Breakbeat, (which led to the emergence of the "Jungle" style). All are modern branches of electronic, dance-driven music using constant, repetitive harmonic/melodic figures. Recent Techno artists (called producers) include Moby, The Crystal Method, The Chemical Brothers, and Fatboy Slim.

TECHNO CHARACTERISTICS

BASS GROOVES: As early Techno used drum machines like the Roland TR-808 and bass sequencers like Roland's TB-303, the use of live musicians (especially bass) is the exception rather than the rule. Because Techno music is usually played by machines, a bass player wishing to create an accurate Techno sound must play perfectly in time and be able to play with a synth track. As with Techno drum patterns, Techno bass lines are generally not intricate, but require great consistency, and usually follow a "four on the floor" bass drum pattern. Techno's tempos are slightly slower than those of Drum n' Bass /Jungle. The bass "pattern" often consists of simply playing the tonic in unsyncopated patterns.

TONE: Bass +9 to + 15 dB, Mid -15 dB @ 500 Hz, Treble -15dB. The use of effects pedals helps simulate the synth-bass tone endemic to Techno, with both extreme bass boost and extreme mid and treble cuts. When using typical instrument/amp setups, an option is to add a sub-harmonic synth effect one octave below the line being played. Distortion can be used. A muted sound with little sustain is typical.

TECHNO CHARACTERISTICS (CONT'D)

GEAR: Techno is computer and sequencer/synthesizer based. The sonic range of 5-string, 6-string and other extended-range basses helps the electric bass to mimic keyboard bass. Upright could be used if amplified and with a lot of effects, but it would not be easy. What's important is to have plenty of power and to be able to cover the wide frequency range of Techno without unwanted distortion. Then add digital effects pedals or rack mounted effects. MIDI pickups to synthesizer or onboard synthesizers can be employed.

TECHNIQUE: Finger style or pick, depending on the tone required. The ability to play with a click track is imperative. You must play with perfect, unwavering tempo.

PROGRESSIONS: Minor keys are the norm in techno as are very simple progressions, with step-wise motion being common. But the progressions are relatively unimportant as the music relies almost entirely on repetitive drum and bass lines with repetitive melody lines on top.

  1) i - bvii/bvi
  2) i - ii - i - biii

QUARTER NOTE = 110 – 184 BPM

TECHNO EXAMPLE 1 (CD 2 TRACK 93, DVD TRACK 91)

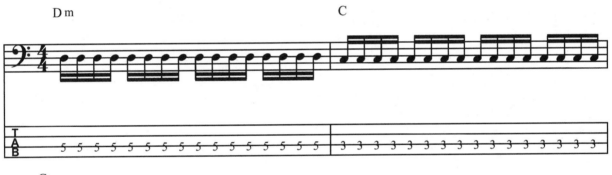

TECHNO EXAMPLE 1 VARIATION 1

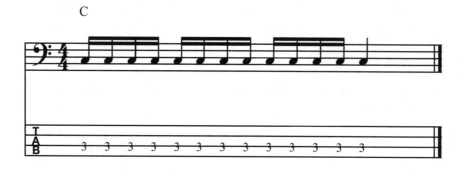

TECHNO EXAMPLE 1 VARIATION 2 (CD 2 TRACK 94, DVD TRACK 92)

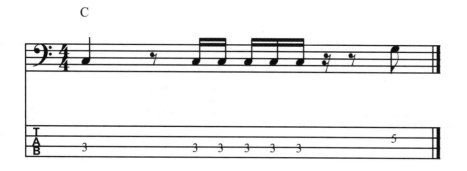

TECHNO EXAMPLE 1 VARIATION 3

Techno Example 1 Variation 4

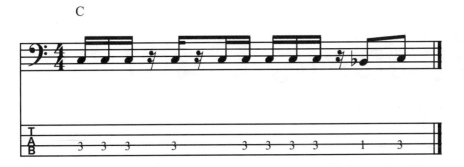

Techno (Disco/House) Example 2 (CD 2 Track 95, DVD Track 93)

Techno Example 2 Variation 1

25 WEDDING DANCES

A knowledge of common wedding dances is a necessity for the working bassist. The following dances are among the most often played.

TARANTELLA

The Tarantella is a dance from southern Italy (Taranto). The dance is basically a march which increases in tempo throughout the song. QUARTER NOTE = 136 BPM

TARANTELLA EXAMPLE

HAVA NAGILA

Hava Nagila is also commonly played at wedding receptions. A Jewish song and dance created in Jerusalem about 100 years ago, it means "Come, Let Us Be Joyful." Similar to the Tarantella, this dance often speeds up and is characterized by celebrants clapping, singing, and dancing in a large circle (a dance often referred to as the "Hora"—not to be confused with the Hora from the Klezmer chapter). QUARTER NOTE = 144 BPM

Hava Nagila Example

NOTE: The bridge section of Hava Nagila usually segues into a double time feel. The most appropriate groove to play in this second section is a standard Polka or Klezmer (Bulgar) pattern.

RUMBA

The Rumba, which originated in Cuba, is another popular wedding dance. Dancers familiar with the Rumba style accentuate the staccato rhythms of the percussion section with vigorous, energetic moves. Rumba rhythms are also frequently used in contemporary pop songs. The following pattern is the same as that of the Blues Rumba. (See Blues chapter.) **QUARTER NOTE = 144 BPM**

RUMBA EXAMPLE 1 (CD 1 TRACK 41, DVD TRACK 18)

Rumba Example 1 Variation 1

G

Rumba Example 1 Variation 2 (CD 1 Track 42)

G

 # Tango

The Tango developed in the brothels and bars in Buenos Aires during the late 1880s. Bass patterns for it are numerous and varied. Most common (though far from universal) seems to be a pattern with an emphasis on beat one and the "and" of beat two, followed by a note on beat three. Other possible patterns include playing whole notes on beat one, laying out (resting) for several measures, or playing more active patterns such as walking or even syncopated arpeggios. **Quarter Note = 128 bpm**

Tango Example

D

VIENNESE WALTZ

From its development in Europe in the 1800s (attributed to both Johann Strauss Sr. and Jr.), the Viennese Waltz remained the most popular European ballroom dance until World War I. It is slightly more syncopated than other Waltzes and often played at brighter tempos. QUARTER NOTE = 152 – 208 BPM

VIENNESE WALTZ EXAMPLE

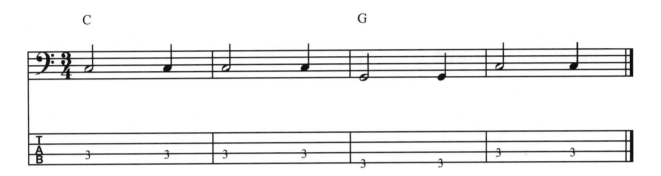

AMERICAN WALTZ

The American Waltz (aka "The Boston," stemming from its development in Boston, Massachusetts) is somewhat slower than the Viennese Waltz and has less syncopation. QUARTER NOTE = 132 – 176 BPM

AMERICAN WALTZ EXAMPLE

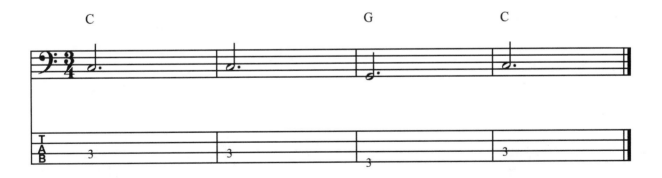

FOX TROT

The Fox Trot was created in 1914 by Vaudevillian Harry Fox "trotting" to Ragtime music. The Fox Trot has become one of the most important dances in ballroom dancing. **QUARTER NOTE = 120 BPM**

FOX TROT EXAMPLE 1

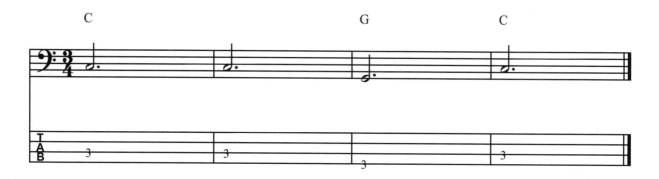

# A STANDUP VS. ELECTRIC

This Appendix Serves Two Purposes. It's an introduction to the standup bass for the electric bassist, and is also intended to help bassists understand the limitations and advantages of both standup and electric. We refer to the upright/standup/double bass as upright or standup. Acoustic bass refers to the guitar-like fretted bass commonly used in "unplugged" Rock n' Roll sessions. Most examples and styles in this book can be played on either electric or standup bass. There are styles, however, in which one or the other is preferable. This tends to be the case especially where a style was developed on one particular type of bass. For instance, early Jazz sounds best on a standup, while Funk sounds best on an electric.

This does not mean that you can't or shouldn't try to cross styles and instruments. It just might not be what the producer, band leader, or composer has in mind.

New music is often derived from combining styles or instrumentation. For example, Acid Jazz, which on the surface seems electronic, is often created using samples of standup basses. An almost opposite approach is to employ an effects unit between a standup bass and its amp, so as to mimic electric or processed tones. Another possibility is to use an e-bow or a volume pedal to simulate arco effects on an electric bass. But emulations are just that—emulations. Almost all styles that call for specific instruments will sound best with the original instruments. Still, there is plenty of room for experimentation, with both electric and standup basses intruding on the other instrument's previously sacrosanct territory.

Standup Bass History and Description

The standup/upright/acoustic/string/double bass was first used in Western classical music. The instrument is not a large violin. It is tuned in fourths (like an electric bass) rather than tuned in fifths like the violin. The sloped shoulders and shape of the body (which give you access to the upper register of the instrument) more resembles a viola da gamba (a six-string, fretted and bowed instrument of the Renaissance, which is also tuned in 4ths) than it resembles a violin. There are two types of bass bow: the familiar German bow and the French bow, which is very similar to a violin bow.

Standup Technique

If you play standup unamplified, there's a danger that you'll be lost in the mix, so you'll usually have to play loudly. Another approach is to learn to play with an amp; this allows more subtle playing and more dynamic range.

Piezo pickups, which became popular in the 1970s, are commonly employed with the standup bass. Because of the high impedance of these pickups, a preamp matched to the pickup is usually required. These produce an authentic standup tone.

Magnetic pickups, which have been around since the 1930s, are also available for standups, but the sound they produce is radically different than that of a piezo pickup—it's more like that of an electric bass than a standup bass.

Feedback is more likely to occur in a standup bass with an amp than with an electric bass, as the hollow body of the standup bass can pick up the vibrations from the amplifier, and some frequencies will resonate (causing feedback). This makes it difficult to get adequate volume with a standup bass. Use of a parametric EQ or an amp with parametric tone controls can help with this problem.

Standup Strings

Round wound strings have been around forever in the standup world, starting with gut wound with silver. They have a bright sound. Flat wound strings are easier to bow and are considered dark. There are many variations of strings with different cores and windings, and opinions vary as to which strings work best with a particular style. In general, bright strings are preferred for pizzicato and dark strings (softer strings that mask the highs) are better for arco.

One example of particular strings being suited to particular styles is Rockabilly, where the slapping technique favors gut strings. Some players use a new type of string called Weedwackers that are simply lengths of the nylon line used in the garden tool of the same name. They're cheap and stable, and if you use them you'll avoid the problems of gut strings (which stretch for a long time). They come in fashion colors such as lime green to go with your shoes.

Standup Limitations

1) "Slap and pop" Funk techniques will not work on standup. There is a "slap" technique often employed in Rockabilly, but it is very different from Funk "slap and pop." In Rockabilly, you slap the strings against the neck of a standup with your fingers. In Funk slapping you use the side of your thumb.

2) Playing with a pick will not work on standup, so playing certain Rock styles will prove difficult.

3) Techno and other electronic styles with its synthesizer-, computer-, and sampler-generated bass lines are much more difficult on standup than electric.

Electric Bass History and Description

Leo Fender introduced the Precision Bass (P-Bass) in 1951. It revolutionized bass playing, displacing the upright as the instrument of choice in many styles (notably Blues, Rock, and Country) within a decade. It's very similar to a typical electric guitar: solid body, fretted bolt-on neck, two electromagnetic pickups, and passive tone and volume controls. It differs from the electric guitar in that it's tuned an octave lower, has only four strings, and has a considerably longer neck (which produces a better tone than a shorter, guitar-length neck would). More than six decades after its invention, the P-Bass remains industry standard.

A large majority of electric basses are very similar to the P-Bass in basic design features. In addition to differences in construction quality, cheap electric basses often are harder to play and have more limited tonal range. High-end basses, in contrast, often have active electronics, which provide better tone shaping and higher output, which helps reduce hum/noise problems. High-end basses sometimes also have both piezo and electromagnetic pickups (in addition to active electronics), which allows them to produce amazing tonal variety.

Electric Technique

Electric bass is normally played finger style, with the middle and index fingers playing alternate notes. Picks are also used in some styles.

Electric Strings

Electric bass strings are normally round wound (that is, you can see and feel tiny, evenly spaced ridges along their length). These are the strings of choice nowadays. They produce a much brighter sound than flat wound (perfectly smooth) strings, and anyone who wants a dull sound while playing round wound strings can simply roll off the mids and highs on their bass's tone control(s) and/or on their amp. Round wound strings can, however, be helpful in getting vintage tones typical of some styles.

Electric Limitations

1) Arco playing (with a bow) will not work on electric bass due to the relatively flat neck. For example, in Klezmer you'll have to play pizzicato if you use an electric. (The style can be played either arco or pizz on standup.) You can also play an electric bass with an e-bow or a volume pedal to simulate the soft attack and smooth dynamics changes you get when playing arco.

2) The slap technique used in Rockabilly, Samba, Western Swing, and Train Beat will not work on an electric bass.

Other Types of Basses

Electric Fretless Bass: The first step an electric bassist often takes when moving towards standup is the fretless electric bass. It gives you the ability to play quarter tones. It also requires you to have perfect intonation. The fretless has a relatively flat neck, like a standard electric bass, so it is relatively easy to play; but you cannot play it with a bow.

Electric Upright Bass (EUB): This instrument is either a solid-body instrument with built-in pickups or a smaller-than-standard upright with pickups. EUBs can have flat fingerboards (which prohibit arco playing) or round fingerboards (which allow arco). Though physically smaller than normal standup basses, they can have added body wings, "false ribs," and a heel on the neck to simulate the feel of a standup instrument. Though similar in many respects to standup bass, EUB is a unique instrument. Playing technique can differ radically, as can the sound, from that of the standup or electric bass.

Standup Piccolo Bass: The acoustic piccolo bass is similar to the standup, but is normally tuned one octave higher. (Ron Carter plays a piccolo instrument tuned a fourth higher: A-D-G-C.) There is also an electric piccolo bass, which is not played upright.

Appropriate Basses for Different Styles

The following list covers all of the styles in this book, indicating the most common instrument used in every individual style. Information on tone can be found in the relevant chapters.

Acid Jazz can be played on standup bass. The sounds in Acid Jazz are typically derived from standup bass sounds, which are sometimes sampled and looped. Amplified standup or EUB can easily be used to effect. It's a wide open style that draws from other styles. Bassists often use effects in Acid Jazz.

African styles were developed on, and are more appropriate for, electric bass. The plentiful use of percussion creates volume issues for standup, although EUB can be used. Standup is more appropriate for some quieter styles, such as African Afro-Cuban fusion (e.g., Orchestra Baobab).

Afro-Cuban can go either way. Standup works well for early Cuban music (e.g., Buena Vista Social Club). Salsa usually calls for an electric or EUB—especially an Ampeg Baby Bass—due to the volume issues caused by competing against horns and percussion. Electric bass is very common.

Blues normally features electric bass. Standup can be used, but it's not common.

Brazilian is well suited to standup bass—especially Samba with its finger slaps (similar to Rockabilly slaps) between notes.

Cajun / Zydeco was developed on standup, but contemporary forms use electric because of volume issues.

Carribbean

Calypso was developed on and is played on standup.

Soca is almost always played on electric.

Reggae and Ska are almost always played on electric. (The climate in Jamaica is hard on acoustic instruments, and electrics are cheaper.) Early Ska was played on standup but quickly moved to electric.

Country was developed on standup, which is still usable in most Country styles.

Western Swing can be played on either electric or standup, although standup is probably better, with pizz and a little slap.

Bluegrass is normally played on standup, with some bassists occasionally playing arco; more recently, electric has become increasingly common, although it's inappropriate.

Train Beat (used in a number of Country substyles) has a specific finger slap technique which is very appropriate to standup, and almost impossible to duplicate on electric.

Country Rock and Modern Country feature electric bass almost exclusively, because of volume issues.

Disco was developed and played on electric. It's not much fun for standup players, and standup is almost never used.

Drum n' Bass consists mostly of computer samples, synthesizer, and sequencer-based patterns, but the style is also played by standup bassists. It's a very open style that employs live musicians as well as computers and samplers, electric bass, EUB, MIDI, and effects.

Flamenco is mostly played without bass, but standup or electric can be used in "pop Flamenco."

Funk was developed on electric, and is played almost exclusively on it. Although most Funk patterns can be played on standup, "slap and pop" is extremely difficult to play on standup.

Gospel was developed on standup, but either standup or electric can be used. Standup is often favored in traditional Gospel (Blind Boys of Alabama), but electric is normally used in contemporary Gospel.

Hip Hop bass lines are mostly computer based. In live situations, electric can be used. Standup, sometimes looped and sampled, is used more than it used to be.

Jazz

Second Line and Dixieland were developed on tuba and standup, and arguably sound better on standup. But you can use electric bass in early Jazz. Certain circumstances (such as a restaurant gig with a small trio) might work better with a standup than an electric.

Big Band Jazz originally featured standup exclusively, although modern Big Band Jazz orchestras use both electric and standup.

Small Band Jazz (Be-Bop, Cool Jazz, and Avant-Garde Jazz) originally employed upright, which is still favored, although electric can be employed in all three subgenres. In Latin Jazz, both upright and electric are common. And in Fusion, electric is almost universal.

Klezmer was developed on upright, which still produces the most authentic sound. Electric can be used and is played pizzicato, often with a pick.

Latin Rock was developed on electric, which is the norm. Occasionally players use standup, especially on recordings.

Metal is played exclusively on electric. Use of a pick and volume issues preclude standup.

Middle Eastern developed without the bass. But standup, fretless electric, or electric can be used in contemporary Middle Eastern. Electric cannot produce quarter tones, but that's not usually a problem as patterns consist primarily of roots, fifths, sevenths, and approach notes.

Polka was developed on upright, but electric is common today. Standup is still used in many traditional ensembles.

Punk was developed on and is almost always played on electric.

Rock was developed on standup in the 1950s, but since then the vast majority of players have used electric.

Rockabilly, with its characteristic slapping technique, is normally played on upright. Electric can be used, but upright is much to be preferred. Bassists in the Psychobilly subgenre (e.g., Rev Horton Heat, Cherry Poppin' Daddies) use slapping on a standup.

Surf developed on electric, but can be played on standup, although that's rare.

Techno is computer and sequencer/synthesizer based. Standup or EUB with effects can be used, but are not at all common.

B EQUIPMENT

BASSES

MODERN BASSES have many configurations. Acoustic basses are made like a traditional 6-string acoustic guitar with a large guitar-like body. They can have onboard pickups and an equalizer. Most solid body-electric basses have passive volume and tone controls. Active solid body electrics have an onboard preamplifier and active equalization. Traditional 4-stringed instruments have been expanded into instruments with 5, 6, 7, 8, 12 and more strings.

Another style of bass is the electric piccolo bass. Its range is an octave above a standard bass with its low E tuned equal to the E located on a standard bass's "A" strings' seventh fret. Two methods are used to achieve this: thinner strings or shortening the scale length (length of the neck.) Strings are also available that turn any standard bass into a piccolo bass.

There are, to put matters broadly, four categories of instruments: 1) Beginners; 2) Basic—minimum necessary for a gigging musician; 3) High end; and 4) Rare.

BEGINNERS INSTRUMENTS are usually made by machines in Third World countries. Workmanship and materials vary considerably. While most are fine for learning purposes, many are not as rugged as one would wish, and are not suitable for gigging. They typically cost in the $100–$300 range (new).

BASIC INSTRUMENTS are often made by machines with perfectly adequate materials. If they are set up correctly and are not flawed (which can make them harder to play), you can play any kind of music on them. They typically cost in the $300–$700 range.

HIGH-END INSTRUMENTS are generally handmade, often in the U.S., with the highest quality materials, craftsmanship, and techniques. They are easier to play, tune, and produce a wider range of sounds than basic instruments. And they're considerably more expensive than basic instruments. They typically cost from about $700 up to several thousand.

RARE INSTRUMENTS are usually no longer manufactured and the stuff of legend. They may (or may not) be easier to play or tune, and they may or may not produce a wider range of sounds than modern instruments; but they are collectors' items and usually produce a very specific sound. Prices for these instruments vary radically, but are generally high.

A lot depends not only on the manufacturer, but also when and where instruments were made. It is now common for manufacturers to reissue older designs, remanufacturing a bass to the original specs using identical or similar materials and processes. These reproductions are usually expensive and probably will not hold their value as well as authentic rare instruments.

AMPLIFIERS AND SPEAKERS

IN GENERAL, when choosing an amp look for one that is at least loud enough to be heard by your bandmates. If they can hear you, most likely the audience will too. It is better to have a little more power than you need so that you can produce clean sounds. An amp run near "10" will likely distort when played hard. At minimum, you need a 1x15, 2x10, or 2x12 speaker cabinet to rise above the drums.

Amplifiers and speaker boxes are a highly subjective matter. A pre-CBS Blackface Fender Bassman may seem a treasure to one player and an underpowered piece of antiquated tech to another. An Ampeg SVT or HiWatt 200 watt bass amp may seem just the ticket for playing a large hall, but is complete overkill for playing in a small club with brick walls, unless you want to drive the audience out of the building. An original 1965 Ampeg Portaflex B-15N "Flip Top" has the sound of James Jamerson, but costs a mint and is probably more appropriate for recording than gigging, depending on the size of the hall and how comfortable you are with the possibility of its being stolen.

Smaller amps, with the amplifier section combined with a speaker box, are called combo amps. But most bass amps consist of a separate amplifier (head) and one or more speaker cabinets. A third type uses a separate preamplifier and a power amp which are usually mounted in a rack case, and are called rack-mount gear. The whole set up is called a rig, as in "What's that horrible buzzing sound?" "It's in your rig, man."

POWER: Amplifiers can best be described in terms of power and tone. Smaller amps range up to 150 watts or so. Mid range amps are roughly 200 to 400 watts. High-powered amps go up from there.

Nowadays, when playing in a large hall with a large PA system, the instruments are run through the sound system, so louder amps are not as necessary as they once were. But basses with five or more strings need high-power amps to reproduce the lower notes cleanly.

For playing average-sized bars, you'll need at minimum a 100-watt combo amp, with 150 or 200 watts being better. However, if you're being miked and everyone is being run through a PA system, you can get by with a smaller amp.

TONE: Tone is also varied by the equalization or tone controls of the amp. Higher quality amps have more flexible tone controls and more power. Clean amps are capable of high volume without distortion. Other amps, most famously Marshall and HiWatt use distortion as an advantage and are designed and "voiced" for a specific distorted sound.

SPEAKER CABINETS: The smallest cabinets for bassists have a single 12-inch speaker or two 10-inch speakers (called a 1x12 or 2x10.) From there, they are commonly configured as 1x15, 2x12, 1x18, 2x15, 4x10, 6x10, and 8x10. Some cabinets also have smaller drivers for the highest frequencies. If you are having trouble being heard, adding a smaller enclosure can help. For example, if you have a 1x15 and add a 2x10 box, the additional midrange adds definition to your sound and allows you to be heard without using too much volume. Of course, that tone works only if it is appropriate for the style you are playing. (Needless to say, you can always ask the drummer and guitarist to play more quietly—and good luck with that.)

BEGINNER'S AMPS are usually made by machines in Third World countries, with as little human labor involved as possible. Workmanship and materials vary considerably. Almost all are combo amps running in the 15-watt to 100-watt range.

While most are fine for learning purposes, almost all are underpowered, many are not as rugged as one would wish, and virtually none are suitable for gigging. They typically cost in the $100–$300 range (new).

BASIC AMPS are often made mostly by machines with perfectly adequate materials. If they are adequately powered, they're fine for most gigs. They're typically combo amps, usually in the 100-watt to 300-watt range, and they typically cost $300–$700.

HIGH-END AMPS are generally handmade, often in the U.S., with the highest quality materials, craftsmanship, and techniques. They're higher powered and have better speakers than basic amps, and some are hand wired. They can be combo amps, but are more often half-stacks or stacks. They're considerably more expensive than basic amps. They typically cost from about $700 up to several thousand.

RARE AMPS are normally no longer manufactured and are the stuff of legend. They usually produce a very specific sound. Rare bass amps from the 1950s, 1960s, and 1970s are almost always underpowered by today's standards. Prices for these amps vary radically, but are generally high.

Some manufacturers now reissue older designs, remanufacturing amps to the original specs using identical or similar materials and processes. These reproductions are usually expensive, underpowered, and probably will not hold their value as well as authentic rare amplifiers.

It's common for older amps to need considerable work. At minimum, they usually need to have their potentiometers (tone and volume controls) and their tubes replaced, which can run up to a few hundred dollars on top of the cost of the amp. As well, it can be difficult if not impossible to find replacement parts (such as unusual tubes or output transformers) for certain rare amps.

C BIBLIOGRAPHY

BOOKS

Modern Reading Text in 4/4, by Louis Bellson. Van Nuys, CA: Alfred Publishing Company, 1985.

The Drummer's Bible: How to Play Every Drum Style from Afro- Cuban to Zydeco (Second Edition), by Mick Berry and Jason Gianni. Tucson: See Sharp Press, 2012.

An Understandable Guide to Music Theory: The Most Useful Aspects of Theory for Rock, Jazz and Blues Musicians (Third Edition), by Chaz Bufe. Tucson: See Sharp Press, 1994.

True Cuban Bass Book, by Carlos del Puerto and Silvio Vergara. Petaluma, CA: Sher Music, 2005.

Building Walking Bass Lines, by Ed Friedland. Milwaukee: Hal Leonard Corp., 1995.

Hal Leonard Bass Method Book, by Ed Friedland. Milwaukee: Hal Leonard Corp., 1996.

Contemporary Country Styles for the Drummer and Bassist, by Brian Fullen and Ron Vogt. Van Nuys, CA: Alfred Publishing Company, 1994.

The Salsa Guidebook for Piano and Ensemble, by Rebeca Mauleón. Petaluma, CA: Sher Music, 1994.

The Latin Real Book, Chuck Sher, ed. Milwaukee: Hal Leonard Corp., 1999.

New Method for Double Bass (Book 1), by Franz Simandl. New York: Carl Fischer, 1958.

New Method for Double Bass (Book 2), by Franz Simandl. New York: Carl Fischer, 1999.

The Latin Bass Book, by Oscar Stagnaro and Chuck Sher. Petaluma, CA: Sher Music, 2005.

The Real Book (Bass Clef and C instrument versions). Milwaukee: Hal Leonard Corp., 2005.

WEB SITES

Bass Talk
www.basstalk.com
(A forum for bassists—very useful)

Chordie
www.chordie.com
(A search engine for song lyrics and chord progressions; very useful, but the accuracy of the lyrics and progressions varies considerably)

Harmony Central
www.harmony-central.com
(A massive site with a huge amount of information on bass playing and gear)

Youtube
www.youtube.com
(A good place to find performances of any style or song you're unfamiliar with)

Reggae Fusion
www.reggaefusion.com
(All things Reggae)

History of Rock n' Roll
www.history-of-rock.com
(A very thorough history of Rock n' Roll)

All Brazilian Music
www.allbrazilianmusic.com
(History of Brazilian styles and much more)

Drummer's Bible
www.drummersbible.com
(Site of our companion volume)

Bassist's Bible
www.bassistsbible.com
(The site for this book—contains a lot of additional useful information)

D LISTENING

We chose these listening examples because they are good representatives of their styles. We've listed them in chronological order because this will help the listener to appreciate how they've developed.

Acid Jazz

Emergency on Planet Earth, by Jamiroquai; Sony Soho2 (1993)
Reachin' (A New Refutation of Time and Space), by Digable Planets; Elektra/Cooltempo (1993)
Brother Sister, by Brand New Heavies; Delicious Vinyl (1994)
Groove Collective, by Groove Collective; Warner Music (1994)
Layin' Low in the Cut, by Alphabet Soup; Mammoth Records (1995)
Crazy Horse Mongoose, by Galactic; Volcano (1998)
Boulevard, by St Germain; PIAS (2002)
In Between, by Jazzanova; Rope a Dope (2002)
Tales from the Beach, by Incognito; Bluey Music (2008)
Full Circle, by Atajazz; 101 Distribution (2008)
The Mirror Conspiracy, by Thievery Corporation; Eighteenth Street (2000)
Radio Retaliation, by Thievery Corporation; Eighteenth Street (2008)
Acid Jazz Complete Anthology1968-2010, by various artists; Music Brokers (2010)

African

West African Styles
Pirates Choice, by Orchestra Baobab; Nonesuch (1982)
Rex Lawson's Greatest Hits, by Rex Lawson; Flame Tree (1997)
Salute to Highlife Pioneers, by West African Highlife Band; Inner Spirit (1998)
Red Hot + Riot: The Music and Spirit of Fela Kuti, by Fela Kuti; MCA (2002)
Best of the Classic Years, by King Sunny Ade; Shanachie (2003)
Live at the Shrine, by Femi Kuti; P-Vine (2004)
Expensive Shit/He Miss Road, by Fela Kuti; Wrasse (2006/2000)
Rhino, by Albino; Mighty Niblet (2007)
E Dide [Get Up], by King Sunny Ade; Atlantic (2008/1995)
Sahara Swing, by Karl Hector & the Malcouns; Stones Throw (2008)

Soukous
Super Guitar Soukous, by Various Artists; EMI (1994)
Mezina, by Tabu Ley; Rounder Select (2004)
Africa Worldwide: 35th Anniversary Album, by Tabu Ley Rochereau; Rounder Select (1996)
Avis De Recherche, by Zaiko Langa Langa; Stern's (1997)
The Rough Guide to Congolese Soukous, by Various Artists; World Music Network (2000)

Bikutsi
Bikutsi Rock, by Les Tetes Bruless; Shanachie (1992)
Bikutsi Pop: Songs of So' Forest, by So' Forest; Naxos (2002)

Le Testament du Bikutsi Vol. 2, by various artists; TJR Prod. (2011)
Le Testament du Bikutsi Vol. 3, by various artists; TJR Prod. (2011)

Afro-Cuban

Dance Mania, by Tito Puente; RCA International (1958)
La Cuna, by Ray Barretto; CTI (1979)
Con Un Poco de Songo, by Batacumbele; Tierrazo Records (1981)
Songo, by Los Van Van; Mango (1988)
Wilfrido Vargas, by Wilfrido Vargas; T.H. Rodven (1991)
Congas Y Comparsas, Vol. 2, by various artists; T.H. Rodven (1993)
Palmas, by Eddie Palmieri; Nonesuch Records (1994)
Master Sessions, Vol. 1, by Cachao; Sony (1994)
Bolero Jazz: Tenderly, by various artists; Sony International (1994)
Ritmo, Sonido, y Estilo, by Libre Conjunto; Montuno Records (1994)
Cubarama: Let's Cha Cha, by Tito Puente; RCA International (1994)
Danzon Cha Cha Cha, Vol. 1 & 2, by Enrique Jorrin; RCA International (1995)
Mambo King 100th LP, by Tito Puente; RMM Records (1996)
Somos Boricuas: Bomba y Plena en Nueva York, by Los Pleneros De La 21; Henry Street (1996)
Puerto Rico Tropical—Quinteto Criollo, by Los Pleneros de la 21; Latitudes (1997)
Plena Libre, by Plena Libre; Ryko Latino (1998)
Senor Bolero, by Jose Feliciano; T.H. Rodven (1998)
Merengue Bomba, by various artists; Sony International (1999)
Merengues, by Luis Kalaff & Los Alegres Dominicanos; International Music Dist. (1999)
Carnaval Habanero, by Various Artists; ANS Records (1999)
Greatest Cumbia Classics, Vol. 1 & 2, by Various Artists; Discos Fuentes (1999)
The Rough Guide to Cumbia, by Various Artists; World Music Network (2000)
Tito Puente: The Complete RCA Recordings; RCA (2001)
Ibraim Ferrer con Los Bocucos, by Ibraim Ferrer y Los Bocucos; Caravelas (2002)
Mambo Mucho Mambo, by Machito and His Afro-Cuban Orchestra; Sony Records (2002)
Nu Latin, by Various Artists; Union Square Music (2004)
Descarga en California, by Rebeca Mauleón; Universal Latino (2006)
Pure Ballroom—Cha Cha Cha Vol. 1, by various artists; Andy Fortuna Productions (2009)
The Best of Perez Prado: The Original Mambo No. 5; RCA (2010)
Saoco: Bomba & Plena Explosion, by various artists; Sony (2011)
Los Mejores del Merengue 2011, by various artists; Sony (2011)
Original Sound of Cumbia, by various artists; Soundway (2011)
Saoco: Bomba & Plena Explosion, by various artists; Sony (2011)

Blues

Paul Butterfield Blues Band; Elektra (1965)
East–West, by Paul Butterfield Blues Band; Elektra (1966)
King of the Blues Guitar, by Albert King; Atlantic (1969)
Hot Tuna, by Hot Tuna; RCA (1970)
Live in Cook County Jail, by BB King; (MCA (1971)
Midnight Son, by Son Seals; Alligator (1976)
Briefcase Full of Blues, by the Blues Brothers; Atlantic (1978)
Texas Flood, by Stevie Ray Vaughan; Sony (1983)
Bad Influence, by Robert Cray; Hightone Records (1983)
Strong Persuader, by Robert Cray; Polygram (1986)
Chess Box, by Willie Dixon; MCA (1988)
In Step, by Stevie Ray Vaughan; Epic (1989)
Too Many Cooks, by Robert Cray; Tomato (1989)
The Complete Recordings, by Robert Johnson; Sony (1990)
The Chess Box—Howlin' Wolf; Chess (1992)
Junior's Blues, by Junior Parker; MCA (1992)
The Last Real Texas Blues Band, by Doug Sahm; Antone's (1994)
The Very Best of John Lee Hooker, by John Lee Hooker; Rhino (1995)
A Ass Pocket of Whiskey, by R.L. Burnside; Matador (1996)
Everlastin' Tears, by Willie Edwards; JSP (1996)
Cruisin' for a Bluesin', by Bad News Blues Band; ARV (1996)
B.B. King's Greatest Hits, by B.B. King; MCA (1998)
Muddy Waters Golden Anniversary Collection; MCA (2000)
Stormy Monday Blues: Essential Collection, by T-Bone Walker; Spectrum (2001)
Burnside on Burnside, by R.L. Burnside; Fat Possum (2001)
Muddy Waters Definitive Collection; Geffen (2006)
Working Man, by Willie Edwards; (2007)
Built for Comfort, by Built for Comfort; (2007)
Definitive Collection, by Robert Cray; Hip-O Records (2007)
Live at Hot Licks, by Bad News Blues Band; ARV (2009)
Queen Bee: The Antone's Collection, by Sue Foley; 101 Dist. (2009)
The Essential Coco Montoya; Blind Pig (2009)
Sugar Thieves Live, by Sugar Thieves (2010)

Brazilian

Samba

Brazil–Roots–Samba, by Wilson Moreira, Nelson Sargento; Rounder/PGD (1989)
Vol. 2, O Samba, by Various Artists; Luaka Bop (2000)
Cafe, by Trio da Paz; Malandro Records (2002)
Let's Dance Samba, by various artists; X5 Music Group (2009)
The Samba Night Club, by various artists; Lola's World (2010)

Baiao

O Rei Volta Pra Casa, by Luis Gonzaga; BMG (1998)
O Doutor do Baiao, by Humberto Teixeira; Biscoto Pino (2003)

Bossa Nova

The Legendary Joao Gilberto, by Joao Gilberto; Blue Note Records (1958)
Getz, Gilberto, Jobim; Atlantic (1963)
Wave, by Antonio Carlos Jobim; A & M Records (1967)
Bossa Nova Around the World, by various artists; Puntamayo (2011)

Cajun/Zydeco

100% Fortified Zydeco, by Buckwheat Zydeco; Black Top Records (1983)
La Musique Chez Mulate's, by Various Artists; Swallow Records (1986)
Silver Jubilee: Best Of Zachary, by Zachary Richard; Rhino (1999)
Zydeco Blowout—Clifton Chenier and His Red Hot Louisiana Band; Blues Factory (1999)
Chez les Cajuns; Narada 1999
Absolutely the Best of Cajun & Zydeco, Vol. 1 & 2, by Various Artists; Varese Records (2001)
Encore Encore the Best of Beausoleil 1991–2001; Rhino (2003)

Best of Steve Riley and the Mamou Playboys; Rounder (2008)
Let the Good Times Roll, by Zydeco A-Go-Go; CDBY (2008)
Up in Flames, by Dwayne Dopsie and The Zydeco Hellraisers; Sound of New Orleans (2009)
Zydeco Junkie, by Chubby Carrier; Swampedelic Records (2010)

Caribbean

Calypso

Calypso, by Harry Belafonte; RCA (1956)
Sing de Chorus: Calypso from Trinidad and Tobago, by Various Artists; Delos Records (1992)
Calypso: Vintage Songs from the Caribbean, by Various Artists; Putumayo World Music (2002)
Calypso Carnival, by various artists; Rounder (2010)

Soca

Soca Carnival, by Various Artists; JW Productions (1994)
Soca Addict, by Ronnie McIntosh; Rituals Records (2001)
Soca Compilation, Vol. 2, by Iwer George, Various Artists; Import (2001)
Socal Gold, by Various Artists; VP Records (2008)
I Am Soca, by Various Artists; Bungalo Records (2012)

Ska

One Step Beyond, by Madness; EMI International (1979)
Special Beat Service, by English Beat; IRS (1982)
Fishbone, by Fishbone; Columbia (1985)
Birth of Ska, by Various Artists; Trojan (1989)
Return of the Ugly, by Bad Manners; Blue Beat (1989)
No Doubt, by No Doubt; Interscope (1992)
Devil's Night Out, by The Mighty Mighty BossTones; Taang (1992)
Offbeats, by Offbeats; Dexter Records (1993)
Undercover S.K.A., by Undercover S.K.A.; Solo Records (1995)
Foundation Ska, by The Skatalites; Heartbeat/PGD (1996)
Fury of the Aquabats, bu The Aquabats; Golden Voice (1997)
Ska Box Anthology, by Various Artists; Big Eye Music (2001)
Rock 'n' Ska, by Offbeats; Dexter Records (2003)
The Police Live; Interscope (2003/1995)
Energy, by Operation Ivy; Epitaph (2007/1991)
Ska Madness, by various artists; Uma (2010)

Reggae

The Harder They Come, by Jimmy Cliff et al.; Universal (1972)
The Best of Toots and the Maytals; Trojan (1979)
Legend, by Bob Marley; Universal (1984)
Ultimate Collection, by Jimmy Cliff; Universal (1999)
Black Uhuru, by Sly and Robbie; Island (2003)
Police & Thieves, by Junior Murvin; Island (2003)
All Rebel Rockers, by Michael Feranti & Spearhead; Anti (2008)
Easy Star's Lonely Hearts Dub Band, by Easy Star; Easy Star (2009)
Best of Reggae, by Various Artists; Sonoma (2011)

Country

Traditional

Ten Years of Hits, by Mickey Gilley; Sony (1984)
The Buck Owens Collection; Rhino (1992)
Hank Williams, Sr.: 24 Greatest Hits; Polygram (1993)
The Essential Johnny Cash; Sony (2002)
Patsy Cline: The Definitive Collection; MCA (2004)
The Definitive Collection: Ernest Tubb; MCA (2006)
21 #1 Hits: The Ultimate Collection, by Buck Owens; Rhino (2006)

Bluegrass

Country Boy, by Ricky Skaggs; Sony (1984)
Ufotofu, by Bela Fleck and the Flecktons; Warner (1992)
Psychograss, by Psychograss; Windham Hill (1993)

Appalachian Stomp: Bluegrass Classics, by Various Artists; Rhino (1995)
16 Gems, Bill Monroe; Sony (1996)
Jam, by Darol Anger-Mike Marshall Band; Compass (1999)
20th Century Masters—The Millennium Collection: The Best of Flatt & Scruggs; Universal (2001)

Western Swing
A Tribute to the Best Damn Fiddle Player in the World, by Merle Haggard; Koch Records (1970)
Last Train to Hicksville, by Dan Hicks; MCA (1973)
The Essential Bob Wills & His Texas Playboys; Sony (1992)
Ride With Bob, by Asleep at the Wheel; Dreamworks (1999)
Western Swing: 40 Bootstompers from the Gold Age, by Various Artists; Primo (2007)
Doughboys, Playboys & Cowboys: The Golden Years of Western Swing, by various artists; Proper (2010)

Western
Gunfighter Ballads and Trail Songs, by Marty Robbins; Columbia (1959)
Cool Water, by Sons of the Pioneers; RCA (1959)
Songs of the Old West, by Roy Rogers & Dale Evans; MCA (1998)
The Ultimate Collection, by Gene Autry; Prism Records (1998)

Country Rock/Modern Day Country
Penitentiary Blues, David Allan Coe; SSS International (1968)
Wanted! The Outlaws, by Waylon Jennings, Willie Nelson; RCA (1976)
Eagles—Their Greatest Hits 1971–1975; Elektra/Asylum (1976)
Man of Steel, by Hank Williams, Jr.; Curb Records (1983)
Guitars Cadillacs Etc. Etc., by Dwight Yoakam; Reprise (1984)
No Fences, by Garth Brooks; Capitol (1990)
The Wheel, by Rosanne Cash; Sony (1993)
Hank Williams, Jr.'s Greatest Hits, Vol.1; Curb Records (1993)
Ten Feet Tall & Bulletproof, by Travis Tritt; Warner Brothers (1994)
Junior High, by Junior Brown; MCG (1995)
The Essential Jerry Reed; RCA (1995)
Losin' Hand, by Al Perry and the Cattle; Addled (1995)
Clint Black—Greatest Hits, Vol.1 & 2; RCA (1996, 2001)
Strange Noises in the Dark, by Austin Lounge Lizards; Blue Corn (2003)
The Drugs I Need, by Austin Lounge Lizards; Blue Corn (2006)
Hag: The Best of Merle Haggard; Capitol (2006)
Straight to Hell, by Hank Williams III; Curb (2006)
Is and Then Some, by Brooks and Dunn; Arista (2009)
The Essential Dixie Chicks; Sony (2010)
Lady & Gentlemen, by LeAnn Rimes; Curb (2011)
This is Country Music, by Brad Paisley; Sony (2011)
Welcome to the Fishbowl, by Kenny Chesney; Sony (2012)

DISCO

Saturday Night Fever: The Original Movie Sound Track, by Various Artists; Polygram Records (1977)
Pure Disco, Vol. 1–3, by Various Artists; Polygram (1996–1998)
Best of K.C. and the Sunshine Band; EMI Gold (2002)
100 Disco Hits of the '70s and '80s, by various artists; Goldenland Records (2010)

DRUM & BASS / JUNGLE

Logical Progression Vol. 1, by LTJ Bukem; FFRR/Good Looking (1996)
Ultimate Drum n' Bass, by Various Artists; Cleopatra (1997)
Hell's Kitchen, by Ming & FS; OM (1999)
Urban Jungle, by Aphrodite, Various Artists; EMD/Priority (1999)
In The Mode, by Roni Size, Reprazent; Talkin' Loud (2000)
System Upgrade, by Dieselboy; Moonshine (2000)
True Colors, by High Contrast; Hospital (2002)
Autopsy: The Dissection of Drum n' Bass, by AK1200 and Gridlok; Project 51 Recordings (2009)

FLAMENCO

Flamenco Rumba Gitana, by Various Artists; ARC (1994)
Live—Gipsy Kings; Columbia (1997)
Gypsy Rumba Flamenco, by Manuel El Chachi; ARC (2001)
Flamenco Virtuoso, by Paco de Lucia; Emarcy Eur/Zoom (2009)
Area 52, by Rodrigo y Gabriela; ATO Records (2012)

FUNK

New Orleans Funk:
Fess: The Professor Longhair Anthology; Rhino Records (1993)
Wild Tchoupitoulas, by Wild Tchoupitoulas; Mango Records (1976)
The Very Best of Dr. John; Rhino Records (1995)
The Very Best of the Neville Brothers; Rhino Records (1997)
The Very Best of the Meters; Rhino Records (1999)
Voodoo Soul: Deep and Dirty New Orleans Funk, by Various Artists; Metro Music (2001)
New Orleans Nightcrawlers; Rounder (2009)
Everybody Want Sum, by Dumpsta Funk; Controlled Substance (2011)
Carnivale Electricos, by Galactic; Anti/Epitaph (2012)

Motown
The Best of Sam & Dave; Atlantic (1969)
Anthology: Martha Reeves and the Vandellas; Motown (1974)
Every Great Motown Hit of Marvin Gaye; Motown (1983)
Wilson Pickett's Greatest Hits; WEA (1987)
The Very Best of Aretha Franklin; Atlantic (1994)
Temptations: The Ultimate Collection (1997)
Essential Four Tops; Hip-o (2000)
Standing in the Shadows of Motown, by Various Artists Hip-o (2002)
The Very Best of Booker T and the MG's; Stax (2007)
The Definitive Collection, by Junior Walker; Motown (2008)

Early Funk
Live at the Apollo, by James Brown; Polygram (1962)
James Brown—20 All-Time Greatest Hits!; Polygram (1991)
James Brown—Foundations of Funk (1964–1969); Polygram (1996)

Later Funk
Funkadelic; Westbound (1970)
America Eats its Young, by Funkadelic; Westbound (1971)
Maggot Brain, by Funkadelic; Westbound (1972)
Headstarters, by Herbie Hancock; Columbia (1973)
Thrust, by Herbie Hancock; Sony (1974)
Mothership Connection, Parliament; Universal (1975)
Gravity, by James Brown; Polygram (1986)
Return of The Headhunters, by The Headhunters; Polygram (1998)
Pickin' Up the Pieces: The Best of Average White Band; Rhino (1992)
Back in the Day: The Best of Bootsy (Collins); Warner Bros. (1994)
Travelling Without Moving, by Jamiroquai; Sony (1997)
What is Hip—Anthology, by Tower of Power; Rhino Records (1999)
Funk on a Stick, by Paul Jackson; Backdoor Records (2005)
Black Octopus, by Paul Jackson; Backdoor Records (2010)

Funk Rock
Sly & the Family Stone—Greatest Hits; Epic/Sony (1970)
Fire, by Ohio Players; Digital Sound (1974)
Songs in the Key of Life, Stevie Wonder; Motown/PGD (1976)
One Nation Under a Groove, by Funkadelic; Piority Records (1978, 2002)
The Best of Earth, Wind & Fire, Vol. 1; Sony (1978)
Thriller, by Michael Jackson; Sony (1983)
The Very Best of Kool & the Gang; Mercury (1993)
Mother's Milk, Red Hot Chili Peppers; Capitol (1989)
The Very Best of Kool & the Gang; Mercury (1993)
Under the Table & Dreaming, by Dave Matthews Band; RCA (1994)
The Ultimate Collection; Motown/PGD (1997)
What It Is! Funky Soul and Rare Grooves (1967-1977), by various artists; Rhino (2006)
Funk Classics Vol. 1, by various artists; DPM Records (2008)

GOSPEL

James Cleveland and the Angelic Choir, Vol. 3: Peace Be Still; Savoy
    Records (1962)
Spirit of the Century, by The Blind Boys of Alabama; Real World (1974)
Taking Flight, by The Gospel Hummingbirds; Blind Pig (1995)
Complete Recorded Works, Vol. 1, Sister Rosetta Tharpe; Document
    (1996)
Very Best of the Blind Boys of Alabama; Collectables (1998)
Al Green, Greatest Gospel Hits; Capitol (2000)
Complete Recordings of Sam Cooke with the Soul Stirrers; Specialty
    (2002)
Down in New Orleans, by Blind Boys of Alabama; Time Life (2008)
Hello Fear, by Kirk Franklin; Gospo Centric (2011)
The Legacy Project, by John P. Kee; Verity (2011)
Gospel's Best Worship, by various artists; EMI Gospel (2011)

HIP HOP / RAP

Rapper's Delight, by Sugarhill Gang; Castle UK (1980)
Raising Hell, by Run D.M.C; Arista (1986)
Straight Outta Compton—N.W.A.; Priority Records (1988)
Please Hammer, Don't Hurt 'Em, by MC Hammer; Capitol (1990)
Mama Said Knock You Out, by L.L. Cool J; Def Jam (1990)
Fear of a Black Planet, by Public Enemy; Def Jam (1990)
The Chronic, by Dr. Dre; Death Row (1992)
Doggystyle, by Snoop Dogg; Death Row (1993)
Blunted on Reality, by Fugees; Sony (1993)
No Way Out, by Puff Daddy; Bad Boy Records (1997)
The Slim Shady LP, Eminem; Interscope (1999)
The Black Album, by Jay-Z; Def-Jam (2003)
La Bella Mafia, by Lil Kim; Atlantic (2003)
The College Dropout, by Kanye West; Def Jam (2004)
Curtis, by 50 Cent; Interscope Records (2007)
How I Got Over, by The Roots; Def Jam (2009)
I Am Not a Human Being, by Little Wayne; Cash Money (2010)

JAZZ

New Orleans Second Line

Mardi Gras Party! New Orleans Second Line, by Various Artists;
    Mardi Gras Records (1995)
Best of New Orleans Jazz, by Olympia Brass Band; Mardi Gras
    Records (1995)
Best of New Orleans Jazz, Volume 2, by Olympia Brass Band; Mardi
    Gras Records (1995)
Ultimate Rebirth Brass Band; Mardi Gras Records (2004)
New Orleans Second Line, by New Birth Brass Bandñ Marti Gras
    Records (2008)
Twenty Dozen, by The Dirty Dozen Brass Band; Savoy Jazz (2012)

Dixieland

Louis Armstrong and King Oliver; Milestone (1923)
When the Saints: Best of Dixieland, by Various Artists; Delta (1990)
The Best of Sidney Bechet; Blue Note Records (1994)
King Oliver's Creole Jazz Band: The Complete Set; Challenge (1997)
Marching Down Bourbon Street, by Preservation Hall Jazz Band;
    Sony Special Project (2001)

Big Band

Complete Decca Recordings—1937, by Count Basie; GRP (1992)
1929–39—Chick Webb; Best of Jazz (1996)
Glenn Miller, Greatest Hits; RCA (1996)
Father of the Big Band, 1925–1937, by Fletcher Henderson; EPM (1999)
The Fabulous Benny Goodman; BMG (1999)
Masterpieces: 1926–1949, Duke Ellington; Proper Box (2001)

Small Band Jazz

Birth of the Cool, by Miles Davis; Capitol (1957)
Giant Steps, by John Coltrane; Atlantic (1959)

The Shape of Jazz to Come, by Ornette Coleman; Atlantic (1959)
Mingus Ah Um, by Charles Mingus; Sony (1959)
Kind of Blue, by Miles Davis; Sony (1959)
Charles Mingus Presents Charles Mingus; Candid Productions (1960)
A Love Supreme, by John Coltrane; Atlantic/GRP Records (1964)
Maiden Voyage, by Herbie hancock; Blue Note (1965)
Cannonball and Coltrane; Polygram (1965)
Unit Structures, by Cecil Taylor; Blue Note Records (1966)
In a Silent Way, by Miles Davis; Columbia (1969)
A Tribute to Jack Johnson, by Miles Davis; Columbia (1970)
Bitch's Brew, by Miles Davis; Columbia (1970)
Science Fiction, by Ornette Coleman; Sony (1971)
On the Corner, by Miles Davis; Columbia (1972)
Conference of the Birds, by Dave Holland; ECM (1972)
Headhunters, by Herbie Hancock; Columbia/Legacy (1973)
Jacaranda, by Luiz Bonfá; Ranwood (1973)
Light as a Feather, by Return to Forever; Polygram (1973)
Hymn of the Seventh Galaxy, by Return to Forever; Polygram (1973)
Where Have I Known You Before, by Return to Forever; Polygram (1974)
Changes One, by Charles Mingus; Atlantic (1975)
Jaco Pastorius, by Jaco Pastorius; Sony (1976)
School Days, by Stanley Clarke; Epic (1976)
Word of Mouth, by Jaco Pastorious; Warner (1981)
Barbecue Dog, by Ronald Shannon Jackson; Polygram (1983)
Money Jungle, by Duke Ellington, Charles Mingus and Max Roach;
    Blue Note (1987)
Best of the Blue Note Years: Thelonious Monk; Blue Note Records (1991)
Small Groups 1945-1950: Night in Tunisia, by Dizzy Gillespie; Giants
    of Jazz (1998)
M2, by Marcus Miller; Telarc (2001)
Boss Bird (Box Set), by Charlie Parker; Proper Box (2002)
Best of Weather Report; Sony (2002)
Legend of Cowboy Bill, by Astral Project; Astral Project (2004)
Dear Miles, by Ron Carter; Blue Note (2006)
Marcus, by Marcus Miller; Concord (2008)
Jazz in the Garden, by Stanley Clark Trio; Heads Up (2008)
Palmystery, by Victor Wooten; Heads Up (2008)
Thunder, by SMV; Heads Up (2008)
Inspiration Information, by Mulatu Astatqe/The Heliocentrics; Strut
    Records (2009)
Four Mf's Playin' Tunes, by Branford Marsalis; Marsalis Music (2012)
Further Explorations, by Chick Corea; Concord (2012)

KLEZMER

Future & Past, by Kapalye; Flying Fish Records (1983)
Klezmer Music, by Brave Old World; Flying Fish Records (1990)
Klezmer Music 1925–56—Dave Tarras; Yazoo (1992)
First Recordings (1976-1978)—Klezmorim; Arhoolie Records (1993)
Master of Klezmer Music: Russian Sher—Harry Kandel; Global Village
    (1995)
The King of the Klezmer Clarinet—Naftule Brandwein; Rounder Select
    (1997)
Blood Oranges, by Brave Old World; Red House (1999)
The Rough Guide to Klezmer, by Various Artists; World Music (2000)
Jews with Horns, by the Klezmatics; Rounder (2002)
Song of the Lodz Ghetto, by Brave Old World; Winter & Winter (2005)
The Klezmer King, by Abe Schwartz; Columbia (2011)

LATIN ROCK

Santana, by Carlos Santana; Sony (1969)
Caravanserai, by Carlos Santana; (Sony (1972)
Pachuco, by Jonny Chingas; Billionaire (1980)
How Will the Wolf Survive?, by Los Lobos; Warner Brothers (1984)
Primitive Love, by Miami Sound Machine; Sony (1986)
Just Another Band from East L.A., by Los Lobos; Warner (1993)
Ricky Martin; Sony (1999)
Marc Anthony; Sony (1999)

Supernatural, by Carlos Santana; BMG/Arista (1999)
Wolf Tracks, by Los Lobos; Rhino (2006)
Jonny Chingas' Greatest Hits; L.A.: Norwalk, (2007)
Los Hermanos Na Fundicao Progresso, by Los Hermanos; Sony (2008)
Las De Ley, by La Ley; We International (2009)
Coliumo, by Los Tres; Sony (2011)
Shakira: EnVivo Desde Pari; Sony (2011)

METAL

Paranoid, by Black Sabbath; Warner Brothers (1970)
Machine Head, by Deep Purple; Warner Brothers (1972)
Number of the Beast, by Iron Maiden; Sony (1982)
Master of Puppets, by Metallica; Elektra/Asylum (1986)
Harmony Corruption, by Napalm Death; Earache Records (1994)
Destroy Erase Improve, by Meshuggah; Nuclear Blast America (1995)
State of Euphoria, by Anthrax; Polygram (1988)
And Justice For All, by Metallica; Elektra/Asylum (1988)
Painkiller, by Judas Priest; Sony (1990)
Led Zeppelin Box Set; Atlantic (1990)
Images and Words, by Dream Theater; Atlantic (1992)
Covenant, by Morbid Angel; Warner Brothers (1993)
Far Beyond Driven, by Pantera; Atlantic (1994)
Universe, by Planet X; Inside Out USA (2000)
Christ Illusion, by Slayer; Sony (2006)
Entity, by Origin; Nuclear Blast (2011)
American Capitalist, by Five Finger Death Punch; Prospect Park (2011)
Midnight in the Labyrinth, by Cradle of Filth; Ais (2012)
Resolution, by Lamb of God; Epic (2012)
Fire from the Sky, by Shadows Fall; Razor and Tie (2012)

MIDDLE EASTERN

The Best of Saiidi & Baladi, by Hossam Ramzy; Arc Music (1997)
Rhythms of the Nile, by Hossam Ramzy; Arc Music (1998)
Sabla Tolo, by Hossam Ramzy; Arc Music (2000)
Desert Roses and Arabian Rhythms, Vol.1, by Various Artists; Ark 21 (2001)
Ayeshteni, by Natasha Atlas; Beggars Banquet (2001)
Arabic Groove, by Various Artists; Putumayo World Music (2001)
Moroccan Spirit, by Moroccan Spirit; Higher Octave (2002)
Greatest Hits, by Nancy Ajram; EMI (2008)
Latisideh, Lawa'ah, by Kadim al-Sahir; Rotana (2011)
Ya Tair, by Hatem Al-Iraqi; Qanawat (2012)

Rai

Kutche, by Cheb Khaled & Safy Boutella; Capito (1989)
Let Me Rai, by Cheb Mami; Tote Records (1990)
C'est Pas Ma Faute: The Father of Rai Music, by Bellemou Messaoud; Wergo (1999)
Meli, Meli, by Cheb Mami; Virgin France (1999)
Rough Guide to Rai, by Various Artists; World Music Network (2002)
Rai Superstars, various artists; Mondo Melodia (2002)
Kasbah Rockers with Bill Laswell, by Pat Jabbar; Barraka El Faratshi (2008)

POLKA

25 Million Seller Polka Hits, Vol. 1,2 & 3 , by Various Artists; Dyno Polkas Records (1994)
Polka Polka Polka, by Various Artists; Madacy Records (1994)
24 Polkas Greatest Hits, by Myron Floren; Polka City (1995)
Vintage Dynatones, by the Dynatones; World Renowned Songs (1995)
Songs of the Polka King, Vol. 1 & 2, by Frankie Yankovic; Cleveland International (1996/1997)
Hardcore 2/4, by Polkacide; Dog Patch Records (2000)
Six Fat Dutchmen: Greatest Hits 2; Polka City (2006)
Polka's Revenge, by Brave Combo; Dentone Records (2007)
The Exotic, Rocking Life, by Brave Combo; Dentone Records (2008)
The Greatest Hits of Polka, by Jimmy Sturr; Rounder (2009)

PUNK

The Velvet Underground & Nico; Polygram (1967)
White Light/White Heat, by Velvet Underground; Polygram (1967)
Kick Out the Jams, by MC5; Elektra/Asylum (1969)
Fun House, by Iggy & The Stooges; Elektra/Asylum (1970)
Never Mind the Bollocks Here's the Sex Pistols; Warner (1977)
The Clash; Sony (1977)
London Calling, by The Clash; Sony (1979)
Wild in the Streets, by The Circle Jerks; Epitaph (1982)
Repo Man Soundtrack, by Various Artists; MCA (1984)
Give Me Convenience or Give Me Death, by The Dead Kennedys; Manifesto Records (1987)
Nevermind, by Nirvana; Geffen (1991)
Dookie, by Green Day; Warner Brothers (1994)
Hey! Ho! Let's Go: The Anthology, by The Ramones; Rhino (1999)
White Blood Cells, by The White Stripes; BMG (2002)
The Black Parade, by My Chemical Romance; Warner Bros. (2006)
Let the Dominoes Fall, by Rancid; Epitaph (2009)
Fever, by Bullet for My Valentine; Zomba (2010)
Cardiology, by Good Charlotte; Capitol (2010)
Damnesia, by Alkaline Trio; Epitaph (2011)

ROCK

Early Rock n' Roll

The Essential Little Richard; Specialty (1985)
Buddy Holly's Greatest Hits; MCA (1996)
The Best of Little Richard; Excelsior (1997)
20th Century Masters: The Best of Bill Haley & His Comets; MCA (1999)
The Anthology, by Chuck Berry; MCA (2000)
Fats Domino Jukebox: 20 Greatest Hits; Capitol (2002)
Elvis 30 #1 Hits, by Elvis Presley; RCA (2002)

Rockabilly

Built for Speed, by The Stray Cats; DCC Compact Classics (1982
Jerry Lee Lewis—18 Original Sun Greatest Hits; Rhino Records (1984)
Carl Perkins—Original Sun Greatest Hits; Rhino Records (1987))
Holy Roller, by Reverend Horton Heat; Sub Pop (1999)

Standard Rock

The Piper at the Gates of Dawn, by Pink Floyd; EMI (1967)
Are You Experienced?, by The Jimi Hendrix Experience; MCA (1967)
Axis Bold as Love, by The Jimi Hendrix Experience; Reprise (1967)
Disraeli Gears, by Cream; Polygram (1967)
The Doors, by The Doors; Elektra (1967)
Strange Days, by The Doors; Elektra (1967)
Surrealistic Pillow, by Jefferson Airplane; RCA (1967)
Wheels of Fire, by Cream; Polygram (1968)
Beggars Banquet, by The Rolling Stones; London (1968)
Electric Ladyland, by Jimi Hendrix; Reprise (1968)
Led Zeppelin, by Led Zeppelin; Atlantic (1969)
Let It Bleed, by The Rolling Stones (1969)
Bless Its Pointed Little Head, by Jefferson Airplane; RCA (1969)
Derek & The Dominos (Eric Clapton, Duane Allman); Polydor (1970)
Raw Sienna, by Savoy Brown; Polygram (1970)
The Who Live at Leeds; MCA (1970)
Twelve Dreams of Dr. Sardonicus, by Spirit; Epic (1970)
Turn It Over, by Tony Williams Lifetime; Polygram (1970)
Morrison Hotel, by The Doors; Elektra (1970)
Smash Your Head Against the Wall, by John Entwistle (1971)
Led Zeppelin IV; Atlantic (1971)
Cry of Love, by Jimi Hendrix; Reprise (1971)
Sticky Fingers, by The Rolling Stones; Virgin Records (1971)
The Allman Brothers Live at Fillmore East; Polygram (1971)
Meddle, by Pink Floyd; EMI (1971)
L.A. Woman, by The Doors; Elektra (1971)
Who's Next, by The Who; Decca (1971)
The Inner Mounting Flame, by Mahavishnu Orchestra; Sony (1971)
Exile on Main Street, by The Rolling Stones; Atlantic (1972)

Whistle Rymes, by John Entwistle; MCA (1972)
Birds of Fire, by Mahavishnu Orchestra; Sony (1972)
1962–1966 and 1967–1970—The Beatles; Capitol (1973)
Spectrum, by Billy Cobham; Atlantic (1973)
Dark Side of the Moon, by Pink Floyd; Capitol (1973)
Toys in the Attic, by Aerosmith; Sony (1975)
Give Me Some Neck, by Ron Wood; Columbia (1978)
Some Girls, by The Rolling Stones; Atlantic (1978)
1984, by Van Halen; Warner Brothers (1984)
Learning to Crawl, by The Pretenders; Sire (1984)
Appetite for Destruction, by Guns N' Roses; Geffen (1987)
Flashpoint, by The Looters; Island (1988)
Tied to the Tracks, by Treat Her Right; RCA (1989)
Nevermind, by Nirvana; Geffen (1991)
Sailing the Seas of Cheese, by Primus; Interscope (1991)
Ten, by Pearl Jam; Sony (1991)
Live, by Col Bruce Hampton and the Aquarium Rescue Unit; Zomba (1992)
Message in a Box, by The Police; A&M (1993)
Superunknown, by Soundgarden; A&M Records (1994)
Yes, by Morphine; Rycodisc (1995)
Devil With a Blue Dress on and Other Hits; Mitch Ryder & the Detroit Wheels; Rhino (1997)
The Fragile, by Nine Inch Nails; Interscope (1999)
Brand New Day, by Sting; A&M (1999)
Morning View, by Incubus; Sony (2001)
Ultimate Collection, by The Who; Polydor/MCA (2002)
Kinks: The Ultimate Collection; Sanctuary (2002)
Brushfire Fairytales, by Jack Johnson; UMVD (2002)
Live, by Leftover Salmon; Compass (2002)
A Rush of Blood to the Head, by Coldplay; Capitol (2002)
Meteora, by Linkin Park; Warner (2003)
Live Dead, by Grateful Dead; Rhino (2003)
Live at Madison Square Garden New Year's Eve, by Phish; Rhino (2005)
Plans, by Death Cab for Cutie; Atlantic (2005)
Only by the Night, by Kings of Leon RCA (2008)
Uplifter, by 311; RCA/Jive (2009)
Isn't Anything, by My Bloody Valentine; Sony (2011)
Here and Now, by Nickelback; Roadrunner (2011)
The King of Limbs, by Radiohead; TBD Records (2011)

SURF

Krill Slippin', by The Mermen; Burnside (1989)
King of the Surf Guitar: The Best of Dick Dale & His Del-Tones; Rhino Records (1989)
Walk Don't' Run: The Best of the Ventures; Capitol (1990)
Aqua Velvets; Heydey (1992)
Wipe Out! The Best of the Surfaris; Varese Records (1994)
Beach Boys Greatest Hits Vol.1; Capitol (1999)
Greatest Surf Guitar Classics, by Various Artists; Big Eye Music (2001)
Rare West Coast Surf Instrumentals, by various artists; Ace (2001)
Lost Legends of Surf Guitar, by various artists; Sundazed (2007)
The Amazing California Health And Happiness Road Show, by The Mermen; Mesa (2009)
The Birth of Surf, by various artists; Ace (2010)

TECHNO

Dew Drops in the Garden, by Deee-Lite; Elektra (1994)
Delusions of Grandeur, by Hardkiss; Universal International (1995)
Northern Exposure I-III, by Sasha and Digweed; Ultra/Unknown (1997–1999)
Movement in Still Life, by BT; Head Space (1999)
Global Underground Series (Nu Breed), by Satoshi Tomiie, Various Artists; Nu Breed (2000)
Global, by Paul Van Dyk; Mute (2003)
Perfect Playlist Techno; Robbin Ent. (2007)

50 Techno Dance Hits, by various artists; Believe Electro (2009)
Secret Weapon Techno Mix Vol. 1, by The Attorney General; Secret Weapon Records (2010)

WEDDING DANCES

Tarantella
25 Favorite Italian Love Songs, by Various Artists; Madacy Records (2000)

Hava Nagila
Hava Nagila & Other Jewish Memories, by Benedict Silverman; Sounds of the World (1996)

Rumba
The Fabulous Ballroom Collection, by Arthur Murray; RCA (1998)

Tango
The Best Tango Album in the World Ever, by Var. Artists; Capitol (2003)

Viennese Waltz
Strictly Viennese Waltz, by Various Artists; Madacy (2000)

American Waltz
22 All Time Favorite Waltzes, by Lawrence Welk; Ranwood (1987)

Foxtrot:
Let's Dance the Foxtrot & Quickstep, by Graham Dalby; Let's Dance (1996)

E GLOSSARY

Acoustic Bass Guitar: An acoustic guitar with, normally, four bass strings. This instrument is most commonly used in Western music, "unplugged" Rock sessions, and Flamenco.

Active Electronics: An onboard preamplifier in the body of the instrument with "active" tone circuits (EQ) that can boost or cut individual bands of frequencies (bass, treble, mids) and can deliver higher output than a passive circuit. ("Passive" controls simply "roll off" or decrease the volume and highs.)

ADSR (Attack Decay Sustain Release): parameters that describe the contours of sound—also known as an "envelope."

Anticipation: Playing a note prior to when you would expect it based on chord movement. Most commonly, in a 4/4 measure, anticipation occurs on either the fourth beat or the "and" of the fourth beat, anticipating the chord that appears on beat one of the following measure.

Arco: Bowed. A term that usually applies only to upright bass.

Arpeggio: Playing the notes of a chord in sequence as individual notes. Arpeggios are normally, but not always, played evenly, with every note having the same duration. (This is in contrast to the normal way of playing a chord, in which all notes are played simultaneously.)

Attack: The speed at which a sound reaches full volume (see "ADSR.")

Baby Bass: An electric upright bass originally made by the Dopyera brothers (makers of the National and Dobro Resonator guitars) and later manufactured by Ampeg starting in 1962.

Backbeat: An informal term describing a strong snare drum stroke/note, usually falling on beats 2 and 4 of a 4/4 measure.

Bass Line: The pattern that a bassist plays. This can vary from a regular, undeviating pattern, to one with large amounts of variation (even from measure to measure) in rhythm and pitch selection.

Before the Beat: Playing just ahead of the drummer. This produces a driving feel, probably most suited to some types of Rock.

Behind the Beat: Playing just behind the drummer. This produces a laid back feel, probably most suited to some types of Blues, Jazz, and other relaxed styles.

Blues Progression: The harmonic chassis upon which a great deal of American popular music is built. A 12-bar pattern which comes in many forms, the most basic of which is I - I - I - I - IV - IV - I - I - V - IV - I - I.

Blues Scale: A scale commonly used in Blues, Rock, Jazz, and related genres. A blues scale starting on C contains the following notes: C, Eb, F, F#, G, Bb.

BPM: Beats Per Minute. The standard way to indicate tempo.

Chart: The musical notation for a song, normally with instrumental parts written out, sometimes including the bass line.

Chord: A fundamental unit of harmony. Chords usually consist of every other note in a major, minor, or modal scale. For example, in the key of C, the C major seventh chord consists of the root (C), third (E), fifth (G), and seventh (B) notes of the C major scale.

Chord Chart: See "Lead Sheet." (See Jazz chapter.)

Chromatic: Movement by half-step, for example movement from E to F.

Clave: A generic term referring to two-measure patterns in Afro-Cuban (and New Orleans) music in which three notes appear in one measure and two in the other. (See Afro-Cuban chapter.)

Combo: An amplifier in which the amplifier section and speakers are enclosed in the same cabinet.

Comping Pattern: An abbreviation of accompanying pattern. The background pattern a guitarist or keyboardist plays during vocals or solos by other instruments. A bassist will sometimes tailor his or her bass line to reinforce the rhythms in comping patterns.

Compressor: An effects unit that reduces the amplitude of the louder notes and increases the amplitude of the softer notes.

Cut Through: Be heard above the rest of the band.

dB: Decibel. The basic unit of loudness.

Dead Note: An unfretted (muted) note that does not produce a harmonic. When dead notes are written, they're normally indicated by an "x" head.

Decay: The speed and rate at which a sound drops to background level. See ADSR.

Delay: A common electronic effect in which a played note will be repeated (via the delay unit) anywhere from a few milliseconds to several hundred milliseconds later.

Diatonic: Stepwise motion, as from C to D. A term also commonly applied to the major scale.

Distortion: A change in the wave form from an instrument (or more generally, any sound source). For our purposes, distortion is normally caused by "overdriving" the preamplifier stage in an amplifier. This causes "clipping" (cutting off the tops and bottoms of waves) and a change in the ratios of the various harmonics, resulting in a rougher sound. Also called "Overdrive" or "Fuzz." Effectively "turning up to eleven"—a phrase uttered by Nigel Tufnel, fictional lead guitarist of the band "Spinal Tap."

Dominant 7th-type chord (also V7-type chord): A 4-note chord consisting of the root, major third, fifth and flatted seventh. For example, a C7 consists of C, E, G, and Bb.

Double Thump: When using the slap and pop technique, having the thumb "slap" twice in a row, often on the same note, using both sides of the thumb in an up-and-down motion.

Downbeat: The first beat in a measure.

Drone: A long, sustained note, normally on the root of the tonic, and usually held throughout, at the minimum, several measures—sometimes throughout an entire song.

Drop D: Tuning the lowest note on a 4-string electric bass to D rather than E. This is sometimes done with a lever on the head of the bass or simply through lowering the note with the tuning peg of the lowest string.

E-Bow: A hand-held, battery-operated device invented by Greg Hall in 1969 which simulates a bowing sound on instruments with magnetic pickups. It uses an electromagnetic field and creates (primarily) overtones.

Effects Box: A piece of electronic hardware that adds sound effects. Typically placed between an instrument and an amp to add sounds such as flange, distortion, delay, chorus, etc. (See "Stomp Box.")

EQ: Equalization. The tone settings.

EUB (Electric upright bass): A fretless type of bass played in the upright position that does not have the acoustic resonating body of a standard upright bass, but instead relies upon pickups and amplification.

Fake Book: A collection of lead sheets in book form. One explanation of the term is that these were unauthorized collections, hence the term "fake." An alternative explanation is that these lead sheet collections help musicians "fake" their way through songs they don't know. (See "Real Book.")

Fifth: The fifth note above the root in a major or minor scale. For example, G is the fifth in the keys of C major and C minor.

Fill: A busy pattern at the end of a song section that drives the song into the next section.

Finger Style: Played with the fingers (as opposed to a pick). On bass, this normally means alternating between the index and middle fingers, although sometimes the ring finger is also used.

Flange. Flanger. Flanging: An audio effect caused by mixing two identical signals together and then delaying one signal slightly and gradually changing that delay. This effect was discovered in the studio by recording one sound to two analog tape machines at the same time, and then feeding the recorded sounds to a third tape machine, while varying the speed of one of the original machines by putting a finger on the tape reel (flange) and varying the pressure. This puts the two signals out of phase. Listen to "Itchycoo Park" by the Small Faces or "Tomorrow Never Knows" by the Beatles for examples. The same effect is now accomplished digitally.

Flat EQ: Reproduction of a wave form as accurately as possible. In standard English, this means adjusting your tone settings to a place where they neither increase nor decrease the prominence of any frequency.

Flat Wound: A type of bass string that is extremely smooth to the touch and that produces a very bassy sound, largely devoid of mid and high frequencies.

Four on the Floor: An informal term that describes a drummer playing all four quarter notes on the bass drum in 4/4 time.

Four to the Bar: Playing four quarter notes in each measure (one bar).

Fretless: An electric bass without frets. This can be a bass designed without frets or (as is the case with Jaco Pastorius's famous P-Bass) a bass where the frets are carefully removed and the resulting troughs filled in.

Ghost Note (also "dead note"): An unfretted (muted) note that does not produce a harmonic, and is normally indicated by an "x" head when written.

Glissando: A slide from one note to another.

Groove: A loose term which refers to a good-sounding pattern played by the bass, drums, and/or comping instrument(s), or all of them together.

Ground Wound: A type of bass string halfway between flat wound and round wound in which the height of the ridges on round wound strings is reduced. This preserves the highs and mids, but reduces wear and tear on fingertips and fretboard produced by round wound strings.

Hammer Off: After executing a hammer on (see next definition), unfretting the second note and then replucking the first note.

Hammer On: Fretting a note and then, as the note sounds, fretting without plucking/picking another note, usually a half-step, whole step, or minor third above the previous note.

Harmonics: Exact multiples of the frequency of the note being played (the tonic). For example, A=440 Hz will have its second harmonic at 880 Hz, its third harmonic at 1320 Hz, etc. These tones are produced along with the tonic and their relative strength defines the timbre (tone color) of an instrument (or any other sound source). On bass or guitar, harmonics can be produced without fretting by touching any string (while plucking or picking) at the 12th, 7th, or 5th frets. (See Slap & Pop section in the Funk chapter.) Harmonics can also be played above other frets but with much less amplitude.

Head: 1) An informal term for the defining melody of a song played in a small band Jazz format; 2) An amplifier head—a pre-amp and power amp in a box separate from a speaker enclosure (as opposed to a combo amp or rack-mounted amp).

Hearing Loss: Something you really don't want. (Please understand that the author is mentioning this from experience. Have you ever played in a Who tribute band? Ahh. You understand.) Anything above roughly 110 dB can produce permanent hearing loss. (Hearing damage after a loud performance is usually indicated by ringing in the ears.) This is a problem, because many loud bands (e.g., Punk and Metal bands) perform at levels of 120 dB or even 130 dB, mandating that anyone playing in such bands who's in his or her right mind use earplugs.

Highs: High frequencies. In bass, this usually refers to everything above roughly one KHz.

Hook: The signature of a tune, usually a repeated riff.

Hz (Hertz): Unfortunately, the standard unit of frequency measurement. Several decades ago, this term displaced the much easier-to-understand term "cycles per second," one of the very few good, descriptive terms in physics.

In the Crack: The typical Reggae and New Orleans Second Line feel that is halfway between straight and swung.

In the Pocket: Playing in perfect sync with the drummer. A term normally used in reference to bassists and drummers.

Jam: To play experimentally or informally, typically improvising on a chord progression, often when much of the band is improvising at the same time, unlike a solo where one musician is improvising with the other musicians comping.

Laying Out: Not playing.

Lead Sheet: A song sheet with the melody written out and chord symbols above it. Using such a chart, a bassist must construct his own bass line based on the placement of the chord symbols in the chart. (See Jazz chapter.)

Legato: Played smoothly.

Loop (See also "Sample"): A short, sampled musical line that plays repetitively. A dedicated effects box called a "Looper" allows a bassist to record and play a musical phrase as a loop and then play along with it while it repeats. It is also common to use computer software such as "Ableton Live" to create and play loops on stage or in the studio.

Magnetic Pickup: The type of inductive pickup normally used in an electric bass, and which produces the characteristic electric bass sound—a sound considerably different from a Piezo pickup or the sound of an upright bass.

Major 7th Chord: A 4-note chord consisting of the root, major third, fifth and natural seventh. For example, a Cmaj7 consists of C, E, G, and B.

Mersey Beat: A variation of the Standard Rock Beat in which the snare plays on both the 2 and the "and" of the 2 (plus, as usual, beat 4).

MIDI (Musical Instrument Digital Interface): A software convention (protocol) that allows different electronic musical devices to "talk" to each other by representing musical notes as defined instructions. (These instructions are also called events, such as Note On, Note Off, Pitch Bend, etc.)

These events can be routed to different sounds or "patches" to play the same pattern of notes on different software instruments. MIDI can also be used as a language for various digital devices to sync to each other and to "map" control devices to "events" so you can push a button (or pedal) and an event happens.

Mids: Midrange frequencies. In bass amps, this normally refers to frequencies between about 300 Hz and 1 Khz.

Minor 7th Chord: A 4-note chord consisting of the root, minor third, fifth and flatted seventh. For example, a Cm7 consists of C, Eb, G, and Bb.

Mode: A type of scale that uses the same notes as the major scale, but starts on a different note. For example, using a C major scale start on its second note: D, E, F, G, A, B, C, D. That is the D Dorian scale. Start on the third note and play E, F, G, A, B, C, D, E, and you have the E Phrygian scale—and onward and upward. The scale starting on the fourth note (F) is the Lydian scale; that starting on the fifth note (G) is the Mixolydian; that starting on the sixth note (A) is the Aeolian (Natural Minor) scale; and that starting on the seventh note (B) is the Locrian scale. The Dorian, Phrygian, and Aeolian are the most commonly used modal scales, while the Locrain scale is almost never used.

Modulation: A change in key center. In most pop music, abrupt modulations—where the key of the music shifts up without preparation, typically up a full step step at the beginning of a new verse—are the norm. In jazz, however, conventional modulations with pivot chords (which are found in two different keys, and which lead to the V of the new key) are probably more common.

Multi-effects Unit: A floor-mounted effects box with multiple effects (wah wah, chorus, auto wah, flange, looper, etc.)

Ninth Chord: A 5-note chord consisting of the root, major third, fifth, flatted seventh and ninth. For example, a C9 consists of C, E, G, Bb, and D. (A ninth chord using a minor third is called a "minor ninth chord." A Cm9 is spelled C, Eb, G, Bb, D.)

Offbeats: The "ands" of beats or "up beats".

Onboard (as in "Onboard Electronics"): A preamp or other electrical device built into the body of a bass or guitar.

On the Beat: Playing exactly on the beat, as opposed to pushing the beat (playing "Before the Beat") or holding back the beat (playing "After the Beat").

On Top of the Beat: (See "Before the beat")

Ostinato: A clearly defined pattern that is repeated consistently throughout a song, or at least a section of a song.

P-Bass: Fender Precision Bass. Without doubt, the most common bass. Like its guitar relative, the Fender Stratocaster, the P-Bass is industry standard in American popular music.

Parametric Equalizer: A tone-altering circuit that allows selection of bandwidth (frequency range), center frequency, and amplitude. Parametric equalizers are normally used to eliminate or greatly diminish a narrow band of frequencies, usually those that produce unwanted feedback.

Pedal: A floor-mounted control/effects pedal such as a volume pedal or a wah pedal.

Pedal Board: A series of individual stomp boxes (or pedals) either in a plywood case (usually created by the musician) or as a self-contained unit produced by a musical equipment manufacturer.

Pentatonic Scale: Literally, any 5-note scale. In practice, usually the first, second, third, fifth and sixth notes in a major scale. In C, that would be C, D, E, G, A.

Piezo Pickup. Piezo-electric pickup: A type of pickup used with standup basses and, occasionally, in electric basses, that gives a much more acoustically accurate tone than the standard magnetic pickup.

Pizzicato (or "pizz"): Literally, "plucked." A sharply played note with a fast attack and quick fade.

Plucking: Using a pick or the fingers to produce a tone (as opposed to using a bow).

Progression: A chord pattern, typically a repeated one that provides the harmonic structure of a song.

Pull Off: Similar to a hammer-off, a pull-off also involves plucking the string with the fretting finger. This sometimes produces a "bent" note.

Rack Mount: A mechanical means of holding effects units (and amp heads) that are built specifically to be mounted in racks. Rack-mounted units are typically higher end than pedals, amp heads, and combo amps.

Real Book: A term used to differentiate authorized song (lead sheet) collections from unauthorized ones ("fake books").

Release: The time it takes for a sound level to decay to zero after the string is released. See ADSR.

Remix: A remixing of a previously recorded song, usually involving changing the volume level of specific tracks or substituting new tracks, especially drum tracks, for existing ones.

Roll Off: To reduce the high (and/or midrange) frequencies.

Root: The first degree of a scale. In C major, the root is C.

Round Wound: The standard type of bass string, with wire wound around a central core, and with slight, regular ridges on the strings as a result. Round wound strings are generally to be recommended, as they produce a much brighter sound than flat wound strings. Some of the first round wound strings for bass were manufactured by Rotosound in 1966 after a visit to the Rotosound factory by John Entwistle, bassist for The Who, who was looking for a more even, piano-like sound than that afforded by flat wound strings.

Rumba: An Afro-Cuban rhythm pattern also used in other styles, especially Latin Rock and Blues. Also a clave pattern in which the third note on the "three side" is played on the "and" of beat 4.

Salsa: A broad term which refers to a large spectrum of Afro-Cuban music, especially dance styles.

Sample: A digitally recorded sound (typically a small section).

Sampler: A dedicated piece of hardware used to record and play samples or software running on a laptop used for the same purpose.

Scale: A sequence of ascending or descending notes.

Second Line: Parade-style ensembles and music from the late 19th/early 20th centuries in New Orleans, inspired by ex-slaves and their descendants. The term originally referred to the line of musicians following a hearse in a funeral procession. Second Line was the predecessor of the Dixieland style, which is the foundation of all modern-day Jazz styles.

Sequencer: A dedicated piece of hardware used to record and play MIDI events.

Shuffle: A four-beats-to-the-measure swung pattern in which only the first and third triplets of a beat are played. The pattern is counted: "one . . . a two . . . a three . . . a four . . . a (one)" etc. See the Blues Chapter.

Slap and Pop: A Funk bass technique in which the thumb slaps strings down against the fretboard and the index and/or middle fingers pull strings up and release them, which results in their "popping" against the fretboard.

Slapping: A Rockabilly bass technique in which the fingers of the right hand slap the strings down against the neck of an upright bass. This technique is only applicable to upright. It is also used in Samba, Western Swing, and Train Beat.

Staccato: Playing note(s) in an extremely sharp, clearly articulated manner.

Stack: An amplifier with the amplifier section and speakers in separate cabinets, with the amp head sitting on top of the cabinet(s). A "full stack" refers to an amp head atop two speaker cabinets, while a "half stack" refers to an amp head atop a single speaker cabinet.

Standard Rock Beat: The most common drum beat in American pop music (in, of course, 4/4 time), in which the bass drum plays on the first and third beats, the snare plays on the second and fourth beats, and the hi-hat plays constant eighth notes on all four beats.

Stomp Box: An effects box with an on/off switch that typically sits on the floor and is operated with the foot.

Straight (time): Time with a duple feeling, with equal spacing between eighth notes, as in "one and two and three and four and."

Sustain: The period of time that sound remains audible. See ADSR.

Swung (time): Time with a triple feeling, as in "one and a two and a three and a four and a." (Note that in most pop music the middle triplet is omitted, resulting in a Shuffle pattern: "one . . . a two . . . a three . . . a four . . . a [one]" etc.)

Swung Eighths: Eighth notes played with a swung feel. These are often written as standard eighths, usually in 4/4 time, but with the words "swung" or "swing" to indicate the feel.

Syncopation: Emphasizing a note (or group of notes) which is not part of the primary rhythmic pulse through the use of accents and/or notes played off the beat or in a manner that emphasizes notes off the beat.

Synthesizer: An electronic musical instrument (often a keyboard instrument) that creates sounds electronically to imitate other more traditional instruments or creates unique sounds using waveforms, filters, and oscillators. There is also a lot of computer software that emulates synthesizers.

Tab, Tablature: An alternative method of musical notion for fretted instruments that indicates where and on what beats to place your fingers on the fretboard.

Tapping: Using the plucking hand to "tap" the strings against the fretboard while simultaneously fretting another note with the other hand. This is often used in conjunction with hammer-ons and pull offs.

Thump: Slapping a string down against the fretboard with the side of the thumb on an electric bass.

Train Beat: A drumset pattern used in Country, Bluegrass, Rockabilly, and Zydeco music characterized by consistent 16th notes on a snare drum with accents on upbeats, simulating the sound of a train. (The Rockabilly Train Beat is swung, in contrast with the other varieties of the beat.)

Tritone: A flatted fifth note (or an augmented fourth). The note in the middle of an octave. For example, the intervals C-F# and F#-C are both tritones.

Tumbao: An Afro-Cuban bass rhythm in which the key notes are the "and" of beat 2 and beat 4 (with beat 1 normally held over from beat 4). This rhythm shows up all over the place in pop music, although often with beat 1 played (as in Latin Rock) rather than held, as in authentic Afro-Cuban music.

Turnaround: A chord pattern in the final two bars of a Blues (or Jazz, or Gospel) verse that leads back to the tonic at the beginning of the next verse. Typically, in a turnaround, chords are played every two beats, with common turnarounds being I/IV - I/V and I/vi - ii/V.

Two Step: A double-time, up-tempo (Polka-like) pattern for the drum set.

Up Beat: A pickup note that occurs immediately before the first beat of a measure.

Vamp: A repeating riff. Also a term for improvising, as in "vamping on a Funk pattern."

Walking Bass Line: A bass pattern consisting of diatonic, chromatic, or arpeggiated quarter notes (that is, playing quarter notes but not staying on the root or playing root-fifth-root-fifth.) Of the three types of movement, diatonic is probably the most common in walking bass lines. (See Walking section in the Jazz chapter.)

Wave Form: The combination of the fundamental frequency and the various harmonics in a note.

F THE UNKNOWN BASSIST

Bassists don't get their due. The average music fan can probably name no more than a dozen: Paul McCartney, John Entwistle, Bill Wyman, and those from a few favorite bands. In all likelihood, most fans could name no more than half-a-dozen bass players.

We're doing our small part here to right that wrong. This appendix gives recognition to hundreds of bassists who play(ed) the styles covered in this book, and who we ran across while researching it. Obviously, this is far from a complete listing, but it at least gives credit to many very good bassists who deserve (often long overdue) recognition.

AC/DC—Mark Evans, Cliff Williams, Neil Smith, Larry Van Kriedt, Bob Bailley

Aerosmith—Tom Hamilton

Alabama—Teddy Gentry

Albino!—Kevin "Bam Bam" Blair, Adam Lowdermilk

Alice In Chains—Mike Starr, Mike Inez

Allman Brothers—Berry Oakley, Lamar Williams, David "Rook" Goldflies, Allen Woody, Oteil Burbridge

Marc Anthony—Carl James, Erben Pérez, Rube Rodriquez, José Gazmel

Anthrax—Danny Lilker, Frank Bello, Joey Vera, Kenny Kushner, Paul Kahn

Aqua Velvets—Michael Lindner

Asleep at the Wheel—Tony Garnier, David Miller, Glen Fukunaga, John Mitchell, David Dawson, Tom Anastasio, Gene Dobkin

Chet Atkins—Steve Wariner, Bob Moore

Austin Loung Lizards—Kirk Williams, Boo Resnick

Average White Band—Alan Gorrie

Ray Barretto—Francisco Centeno, Andy González, Sal Cuevas, Jaime Moreno

Count Basie—Walter Page, John Clayton, Cleveland Eaton, James Leary,

Beach Boys—Brian Wilson, Carol Kaye

Beastie Boys— Adam Yauch

Beatles—Paul McCartney

Chuck Berry—Willie Dixon

Clint Black—Jake Willemain

Black Flag—Chuck Dukowski, Kira Roessler, Raymond Ginn, Glen "Spot" Lockett, C'el Ruvuelta

Black Sabbath—Terence "Geezer" Butler, Dave Spitz, Bob Daisley, Neil Murray

Blind Boys of Alabama—Tracy Pierce

Blind Faith—Rick Grech

Blink 182—-Mark Hoppus

Blondie—Chris Stein, Leigh Foxx, Gary Valentine, Frank Infante, Nigel Harrison, Fred Smith,

Blue Cheer—Dickie Peterson

Body Count—Mooseman, Griz, Vincent Price

Buddy Bolden—James Johnson, Bob Lyons

Luis Bonfa—Mark Drury

Booker T and the MG's—Donald "Duck" Dunn, Lewie Steinberg

David Bowie—Trevor Bolder, George Murray, Gail Ann Dorsey

Brave Combo—Ann Marie Harrop, Cenobio ("Bubba") Hernandez, Lyle Atkinson, Little Jack Melody

Garth Brooks—Mike Chapman, Mark Greenwood, Betsy Smittle

Brothers Johnson—Louis Johnson

James Brown—Bernard Odum, William "Bootsy" Collins, Fred Thomas, Tim Drummond, Charles Sherrell, Ray Brundridge

Junior Brown—Bob Moore, Steve Layne, Spencer Starnes

Buggles—Trevor Horn

Paul Butterfield—Jerome Arnold, Billy Rich

Byrds—Chris Hillman, John York, Skip Battin

Cake—Shon Meckfessel, Gabriel Nelson, Victor Damiani

Canned Heat—Stuart Brotman, Larry Taylor, Antonio de la Barreda, Richard Hite, Richard Exley, John Lamb, Ernie Rodriguez, Skip Jones, Ron Shumake, Greg Kage

Cannibal Corpse—Alex Webster

Carcass—Jeffrey Walker

Cars—Benjamin Orr

Johnny Cash—Marshall Grant, Dave Roe, Bob Moore

Chantays—Warren Waters, Gil Orr, Brian Nussle

Ray Charles—Frank Fields, Paul West, Curtis Ohlson, Carol Kaye, Steve Beskrone, Roger Hines, Tom Fowler

Chemical Brothers—Tom Rowlands, Ed Simons

Kenny Chesney—Larry Paxton, Buddy Cannon, Michael Rhodes, Steve Marshall

Chicago—Peter Cetera, Jason Scheff

El Chicano—Freddie Sanchez, Brian Magness, Joe Perreria

Circle Jerks—Roger Rogerson, Zander Schloss, Earl Liberty,

Eric Clapton—Jack Bruce, Carl Radle, Nathan East

Clash—Tony James, Paul Simonon

James Cleveland—Andrew Gouche

George Clinton and Funkadelic— William "Bootsie" Collins, "Billy Bass" Nelson, Cordell "Boogie" Mosson

David Allan Coe—Danny Sheridan

Ornette Coleman—Don Payne, Charlie Haden, Scott LaFaro, David Izenzon, Jimmy Garrison, Gregory Cohen, Tony Falanga

John Coltrane—Steve Davis, Reggie Workman, Jimmy Garrison

Commodores—Ronald LaPread

Sam Cooke—Ted Brinson, Red Callender, Frank Fields, Clifford Hils, Milt Hinton, Adolphus Ashbrook, Clifford Hils, Ray Pohlman

Chick Corea—Carlos Benavent, Stanley Clark, Bunny Brunnel, Miroslav Vitous, John Patitucci, Jeff Ballard, Christian McBride

Alice Cooper—Dennis Dunaway, Prakash John, Tony Levin, Babbitt, Russell Powell, Dee Murray, Chuck Garric

Count Five—Roy Chaney

Counting Crows—Matt Malley, Millard Powers

Robert Cray—Richard Cousins, Karl Sevareid

Cream—Jack Bruce

Crystal Method—Ken Jordan, Scott Kirkland

Dick Dale—Steve Soest, Ron Eglit

Charlie Daniels—Charlie Hayward

Miles Davis—Dave Holland, Darryl Jones, Paul Chambers, Ron Carter, Harvey Brooks, Michael Henderson, Marcus Miller, Benny Reitveld, Joe McCreary aka "Foley"

Dead Kennedys—Klaus Flouride (Geoffrey Lyall), Greg Reeves

Deep Purple—Roger Glover, Glenn Hughes Nick Simper

Def Leppard—Rick Savage

Derek and the Dominos--Carl Radle

Devo—Gerald Casale

Bo Didley—Roosevelt Jackson, Gus Thornton, Debby Hastings

Dixie Chicks—Laura Lynch, Sebastian Steinberg

Dokken—Jeff Pilson, Juan Croucier, Barry Sparks

Fats Domino—Alvin "Red" Tyler, Billy Diamond, Frank Fields, Papa John Joseph

Dominoes—Bill Brown

Dr. John—Earl Stanley, Bob Frasier, Bob West, Ron Johnson, Jimmy Calhoun, George Porter Jr., Julius Farmer, Abe Laboriel, Dave Barard, Chris Severin, Essiet Okon Essiet, Marcus Miller

Doors—Kerry Magness, Leroy Vinnegar, Harvey Brooks, Ray Neopolitan, Lonnie Mack and Jerry Scheff

Drifting Cowboys—Howard "Cedric Rainwater" Watts, Herbert "Lum" York, "Cannonball" Nichols

Paquito D'Rivera—Carlos del Puerto, Oscar Stagnaro

Eagles—Randy Meisner, Tim Schmidt

Earth, Wind and Fire—Verdine White, Louis Satterfield

Steve Earle—Kelly Looney

Willie Edwards—Larry Vigneault, Jesse Howes

Duke Ellington—Jimmy Blanton, Oscar Pettiford, Wellman Braud, Billy Taylor, Hayes Alvis, Junior Raglin, Joe Benjamin

Emerson, Lake & Palmer—Greg Lake

Emperor—Ihsahn (Vegard Sverre Tveitan)

Udoh Essiet—Ahmed Barry, Wilbur Bascomb, Greg Edick, Hilaire Penda

Fatboy Slim—Quentin Leo Cook

Maynard Ferguson—Linc Milliman, Rick Petrone, Jimmy Rowser, Lou Carfa, Phil Palombi, Paul Thompson, Chris Berger, Red Callender, Arnold Fishkin, Milt Hinton, Gordon Johnson, Gary King, Will Lee, Curtis Counce

Flatt and Scruggs—Howard "Cedric Rainwater" Watts, Bob Moore

Fleetwood Mac—John McVie, John Brunning

Flying Burrito Brothers—Chris Ethridge, Chris Hillman

Generation X—Tony James

Genesis—Mike Rutherford, Daryl Stuermer

Germs—Lorna Doom (Teresa Ryan), Diana Grant

Stan Getz—Gene Cherico, Tommy Williams, Don Payne, Keter Betts, Tommy Potter, Ray Brown

Dizzie Gillespie—Oscar Pettiford, Ray Brown, Slam Stewart, Gene Ramey, Israel Crosby, Bam Brown, Nick Fenton, Milt Hinton, Curly Russell, Murray Shipinski, Dick Fullbright, Al McKibbon

Gipsy Kings—Gerard Prevost, Gildas Bolce, Fernando Padilla-Delgado

Benny Goodman—Artie Bernstein, Harry Goodman

Al Green—Leroy Hodges

Grateful Dead—Phil Lesh

Green Day—Mike Dirnt

Guns n' Roses—Ole Beich, Duff McKagan, Tommy Stinson

Buddy Guy—Davey Faragher, Orlando J. Wright

Bill Haley and the Comets—Al Thompson, Al Rex, Al Rappa, Marshall Lytle,

Herbie Hancock and the Headhunters—Paul Jackson

Havana Philharmonic—Israel "Cachao" López

W.C. Handy—Archie Walls, "Pops" Foster

Isaac Hayes—James Alexander, Ronald Hudson

Joe Henderson—Nilson Matta, Ron Carter, Tony Dumas, Richard Davis

Jimi Hendrix—Billy Cox, Noel Redding

Woody Herman—Chuck Andrus, Joe Mondragon, Chubby Jackson

Dan Hicks—Jaime Leopold, Kevin Smith, Tony Garnier

Faith Hill—Leland Sklar

Hives—Dr. Matt Destruction (Mattias Bernwall)

Buddy Holly—Joe B. Mauldin, Larry Welborn, Don Guess, Waylon Jennings

Hot Tuna—Jack Casady

Howlin' Wolf—Willie Dixon

Human League—Ian Burden

Incubus—Ben Kenney, Alex "Dirk Lance" Katunich

Invisible Surfers—Johnny Ted

Irakere—Carlos del Puerto

Iron Maiden—Steve Harris

Michael Jackson—Steve Lukather, Bryan Loren, Terry Jackson, Louis Johnson, David Paich, Alex Al, Nathan Watts, Chuck Rainey, Nathan East

Elmore James—Ransom Knowling, David Miles, Ralph '"Chuck" Hamilton, Frank Fields, John A. Williamson "Homesick James", Lee Bully, Leonard Ware

Jan and Dean—Carol Kaye

Jefferson Airplane—Jack Casady

Waylon Jennings—Jerry "Jigger" Bridges, Robby Turner, Duke Goff

Jethro Tull—Glen Cornick, Jeffrey Hammond, John Glascock, Tony Williams

Antonio Carlos Jobim—Tommy Williams, Bob Mondragon, Luiz Mala

Louis Jordan—Charlie Drayton, Dallas Bartley, Henry Turner

Juanes—Shawn Davis, Fernando Tobon, Felipe Navia

Judas Priest—Ian Hill, Bruno Stapenhill

Kanda Bongo Man—Shaba Kahamba

Shaba Kahamba—Shaba Kahamba, Mokonkole Makangu Master

Kansas—Billy Greer, Dave Hope

Khaled Hadj Brahim—Bernard Paganotti, Benji Meyers, Abe Laboriel

Albert King—Donald "Duck" Dunn, George Proter Jr., Charles Rainey, Anthony Willis, James Alexander

B.B. King—Tuff Green, Willie Weeks, Ray Brown, Gerald Jemmott, Nathan East

Freddie King—Benny Turner

King Crimson—Peter Giles, Greg Lake, Gordon Haskell, Boz Burrell, John Wetton, Tony Levin

King Sunny Ade—Ken Okulolo, Remi Abegunde, Jelili Lawal

Kinks—Pete Quaife, John Dalton

Kiss—Gene Simmons

Kool and the Gang—Robert Bell

Korn—Reginald "Fieldy" Arvizu

Lennie Kravitz—Jack Daley, Lebron Scott

Fela Kuti—Ayo Azenabor, Franco Aboddy, Oghene Kologbo

Led Zeppelin—John Paul Jones

Les Tetes Brulees—Atebass

Jerry Lee Lewis—J.W. Brown, Bob Moore

Limp Bizkit—Sam Rivers

Little Richard—Frank Fields, Lloyd Lambert, Olsie Richard Robinson

LL Cool J—Kern Brantley, Erik Sermon

Los Lobos—Conrad Lozano

Los Straitjackets—E. Scott Esbeck, Pete Curry

Lyle Lovett—Viktor Krauss

Lynyrd Skynyrd—Larry Junstrom, Leon Wilkeson, Greg T. Walker

M.C. Hammer—Oscar Alston

Mahavishnu Orchestra—Rick Laird

Malo—Pablo Telez, Julina Molina, Ramiro Amador

Cheb Mami—Jerry Barnes, Desmond Foster, Youcef Boukella, Renaud Garcia-Fons

Ricky Martin—Reggie Hamilton, Kari Cameron, Mike Porcaro, Hugh McDonald, Ricardo Suarez

Dave Matthews—Stefan Lessard

John Mayall—John McVie, Jack Bruce, Stephen Thompson, Larry Taylor, Bobby Haynes, Tony Reeves, Rick "RC" Cortes, Greg Rzab, Hank Van Sickle

Curtis Mayfield—Joseph "Lucky" Scott

Tim McGraw—Mike Brignardello

MC5—Pat Burrows, Michael Davis

Reba McEntire—Chopper Anderson, Leland Sklar, Larry Paxton, Spady Brannan

MDC—Michael "Offender" Donaldson

Megadeth—David Ellefson

Sergio Mendez—Tiao Neto, Bob Matthews

Mermen—Allen Whitman, Jennifer Burnes

Meshuggah—Dick Lövgren

Metallica--Ron McGovney, Cliff Burton, Jason Newsted, Robert Trujillo

Meters—George Porter, Jr.

Miami Sound Machine—Juan Marcos Avila, Jorge Casas

Moby—Alistair "Ali" McMordie, Greta Brinkman

Bill Monroe—Amos Garren, "Cousin" Wilbur Wesbrooks, Howard "Cedric Rainwater" Watts

Jelly Roll Morton—John Lindsay, Wellman Braud

Motley Crue—Nikki Sixx

Muddy Waters—Ernest "Big" Crawford, Willie Dixon, Charles Calmese, Calvin "Fuzzy" Jones

Napalm Death—Graham Robertson, Finbar Quinn, P-Nut (Peter Shaw), Nicholas Bullen, James Whitley

Willie Nelson—Bee Spears, Chris Etheridge, Garry Tallent

Neville Brothers—Tony Hall, Milton Davis, Ivan Neville

New York Dolls—Arthur Kane

Nirvana—Chris Novoselic

Offbeats—T. Boomer

Ohio Players—Marshall Jones

Joe "King" Oliver—Bill Johnson

Manny Oquendo—Andy González

Orchestra Baobab—Charlie N'Diaye

Buck Owens—Merle Haggard, Doyle Holly, Doyle Curtsinger

Ozomatli—Wil-Dog Abers

Charlie Palmieri—Bobby Rodriguez

Eddie Palmieri—Andy González, Dave Perez

Pantera—Tommy Bradford, Rex Brown

Charlie Parker—Curly Russell, Vic McMillan, Al McKibbon, Tommy Potter, Charles Mingus, Ray Brown

Junior Parker—Kenneth Banks, Hamp Simmons, Otto Jackson, Al Smith

Parliament—William "Bootsie" Collins

Pearl Jam—Jeff Ament

Carl Perkins—Clayton Perkins

Pinche Blues Band—Jaime de Zubeldia, Michael "Did'r" Zubay

P.O.D.—Traa Daniels

Poison—Bobby Dall

Police—Sting (Gordon Matthew Thomas Sumner)

Polkacide—Alistair Shanks aka Lance Boyle aka Murder'r Bob

Polkaholics—Jolly James Wallace

Elvis Presley—Bill Black, Meyer Rubin, Jerry Scheff, Ray Siegel, Bob Moore, & Elvis himself on some of his later tracks

Ray Price—Bob Moore, Willie Nelson

Primus—Les Claypool

Prince—Andre Cymone, Mark Brown, Levi Seacer Jr., Rhonda Smith

Prince Nico Mbarga—Andy Morris

Professor Longhair—Will Harvey Jr., George Davis

Public Enemy—Brian Hardgroove

Tito Puente—Bobby Rodriguez

Louie Ramirez—Bobby Rodriguez

Ramones—Dee Dee Ramone (Douglas Colvin)

Lou Rawls—Carol Kaye, Jimmy Bond, Brian Bromberg, Curtis Robertson

Red Elvises—Oleg Bernov

Red Hot Chili Peppers—Michael "Flea" Balzary

Buddy Rich—James Gannon, Tom Warrington, Dave Carpenter, Phil Leshin

Max Roach Quintet—Bobby Boswell

Marty Robbins—Hillous Butrum, Colin Cameron

Rolling Stones—Bill Wyman, Darryl Jones, Chuck Leavell, Dick Taylor

Sonny Rollins—Doug Watkins, Donald Bailey, Oscar Pettiford, Leroy Vinnegar, Bob Crenshaw

Linda Rondstadt—Bob Glaub, Kenny Edwards, Randy Meisner, Mark Schatz

Rush—Geddy Lee

Doug Sahm—Jack Barber, Louie Terrazas

Arturo Sándoval—Carlos del Puerto

Mongo Santamaria—Andy González

Santana—Dave Brown, Douglas Rauch, David Margen, Alfonso Johnson, Benny Rietveld

Savoy Brown—Tony "Tone" Stevens

Son Seals—Johnny B. Gayden, Harry "Snapper" Mitchum, Noel Neal, Bay WIlliams

Seeds—Sky Saxon

Brian Setzer Orchestra—Bob Parr

Sex Pistols—Glen Matlock, Sid Vicious

George Shearing—Al McKibbon

Paul Simon—Vincent Nguini, Bakithi Kumalo

Ricky Skaggs—Mark Fain

Skid Row—Rachel Bolan

Slayer—Tom Araya

Slipknot—Paul Dedrick Gray, Donnie Steele

Smashing Pumpkins—D'arcy Wretzky

Bessie Smith—Billy Taylor, William Oscar Smith

Soundgarden—Hiro Yamamoto, Ben Shepherd

Spinal Tap—Derek Smalls (Harry Scherer)

Sons of the Pioneers—Bob Nolan, Pat Brady

Spirit—Mark Andes

Bruce Springsteen—Garry Tallent

Staple Singers—David Hood

Steely Dan--Walter Becker, Wilton Felder, Chuck Rainey

Angie Stone—Larry Peoples Sr., Jackie Clark, Alex Al, Chucky T

Stooges—Dave Alexander

Stray Cats—Lee Rocker

Strokes—Nikolai Fraiture

Styx—Chuck Panozzo

String Cheese Incident—Keith Moseley

Super Mezembe—Atia Jo, Mwanza wa Mwanza Mulunguluke

Surfaris—Pat Connolly

Tabu Ley—Shaba Kahamba

Talking Heads—Tina Weymouth

Cal Tjader—Al McKibbon, Andy González

Toto—David Hungate, Mike Porcaro, Leland Sklar

Tout Les Soir—Butch Landry

Tower of Power—Rocco Prestia

Marshall Tucker—Tommy Caldwell, Franklin Wilkie

Shania Twain—Andy Cichon

Richie Valens—Buddy Clark, Carol Kaye, Waylon Jennings

Van Halen—Michael Anthony, Wolfgang Van Halen

Los Van Van—Juan Formell

Stevie Ray Vaughan—Tommy Shannon

Velvet Underground—John Cale, Walter Powers

Venom—Conrad "Cronos" Lant, Tony Dolan

Ventures—Bob Bogle, Nokie Edwards, Earl Herbert

Vines—Patrick Matthews

T-Bone Walker—Billy Hadnott, Ransom Knowling

War—Morris "B.B." Dickerson

Weather Report—Miroslov Vitous, Alphonso Johnson, Jaco Pastorius, Victor Bailey

Papa Wemba—Boss Matuta

Barry White—Nathan East

Whitesnake—Neil Murray

Who—John Entwistle, Pino Palladino

Maurice Williams—Norma Wade

Bob Wills—Billy Jack Wills

Stevie Wonder—Scott Edwards, Nathan Watts, Scott Edwards, Reggie McBride, James Jamerson

Yes—Chris Squire

Dwight Yoakam—Dave Roe, J.D. Foster, Taras Prodaniuk

Zaiko Langa Langa—Bapius Muaka

Frank Zappa (and the Mothers of Invention)—Roy Estrada, Jim Pons, Jeff Simmons, Bruce Fowler, Patrick O'Hearn, Tom Fowler, Scott Thunes

Zélé le Bombardier—Atebass, Sossu

As my guitarist Jay said to me in 1995 in response to an email, "Hello from the Internet. Say good bye to everything else." I am indeed on the 'Net.

You can find additional material on the books's website at www.bassistsbible.com, and if you search on Youtube and Facebook you will also find content related to the book and to yours truly as a bassist.

I play in a number of bands. After 27 years, my originals band, Offbeats, is still alive. At this point, playing with the other guys in it is instinctive. We have been playing each others' material since we were young. We're at www.offbeats.com.

You can also find more at www.timboomer.com and on youtube, facebook, twitter, and all that.

See you out there.